Women's College
Softball on the Rise

D0584370

Women's College Softball on the Rise

A Season Inside the Game

MARK ALLISTER

Foreword by Carol Hutchins

McFarland & Company, Inc., Publishers
Jefferson, North Carolina

LIBRARY OF CONGRESS CATALOGUING-IN-PUBLICATION DATA

Names: Allister, Mark Christopher, 1956– author. | Hutchins, Carol, 1957–
    writer of foreword.
Title: Women's college softball on the rise : a season inside the game /
    Mark Allister ; foreword by Carol Hutchins.
Description: Jefferson, North Carolina : McFarland & Company, Inc., 2019 |
    Includes index.
Identifiers: LCCN 2019011174 | ISBN 9781476676166 (paperback :
    alk. paper) ∞
Subjects: LCSH: Softball for women—United States. | Softball for women—
    Social aspects—United States. | Softball for women—Economic
    aspects—United States. | College sports for women—United States. |
    College sports for women—Social aspects—United States. | College
    sports for women—Economic aspects—United States.
Classification: LCC GV881.3 .A55 2019 | DDC 796.357/8082—dc23
LC record available at https://lccn.loc.gov/2019011174

BRITISH LIBRARY CATALOGUING DATA ARE AVAILABLE

ISBN (print) 978-1-4766-7616-6
ISBN (ebook) 978-1-4766-3586-6

Front cover: Jessie Warren, Florida State University third baseman,
connecting on a home run (photograph courtesy Brendan Maloney/
Florida State Athletics)

Printed in the United States of America

McFarland & Company, Inc., Publishers
    Box 611, Jefferson, North Carolina 28640
    www.mcfarlandpub.com

To all the female softball players and coaches—
past, present, and future
And to Derek and Joann Allister

Acknowledgments

Thousands of books have been written on baseball over the last century, and baseball players, as well as the game itself, have been amply celebrated. Not so softball, and my biggest debt is simply to all those over the years who have helped make softball the marquee sport it has become: the players, coaches, parents, media members, and so forth. May the special culture of this sport remain.

I'd like to thank all those people who granted me interviews and were quoted in the book. Others of you talked to me about the sport, your teams, or your own performances, and though I couldn't work your words or point of view into my narrative, you furthered my knowledge of women's softball and this season's events. Thank you. The work of umpires is necessary and often overlooked, and I appreciate the time and insights they gave me. I owe a special thanks to Carol Hutchins, head coach at Michigan, for writing the foreword to the book, and for being such a positive presence in the sport.

Every university has sports information directors who work hard behind the scenes to distribute information for the media, to arrange interviews, to run social media, and even occasionally to call a game on the radio. I am so grateful for the help that I was given by the SIDs of all these teams; this book could not have been written without them. There are too many to name individually, but thank you, one and all.

Thanks to St. Olaf College who gave me a necessary leave of absence to write and thanks to FastPitch News and FastPitch Delivery for giving me outlets for my work. Thanks to Gary Mitchem, my editor.

Writing and re-writing a book-length manuscript becomes an emotional roller-coaster, where one week you feel like you're making progress and the next week you're not sure if anyone will ever want to read past the first chapter. It helps to have critical feedback, and I was lucky to have four such readers who helped make the manuscript better and kept me positive. Thank you to Tanya Spishak, Kayla Hatting, Carol Holly, and Heather Allister for reading all or parts of the manuscript.

My wife, Meredith Allister, attended numerous softball games with me, watched them on television, and listened to my talk throughout the season. It's a gift for a writer to have someone so supportive. Meredith also gave feedback on the entire manuscript and helped me choose photos. I owe her much, as well, for the life we have beyond the writing of this book.

My final thanks to my brother and sister-in-law, Derek and Joann Allister, who have themselves contributed so much to the sport of softball. I would never have gotten immersed in the sport without them.

Table of Contents

Foreword by Carol Hutchins

My first memories of playing softball are from the sixth grade. I was asked to play for the neighborhood Baptist church in a girls' church league. I wasn't a member of the church, but I wanted to play on a team! This experience lasted one month and ultimately ended when my strict, state trooper father forced me to leave the team because our catcher made a habit of fighting with our opponents. He did not think that fighting was "ladylike" behavior. I was heartbroken, but I had discovered a passion for playing softball.

I grew up idolizing a local women's softball team, the Lansing Laurels. They were a semi-professional team that traveled the country at a time when it was fairly uncommon for women to participate in athletics. Locally, the Laurels were treated as celebrities. I would go to the games with my best friend and her father, who was himself a fastpitch player. I dreamed of being a player of the Laurels' caliber, and when they had an open tryout and clinic, I jumped at the opportunity to participate. Despite my very short-term organized competitive experience with the Baptist church league, I earned a spot on the "farm team," the Lansing Lassies. That was the beginning of my life in softball.

I was surrounded by actual coaches and a competitive environment, and my skill level increased at a rapid pace. I was elevated to play with the Laurels the next year. At the age of 16, I played softball with women whose ages ranged from 20 to 49. Our coach was Kay Purves, a fierce and demanding leader who assumed the role of catcher-manager at the age of 49. One of my new teammates, Mary Nutter, was a good ten-plus years my senior and educated us daily on the subjects of softball excellence on the field and personal excellence off it. We traveled the country playing against teams with players such as Margie Wright, Linda Wells, Joan Joyce, Joyce Compton, Carol Spanks, and Shirley Topley, among others, who quickly became my idols and heroes. All of these women had one thing in common that a kid like myself could palpably sense: they were passionate competitors. When I had an opportunity to either compete against them or just sit in the stands and observe, they always inspired me to play with passion.

1

Back then, softball existed largely in a world known only to those who actually participated in that arena. There were varied rates of participation at the high school and collegiate levels. My high school in Lansing, Michigan, did not sponsor softball, and it was not until I enrolled at Michigan State University that I had my first opportunity to represent my school in the sport. The NCAA did not sponsor college softball until 1982, but the Association for Intercollegiate Athletics for Women (AIAW) did, and Michigan State won the AIAW College World Series in 1976, my freshman year. That 1976 championship was as important to my teammates and me as any championships won by players today. It was the pinnacle of our sport at that time and no less significant to us. The pure joy of working to get to the "top of the mountain" was our reward. That joy can still be seen as victors hoist the championship trophies, but today vast resources and support networks help to create the experience. We have come a long way in our sport.

There have been many books written about baseball but very few about softball. When Mark Allister asked if I would participate in this project, I was elated to do so. Many Americans love baseball, but over my 40-year coaching career, thousands of these same fans have told me that they were captivated by college softball too. Mark Allister writes about where we have come from and provides insight into today's remarkable college game. He conveys the intensity and passion of our sport, and through his conversations with many of the game's great coaches, he is able to show how softball continues to grow and even to thrive on major television networks.

One of the topics that Mark touches on is the implementation of Title IX. No single piece of legislation has had greater impact on social change than those 37 words added, within the Education Amendments of 1972, to our constitution. This is a significant part of our history, and no doubt enhanced the athletic opportunities for our talented women on the diamond. Those of us who are involved in the education of today's athletes need to ensure that their generation understands the history that led to the creation of this law. I was recently asked what, besides Title IX, is the most important thing that has ever occurred in women's athletics? There is *nothing* in our history that is more significant than the passage of Title IX. Without it, women's sports as we know them would not exist. Before Title IX there were fewer women involved in higher education as students and far fewer women involved as teaching faculty. To ensure opportunities for today and for tomorrow, those who lead women must remain vigilant in promoting equity and opportunity for women.

I look back on the more than 40 years since my days of church league and realize that I could never have envisioned college softball as we know it today, and certainly not the multi-million-dollar stadiums and the crowds that fill them. Visibility and attention continues to mount for the game that we all love, as major television networks now showcase the game's tremendous athletes. Softball is no longer a sport known only to those who participate. Young girls and boys flock to get players' autographs and pictures. Young girls have an abundance of role models to emulate. Coaches and players are rock stars on their college campuses and in their hometowns. Young women from ages 8 to 18 travel the country playing softball with the hopes of earning a scholarship. Excitement for the game is at an all-time high, and on many campuses, it is the priority female sport.

In this book, Allister conveys the excitement and passion of college softball today while reminding all of us that women tend to play best when they are happy and having fun. He also reminds us that women are as competitive and intense in their game as males who play their sport. He shares details from conversations with college coaches at all levels, and the common theme is that these coaches care deeply about their athletes as people. To these leaders, the personal growth of the individual athlete is as important as talent; most coaches, in fact, would say developing young women into strong, responsible women is the most important thing they do. College softball and the cottage industry surrounding it has become a booming business, yet at the highest levels, the coaches in our sport are committed to the welfare of the entire athlete. This connection between coach and athlete is the most fulfilling part of the picture. It creates the best experiences and often the most productive and successful environments.

Softball is America's hottest game right now. It is wildly successful largely because television, and in particular ESPN, has fallen in love with the college game. Players and coaches are accessible to the fan bases and the field dimensions allow the spectators to feel as if they are right in the dugout with the teams. Television captures the passion and intensity of every pitch. And viewers respond: ESPN has ratings that regularly outdraw the NHL and NCAA baseball. The 2017 Women's College World Series championship, which pitted Florida against Oklahoma and lasted an astonishing 18 innings, even preempted the NBA playoffs.

Softball is a game that people readily identify with because of its similarity to baseball, but the uniqueness of the game also appeals. To quote one of the greatest coaches in the college game, Sue Enquist, "If you take care of the game, the game will take care of you!" The game will continue to grow, reaching new audiences and heights. It will continue to teach us and to reach us.

Carol Hutchins played varsity basketball and softball at Michigan State University from 1976 to 1979. Head coach at the University of Michigan since 1985, Hutchins has won more games than any other softball coach in Division I history (a number she adds to yearly), and she led her 2005 Michigan team to the national championship, a first for a team located east of the Mississippi River. Hutchins is in the National Fastpitch Coaches Association Hall of Fame.

Prologue

Championship sporting events are often decided by one pass in the Super Bowl, one three-pointer from the corner during March Madness, one putt at the Masters golf tournament. At least that's how we label such moments. Players, coaches, sportswriters, and fans distill a season into a single play that makes the difference between winning and losing, between being remembered or forgotten.

I'm in Oklahoma City watching the Women's College World Series (WCWS), the most important yearly event in American softball. After four days of play and the elimination of six teams, the best-of-three championship series has come down to the University of Washington and Florida State University. Game one went to FSU, 1–0, when catcher Anna Shelnutt homered in the sixth inning. In game two, Washington jumps out to a quick lead, scoring three runs in the top of the first. One of their two pitching aces, Taran Alvelo, strolls into the circle, looking to shut down the Seminoles hitters and get her defense off the field quickly.

Jessie Warren, FSU's do-everything third baseman, opens with a single. Alvelo strikes out the next two batters. Shelnutt steps up to the plate. Everyone is tense—the 9,000 spectators at OGE Energy Field in the USA Softball Hall of Fame Stadium, the 1.5 million viewers watching on ESPN. With a count of 1–2, Alvelo throws a sixty-eight-mph riseball that she believes is a strike. She pumps her fist and begins to walk toward the dugout. The umpire calls it a ball. Replay shows that it was a borderline call. Alvelo begins her windmill motion and delivers the next pitch. Shelnutt swings and, almost unbelievably, the ball once again jumps off her bat. Fans roar.

Despite the excitement created and athleticism displayed, women's sports get scant coverage in traditional media, with the few exceptions of women's basketball, women's tennis, and Olympic years coverage of gymnastics, ice skating, and skiing. In "It's Dude Time," the summary of their twenty-five-year longitudinal study of gender in televised sports news, Cheryl Cooky, Michael Messner, and Michela Musto reveal that the tremendous growth of women *playing* sports hasn't transferred over to media coverage.

ESPN's SportsCenter, for example, gave only 2 percent of its airtime to women's sports in 2014. Local outlets did little better. While the decision makers at television stations and city newspapers justify the lack of coverage by saying that the interest isn't there, their logic is self-serving, in that more coverage would generate more interest. Even without the general coverage, the Women's College World Series beats the television ratings for the College Baseball World Series.

An amazing play in softball might end up on ESPN's Top Ten Plays of the Day, but analysis of a game or a profile on a female athlete* rarely does. City newspapers will cover their local team, if they have one playing in the tournament, but won't cover the tournament in general. Baseball gets the attention, at whatever level it's played. Welch Suggs, author of *A Place on the Team: The Triumph and Tragedy of Title IX*, tells of having no answer when his nine-year-old daughter asked why girls play softball and boys play baseball. "Most of the vestiges of separate sports for men and women have fallen away," he writes. "Women no longer play six-on-six basketball.... Women compete in all the same events in track with the exception of the multi-events (heptathlon for women, decathlon for men) and cross-country distances. Soccer teams play under the same rules. So why no baseball for girls now?"

Fans of the women's game have an easy answer to Suggs' question: softball is the more interesting sport. The shorter distances for base paths ensure that the game's speed is greater, and the strategies attempting to deal with this speed create high interest. Without the incessant number of times that batters step out of the box or that pitchers throw over to first base, softball games move at a faster clip, your typical college game lasting about two hours, compared to a baseball game's three hours. The amount of proportional action is greater in softball. Fewer players get injured. Star pitchers can throw every day, because the underhand windmill motion of pitching doesn't place the stress on the elbow and shoulder that overhand pitching does. Fans of softball can add their own reasons to my list of what makes the sport so compelling.

If we aren't comparing baseball and softball abstractly as sports but comparing the experience of watching them, the biggest difference is how the

---

*Language use connected to gender is potentially fraught—not just about pronouns, but adjectives. I understand the point of view of those who write "women engineers" rather than "female engineers," the latter of which in a patriarchal world can seem disrespectful and referencing only biology. In this book, however, I use "female" as the preferred adjective when the noun refers to people (I will say "women's softball," of course). Perhaps my decision to use "female" comes because I teach writing and "woman" and "women" are nouns, not adjectives. Perhaps I'm simply using what sounds right in my ear; if we are unlikely to say "man athlete" then "woman athlete" sounds wrong to me. The athletes I'm writing about are challenging the patriarchal world, and so I prefer "female athletes," which to me implies equality. Based on what I read in sports journalism, many disagree, as do those in the non-sports world. There is no consensus on this matter; we all must simply make a choice and explain ourselves.

women perform their gender, which is an academic way of discussing the particular vibe that the participants of each sport create. Men, on the baseball field, are cool and mostly unemotional; the masculine code dictates that they act as if they're in control. In a few men's sports, football, let's say, some emotion is encouraged—players engage in trash talking or glorifications of ego as they pump their chests and point a finger to God. Female softball players show their emotions constantly, but it's a different performance of emotion. They cheer on their teammates with self-created chants and motions; they are cute and goofy for the team; individual ego isn't on display as much as expressions of team unity. There is little grandstanding in women's softball.

I grew up an athlete in Southern California playing sports year round, and I followed my local university and pro teams then and after college: reading about them in newspapers and magazines, viewing them on television, occasionally attending games. I believed that playing sports builds character. In recent decades I have become disillusioned, however, by behaviors that counter the potential character-building inherent in sports. The widespread doping that emerged in the Olympic track world in the 1980s, the steroids era of major league baseball in the 1990s and 2000s, and all the subsequent drug scandals that have followed make me skeptical of amazing performers I might have otherwise admired. The academic and cheating scandals of college sports have made the phrase "student-athlete" ring hollow, scandals that have hit particularly close to home because I'm a college professor. As the money in pro sports has skyrocketed, I find myself half angry and half amused when a pro athlete bolting his organization and city claims that "it's not about the money" as he turns down twelve million dollars a year from his local team to play for someone else for fourteen million dollars a year. Perhaps most disturbing to me has been the physical and sexual abuse that goes unpunished, or is even condoned, when a pro or university team believes that they need that offending individual.

When I began to be skeptical of men's sports and male athletes, the trash-talking and displays of ego turned me off further. I'm not suggesting that watching football or men's basketball isn't interesting. I like the game of chess and football is a chess game that has infinite variety because the "pieces" (the players) adapt and improvise and do marvelous things in front of our eyes. Basketball was always my favorite sport, with its fluidity and athleticism, and a team such as the 2017–18 Boston Celtics can still catch my attention. But these sports' negatives outweigh their positives for me. Sport does not *necessarily* build character—witness the lack of it in so many of our athletes, coaches, and owners—but my belief remains that sport can be transformative because I now follow women's sports. I see what the female athletes can do on a field. I've learned about their tremendous successes off the field: as students, as community members, as leaders in their professional lives.

The University of Alabama's Haylie McCleney, one of college softball's greatest power slappers, exhibits her speed and defensive skills. Making this catch, McCleney counters social constructions of femininity and shows us the inadequacy of a condescending phrase such as "throws like a girl." Perhaps this is what it means to "field like a girl." Courtesy Kent Gidley.

Since I began writing this book, I've heard repeatedly a catchy phrase that sums up the difference between the two sexes when it comes to sport: *Boys have to win to have fun. Girls have to have fun to win.* These women I'm watching, and high-powered female athletes everywhere, want to win very much. But individual athletes and coaches of women's teams believe that there's more to sport: life lessons to be learned, value systems to be established, traditional notions of gender to be challenged, friendships to be made. Female athletes enact, on and off the fields and courts, a visibly inspiring selfhood, a selfhood that can serve as an aspirational model for girls, boys, and adults as well. Women's college softball shows us why the popular phrase "Winning isn't everything; it's the only thing" is wrong. Winning is just part of what's important about competing. Thousands of events and specific moments over the course of the season have created this championship series between Washington and Florida State, and what the 2018 season means for coaches, fans, and the female athletes has been far greater than simply determining a champion. The season will *not* come down to one pitch or swing of the bat.

In 2014 the award-winning filmmaker Lauren Greenfield produced a three-minute video, #LikeAGirl, for Always, the feminine hygiene brand owned by Procter & Gamble. The video brilliantly shows cultural stereotypes about performing gender in the sports arena. As a social experiment, Greenfield held a fake casting-call with young women and men, with boys and girls, asking them to run, throw, and hit "like a girl." The women, men, and boys all perform in a silly, badly-done way, as if the phrase is simply derogatory. But the young girls run, throw, and hit as hard as they can, with pride and confidence and athleticism. Doing something "like a girl," for the girls, means doing it well and as best they can. When the women, men, and boys are brought back in front of the camera and shown how the young girls responded, they realize their mistake. When the director asks one young woman if she'd like to re-do what she believes a girl does, she says yes.

A sixty-second advertisement for the "Like a Girl" campaign debuted at the 2015 Super Bowl, and the ad won the 2015 Emmy award for the outstanding commercial of the year. The video, which has had well over a hundred million views, touched a chord (as did the ad), perhaps because it embarrasses those who know they perpetuate the stereotype of "you throw like a girl" as well as inspires them to re-think what girls, and women, can do. A college women's softball game does something similar to the video and advertisement. Watch a game and you'll see what I mean, particularly if you attend in person, where you get to witness up close that women throwing, running, sliding, and hitting look powerful, graceful, athletic.

In all ways, on the field and off, the female athletes simply crush it.

ONE

Play Ball

A stock market slump, post–Super Bowl hangover, and major snow storms may have marked early February for most Americans, deepening the blahs of winter, but excited softball fans were readying for the first weekend of Division I play, when coaching staffs, teams, and fans of those teams could all hope for success. Early-season losses might temper expectations by March, so this was the weekend to dream, or simply to rejoice that the women's college softball season was beginning once again.

When an outdoor sport opens in early February, most teams travel to play at warm-weather sites. At the Kajikawa Classic in Tempe, Arizona, on a perfect day for softball—temperatures in the 70s, light winds, sunshine—Brittany Gray of the University of Georgia delivered the first pitch of the season to Kiera Wright of San Diego State University. It was Thursday, February 8. On June 5, 118 days later, the 2018 Division I softball champion would be crowned.

A thousand miles south of Tempe, the Puerto Vallarta Challenge (PVC) opened thirty minutes later when Louisiana Tech took the field to play Nevada. The inspiration of Dave King, the founder of Fort Collins–based Triple Crown Sports, the PVC has a short and long history simultaneously. In 1996 Triple Crown Sports built a fastpitch softball field in Puerto Vallarta, desiring to put on a college tournament, but their planning got interrupted by the terrorist attacks on September 11, 2001. Having put the tournament on hold, Triple Crown decided in 2008 to try again, only to have the economy fall apart in the Great Recession. But King was patient, and in 2015 he got four teams—BYU, Nevada, Northern Colorado, and Southern Illinois—to come down to Puerto Vallarta, try it out, and give him some feedback. They liked it. "That first year," King said, "we had the tournament during the third week of February, and the schools suggested that the PVC should be on the first weekend. So then we started putting the word out that we would be hosting a two-weekend tournament for 2017. We had a great response and started the season with #1 Oklahoma versus #2 Auburn. ESPN decided that they should cover it, and the next thing we knew we had ESPN in Mexico."

Success for a specific college tournament can be measured by television

In the Puerto Vallarta Challenge, an event created by Colorado's Triple Crown Sports, U.S. college teams play on this Puerto Vallarta field that Triple Crown built and maintains. Local community teams play the rest of the year. Internationally, women's fastpitch softball is gaining popularity, and the return of softball to the 2020 Olympics in Tokyo will raise visibility. Courtesy Nate Chu.

exposure or attendance, but success can also be measured by intangibles. "If you go to the park at night during our college tournament," King said, "it has the atmosphere of America forty years ago. Kids, dogs, vendors, and fans wander around. The tournament is part of Puerto Vallarta's social fabric now." The community engagement extends far past the tournament's two weekends. King is particularly proud of Triple Crown's involvement with Puerto Vallarta itself: "We have maintained several fields down there for all these years, and we put in all the amenities: new lights, dugouts, and batting cages. We pay a full-time maintenance employee. We train all the officials for Puerto Vallarta's community leagues. Eighty-five community teams played there last year, in leagues for kids, for women, and for men. It's been a very successful outreach." As in the United States, women's fastpitch softball in Mexico has become increasingly popular. Their national women's team is currently ranked seventh in the world by the World Baseball Softball Confederation, and Mexico will have a shot at medaling when softball returns to the Olympics in 2020.

The 2018 Puerto Vallarta Challenge wasn't as glitzy as the 2017 version that paired the two preseason top-ranked teams. This time around, the field's highest ranked team was James Madison University, a program that emerged as a mid-major national power when they hired Mickey Dean as head coach in 2012 and won 237 games in the next five years. In 2016 they reached #7 in the late-season rankings and missed the Women's College World Series by a whisker: in the bottom of the seventh inning, down 3–2 to Louisiana State University in the deciding game of the super-regionals, JMU left the bases loaded. In 2017 JMU was 50–6 and thirteenth in the Ratings Percentage Index

(RPI) when the NCAA committee, in an insult to mid-major programs, denied the Dukes a chance to host a regional. In an eventful off-season, Mickey Dean had been hired away by Auburn University, a perennial national contender who plays in the powerful Southeastern Conference (SEC). Dean's long-time associate, Loren LaPorte, was promoted to head the JMU program.

Despite the off-season upheaval, fall ball for JMU, according to LaPorte, actually went great: "We only had three days after Coach Dean left before we began practice. We had games in two weeks. Our team was shocked, I will say that, and it wasn't what they prepared for in the summer, but as I told them, things like this in life happen. You have sudden change and adversity and you have to figure it out and move on." JMU had much to look forward to, with five of their top six hitters returning, as well as their top pitchers. And any team returning a star player such as Megan Good, the Schutt Sports/National Fastpitch Coaches Association Division I National Player of the Year for 2017, could be excited about their prospects. Good led the nation in victories in 2017 with a 38–3 record, shutting out fourteen teams on her way to being ranked third nationally with a 0.63 ERA. She also hit .383, with twelve home runs and fifty-eight RBI.

Megan Good exemplifies something that makes women's college softball so compelling, and that's the character issue. At Fort Defiance High School in Virginia, she played four years of varsity basketball and softball, but her best sport and first love was volleyball. Under Armour named her Honorable Mention All-American as a senior, but at 5'11", Good was undersized as an outside hitter for the top college volleyball programs. In softball, she was under-recruited because she didn't play on a high-profile travel ball team. But a mere sixteen miles away from her high school, at James Madison, Mickey Dean knew that Good's ceiling in softball would be high if she focused on it. He recruited her hard and she came to play for him, making an immediate impact when she was Second Team All-American as a freshman. But everyone who knows Megan Good says she's an even better person than an athlete.

Dick Halterman, the public address announcer for Fort Defiance High School's volleyball and basketball games, said of Good, in a story by Patrick Hite, that Good was the school's best athlete during her years there. But what really impressed him? "She was and still is an animal on the outside and a little kitten on the inside. Her heart is way bigger than those pitching muscles." Being a great athlete and a lovely person doesn't necessarily keep bad luck away, however, and JMU's off-season of drama worsened when in late January Megan Good was declared out for the season.

"We found out about her injury in November," LaPorte said. "It was a bone injury related to her knee, not an ACL or MCL." Uncertain about a prognosis, Good did rehab for two months, but in January the decision was made for surgery. "Doctors felt like it was going to be tough for Good to get

The impact of injuries: 2017 Schutt Sports/NFCA Player of the Year, James Madison University's Megan Good, was declared out for the season in January 2018, dashing JMU's hopes for a WCWS berth. Good is both an excellent hitter and dominant pitcher. The program looks forward to her return in 2019. Courtesy JMU Athletics.

through the entire season," LaPorte said, "and given that she is a senior, we didn't want her to go down during the season and have her career end that way. She opted for the surgery and a redshirt, so that she could come back and play in 2019." In any one-game showdown, JMU with Good in the circle would have an excellent chance to win, but now the team went from one likely to be a regional host in May to one likely not.

In any college softball season, twists and turns occur, and most of these are unknown in early February. Many teams don't have to count on one player, so they might be less impacted than James Madison if a star goes down. But twists and turns don't come just from injuries. No one can predict the freshman who becomes an All-American, or a seeing-eye single that sinks a favorite in a super-regional and boosts an underdog to the Women's College World Series. Coaches don't know yet how their players might or might not improve, or how the players will hold up under pressure, or whether the team will jell or fall apart under adversity. The season always brings surprises.

*   *   *

Pre-season rankings are mostly for publicity and fun. Some teams will be too highly regarded and others will fly under the radar. People make pre-season rankings by looking at who returns from the previous year's team and whether incoming freshmen might contribute immediately. But much happens to a team from June to January, particularly during the six weeks of practice and exhibition games called fall ball, which helps set the tone for the season.

Much of fall ball concerns individual skill building. Pitchers and hitters focus on mechanics, using the time to re-tool a swing or to understand how to get more spin on a breaking pitch. Freshmen discover that weight room workouts will be grueling. The team will scrimmage, which allows coaches to see individual skill improvement for their returnees, as well as to see how their newcomers stack up against college competition. Exhibition games continue the experiments, with coaches often moving players around, trying them in different positions on the field and in the batting order.

Skills cultivated during fall ball are also of the team-building kind; many coaches stress the importance of these skills for the success of their team the following spring. Tim Walton, who has shaped the University of Florida into one of the country's top programs, said in an interview with Eric Lopez that fall ball is important in that the returning veterans teach the young players the day-in, day-out work ethic. Walton emphasized how tricky this can be. "You want to recruit and develop the most competitive players that you can," he said, "but there's a fine line between their competitiveness and their ability to mesh and receive teammates for who they are, to show them the way without wrecking chemistry or ruining self-confidence." At Florida, and nearly all programs, the on-field and weight room activities are balanced by community service events. Last fall the Florida team delivered Thanksgiving baskets, visited the children's hospital, and volunteered at Special Olympics events on campus. The players had dinners weekly at Walton's house.

Walton emphasizes healthy eating, and fall ball is when the returning players are reminded of these lessons and newcomers are introduced to them. "What do you have to do to be an elite program? The little things," Walton said. "Nutritional excellence is key nowadays with the amount of pressure and stress on the bodies to play this game at such a high level. You're going to have to train yourself not only physically but mentally. You're going to have to sacrifice yourselves with some of the things you eat or drink and you're going to have to do a good job of putting that time into your bodies."

The University of Maine is decidedly not a national power like Florida, but their head coach, Michael Coutts, sounded remarkably like Walton when he described his goals for fall ball. Much time on the field, Coutts said, is spent on fundamentals and approaches—how the coaching staff likes to hit, pitch, play defense, and run the bases. Skill improvement is a priority. But fall ball is also used to familiarize freshmen with how the Maine program does things on and off the field.

Like every college softball coach I talked to, Coutts stressed that college is about growing the whole person. "On Mondays," he said, "players cannot wear any clothes that say Maine softball. We want them to wear normal clothes and be someone their peers see as not just an athlete. The girls are here to learn about life and become strong, energetic people who have a positive impact on their teammates and friends and in the community. We talk a lot about being the best teammate ever. That includes on and off the field." Coutts forms a Leadership Team to serve as mentors.

Because Orono, Maine, is a small town, the players are visible in the community. "They represent our school, the team, their parents, and themselves every minute of every day," Coutts said. "There is a certain way that we expect them to interact when they are not at practice. Who they are is really determined by how they act away from the softball field. I'm an old school person—I'll give you everything I have and in return I want the same from you. As I tell them, I want to be around good, positive people that I can trust. Winning isn't that important to me." By the way, the University of Maine sometimes wins, and always contends in, the America East Conference.

Tim Walton praised the senior leadership on his team this year and how they brought the team along through the fall. In the pre-season rankings, Florida came in at #2 in everyone's poll, right behind defending champion Oklahoma, who beat Florida in the title series last June. Oregon was the consensus #3, and different polls scattered the usual suspects—UCLA, Arizona, LSU, Florida State, Washington, Texas A&M—further down the top ten. In every year, some teams highly regarded in January drop by the wayside due to injury or lack of team cohesion or simply not being as good as people thought. In every year, new teams emerge.

*   *   *

In the America East, the Patriot League, the Summit League, and numerous other small conferences across the country, the conference tourney winner in May receives an automatic bid to the postseason NCAA tournament, but runner-up teams are not strong enough nationally to be given an at-large bid to the tournament. For Maine and hundreds of other schools who play in these conferences, these early weekends are about the joy of playing softball games again and about working on individual and team developmental skills. Experimenting with their lineups and their pitching staffs, coaches stress that they want to see improvement over these first eight weeks of the season, before league play begins.

For teams from the Power Five conferences—athletic conferences in the Football Bowl Subdivision whose member schools have the biggest budgets—or for mid-major teams who hope to gain an at-large bid if they don't win their conference tournament, opening weekend matters a great deal.

Some teams play five or six games, which may be 10 percent of their schedule. The Ratings Percentage Index (RPI) doesn't account for whether wins or losses come early or late, and the RPI come May is a big factor in determining at-large bids as well as seedings for the NCAA tournament. But here's an unacknowledged fact. If you play six games on opening weekend, it counts for far more than 10 percent of your RPI, because by the time conferences begin play in mid to late March, each conference has, more or less, an RPI. If you win or lose within your conference, therefore, the needle won't move much on your own RPI. That is, if you're in a powerful conference for softball such as the SEC or Pac-12, your winning or losing within the conference is relatively inconsequential. Your conference's overall play will already have largely determined your RPI.

The RPI is a source of controversy in all NCAA sports. A softball team's RPI is constructed in the following way: 25 percent of the ranking comes from a team's won-loss record; 50 percent comes from their opponents' won-loss records; 25 percent comes from the opponents' opponents' won-loss records. Such a formula is designed to factor in strength of schedule. But the RPI is only a formula based on numbers—a win is a win, and so beating a team 15–0 or 2–1 means the same; beating convincingly a team ranked #25 in the RPI actually can do less for you than playing the #3 ranked team in the RPI and losing 12–0. Numbers, in other words, don't necessarily show how well a team has played. There's widespread agreement in college sports that this 25–50–25 formula favors schools in powerful conferences and is meant to do so, because of the outsized power such conferences wield in the NCAA.

Climate determines softball's strongest conferences in a way that is not true of indoor sports such as basketball or volleyball. Warm-weather schools, early in softball's season, have an upper hand by being able to practice outdoors in January. Playing at home before league play begins is likewise a huge edge. Let me explain. Georgia won four of their five games at the Kajikawa Classic, losing only to Oregon, 8–3. The #25 ranked Bulldogs would surely rise in the rankings off such a weekend. They were scheduled to play twenty-four of their next twenty-six games at home, with only one away doubleheader at a mediocre Winthrop team. If you're a northern team, you don't really have a choice about scheduling home or away because for the first six or seven weeks your field is unplayable. You play teams at neutral sites, or you play away games. In 2017, on their way to a 54–3 record before the tournament began, the University of Minnesota played thirty-three straight away games, including eighteen as a true visiting team and fifteen at neutral sites. Men's college baseball, as a way to get around the advantage that playing at home confers, adjusts the numbers for the RPI, giving .7 points for a home win, 1.0 for a neutral site win, and 1.3 points for an away win. Softball has yet to follow that baseball model, but imagine how doing so would have changed

Minnesota's already high RPI if their fifteen wins in those games counted as 1.3 points each. Moreover, it would change the RPI of every team that they played, and the same would be true of all their Big Ten opponents who play constantly on the road. If Georgia, Texas A&M, Arizona, or other national contenders who play almost their entire non-conference schedule at home were only getting .7 points for their home wins, the teams would adjust their schedules.

A way to partially neutralize the weather issue would be to move the softball schedule, which is the earliest for any college sport played outdoors in the spring. Amanda Lehotak, head coach at Penn State University, thinks a change in the calendar would reap numerous benefits. "Moving the schedule back three weeks or so would help the kids, body-wise and education-wise," Lehotak said. "And you could then have some super-fun matches. UCLA at Michigan for a three-game series in April would be a blast. Or Florida at Minnesota. The fans in those communities deserve to see glamour programs come to them."

Carol Bruggeman is the executive director for the National Fastpitch Coaches Association (NFCA). Asked about weather issues and competitive balance, Bruggeman also talked about changing the calendar, but she brought up the risks. "ESPN isn't going to cover the Women's College World Series the same way if it's moved back several weeks, and college administrators might be reluctant to keep players on campus if they believe their schools can't afford it." Bruggeman may be correct about ESPN. Such a view gives, however, tremendous power to a sports broadcasting network, even if that entity has helped grow the sport.

The College Baseball World Series concludes three weeks after the softball season ends; in essence, the men have the desirable calendar. ESPN televises baseball's NCAA tournament—regional sites, super-regionals, the championship—much as they do women's softball, and so to run baseball and softball concurrently would not work for television. Is there a solution? Gender equity advocates might suggest that women's softball and men's baseball should alternate beginning early, even with the hassle that changing dates would bring.

Arguments against change—in nearly any scenario—usually focus on present-day success and are supported by those who benefit from the status quo. The inequity in college softball between southern and northern conferences is real, and not just because of issues such as whether a team practices indoors or out, or has to travel or gets to play non-league home games, but because all those issues strongly affect recruiting—highly recruited players from northern states are much more likely to go south to play outdoors and somewhere warm, than girls from warmer climates are likely to head north.

Softball's claim to develop the whole person and to emphasize the ac-

The University of Maine plays a home game, finally, in April. Note the snow piles, the heavy jackets, and the artificial turf necessary to get a field ready under such conditions. Softball is an outdoors "spring" sport that begins the second week of February, making for much travel and few home games for northern teams. Molly Flowers pitches for Maine. Courtesy Maine Athletic Department.

ademic as well as the athletic strongly argues for moving the calendar to a later date. In men's college sports, progress for a team is measured primarily by wins or a team's competitiveness on the field. But because softball coaches stress to their players that excellence happens not just on the field but in all areas of life, academics matter greatly in softball culture. Academic rankings for all college sports teams are publicized, and the results might surprise fans who only follow men's sports. Upper Iowa University, whose softball program plays in DII, posted a team GPA of 3.813! The University of Alabama's softball team not only reached the super-regionals in 2017, but the players combined for a 3.647 GPA. Coaches' bios on their university websites routinely mention the academic success of their teams and individual players. Here's one of my favorite examples of softball's priorities. Under "Career Honors" on the team roster page for Tennessee shortstop Meghan Gregg, the following are the first three lines: SEC Spring Academic Honor Roll—2017; Easton/NFCA Scholar-Athlete—2017; CoSIDA Academic All-American (3rd Team)—2017. It's not until line four that you discover she was a USA Softball Player of the Year Finalist last year, and subsequent lines tell us she was First Team All-American and the reigning SEC Player of the Year.

Maurice Williams, the Sports Information Director for softball at Tennessee, is responsible for the program's website, but he modestly took no credit for the priorities demonstrated on these bio pages, saying that he "just followed the folks who were here before me." If you're a young girl playing on a travel ball team, and you idolize Meghan Gregg and see her academic achievements listed before her athletic achievements, how motivating is it to study? Very motivating, I would guess, particularly when academic achievement is stressed by everyone around you as part of softball culture. And it's not just Tennessee or one SID writing bios that creates this culture. It's everyone. In public and in private. Kate Drohan, head coach at Northwestern, once shrugged off my comment about a particular player's performance by saying, "yes, she's not having her best year, but she's a great person, she's been accepted to med school, and she's going to be a great surgeon. It's ok."

With a later calendar, players wouldn't have to be studying on the road week after week, if they could occasionally play at home or travel regionally. In this second week of February, freshmen were learning and returning players were being reminded about the demands of traveling, playing multiple games, and still doing all their schoolwork. If they had essays due or tests to take on Monday or Tuesday, they had to compartmentalize and get that work done. Northern teams were going to have to balance this travel and academics for numerous straight weeks to come.

*   *   *

Traditionally strong programs dominated on opening weekend. Of the top-ten teams, only Arizona dropped a game, and that was to #21 ranked Oklahoma State. The top-ranked Oklahoma Sooners, two-time defending champions with nearly their entire roster returning, rolled through five games at the Grand Canyon Kickoff Classic in Phoenix. The second-ranked Florida Gators shut out their first four opponents, including an exciting 2–0 win against #16 Michigan, and ended the weekend with a 14–3 romp over a good University of South Florida team.

If any top-ten team surprised, it was Oregon because of how they won. In 2017 Oregon played a relatively weak non-conference schedule; Head Coach Mike White didn't know what he had with his pitching staff, having graduated Cheridan Hawkins, who exited the Oregon program as a three-time All-American and three-time Pac-12 Pitcher of the Year. Sophomore Megan Kleist had shown promise, and White was bringing in two highly touted freshmen pitchers in Maggie Balint and Miranda Elish, but no coach wants to see untested freshmen getting rocked—they didn't, and Oregon won its first thirty-five games. But this year, returning a staff among the nation's best, Oregon stepped up the quality of competition, and at least for one weekend they showed that their bats might be even better than their pitching. Even though they graduated two hitting stars in Nikki Udria and Danica Mercado, Oregon scored seventy-three runs in their six wins, which included two against SEC teams Georgia and Missouri and a win over a good Fresno State team. As a team, they hit .472 with seventeen home runs (including five by Gwen Svekis and four by DJ Sanders). But their most amazing stat for the weekend was their OnBase + Slugging Percentage (OPS), the statistic that is usually considered the most significant for hitting. Baseball's individual major league leader for OPS is usually around 1.0; as a team, Oregon had an OPS for the weekend of 1.328.

The results from the opening weekend didn't suggest, however, that Oregon was going to dominate the Pac-12 conference. Fifth-ranked University of Washington Huskies outscored their five overmatched opponents 70–3. Last year they rode the arm of Taran Alvelo to a high ranking and a top finish at the WCWS, but didn't have the pitching depth to win the title. Head Coach Heather Tarr brought in an Australian with international experience, Gabbie Plain, to bolster the staff, and she looked like the real deal, giving up no earned runs in two games. Sophomore Samantha Manti was also strong, looking to improve upon her freshmen campaign. Equally impressive as the Huskies was fourth-ranked UCLA, a storied program with eleven NCAA softball championships, though most of them were before the SEC emerged as a conference to challenge the Pac-12. UCLA's key 2017 graduate was Second Team All-American shortstop Delaney Spaulding; they were also looking in 2018 to bolster their pitching staff, which lacked some depth past Rachel Garcia. UCLA always recruits great classes, and the new freshmen were no exception, led by shortstop Brianna Perez and pitcher Holly Azevedo. On the weekend, Perez went 11–18 with two homers, a triple, and two doubles, for a slugging percentage of 1.167. In the circle Azevedo went 3–0, giving up only one earned run. Two other freshmen, Kinsley Washington and Aaliyah Jordan, started and contributed. With play like that from their freshmen, UCLA looked already like a team that could have a deep playoff run, or even win it all.

For geeky softball fans, opening weekend is the first chance not only to follow your favorite team or see how dominant the top programs are, but to compare conferences for the new season. The Pac-12 looked deep, and not only with Oregon, UCLA, Washington, and Arizona. #19 Arizona State won five of its six games, including a win against a resurgent Nebraska program; unranked Oregon State beat ranked teams BYU and Oklahoma State, as well as Missouri, losing only to Georgia in a 4–1 weekend; California won its four games, though against lesser opponents. The SEC flexed its muscles, as usual. Florida, Texas A&M, LSU, Alabama, Tennessee—all teams ranked in the top eleven—swept their games, and Georgia, South Carolina, and Mississippi State got off to hot starts. But perhaps the biggest surprise in the SEC was the performance of Auburn University.

Women's sports have relatively few scandals, but one did occur in 2017 at Auburn, a scandal that culminated when NFCA Hall of Fame coach Clint Myers grudgingly retired. In March during the season, his son Corey, an assistant coach with the team, had abruptly left the program, citing personal reasons that included spending more time with his family. But Auburn's own investigation of its softball program led it to ban Corey Myers from campus for pursuing inappropriate relationships with members of the team. Several players alleged in a Title IX complaint that Clint Myers had created an atmosphere to protect his son. Clint's retirement soon followed. After a coaching search, Mickey Dean from James Madison University was hired.

The off-season coaching changes meant no one was sure how Auburn's season might begin. Under Myers, Auburn was known first for their hitting, second for their defense, and last for their pitching, one reason being, perhaps, that they never had a true pitching coach. Wanting to keep pitch counts low, Myers' staff had preached a "pitch to contact" strategy, trying to make batters hit slower speed offerings or hit weak grounders or fly balls because of location. Dean serves as his own pitching coach, and he brought in a different philosophy, a "strike them all out" mentality. He wanted his pitchers to develop arm strength and speed, as well as to have a strikeout pitch that they could rely on. Led by returning veterans Kaylee Carlson and Makayla Martin, Auburn's pitching staff on the weekend threw five straight shutouts and gave up only one unearned run in six games. Dean's new philosophy was off to a strong start.

It's become a cliche to emphasize the journey, to stress adherence to a process, but simple wisdom only turns into social cliche when it's useful and right. "Sports remain a great metaphor for life's more difficult lessons," wrote Susan Casey, when she was editor-in-chief of *Sports Illustrated Women*. "It was through athletics that many of us first came to understand that fear can be tamed; that on a team the whole is more than the sum of its parts; and that the ability to be heroic lies, to a surprising degree, within." Whatever the record on opening weekend, players and coaches had more tournaments and the start of league play to look forward to. Players and coaches together would tackle how to tame fear and nerves, how to tamp down individual ego for the betterment of the team. College softball's 2018 journey had begun.

Two

It's the Speed, Stupid

In the iconic if schmaltzy 1989 film *Field of Dreams*, an Iowa farmer hears a voice repeatedly saying "If you build it, he will come." In his corn fields, Ray Kinsella builds a baseball diamond, hoping that it might connect him to his father, John, a devoted baseball fan but not a devoted father. Shoeless Joe Jackson and other dead baseball players emerge from the cornfields to play, and Ray's father, eventually, shows up to have a game of catch with his son.

The *Field of Dreams* film set is now an Iowa tourist attraction. In the mid–1990s two brothers, Rick and Jeff Odekirk, both former baseball players, had a dream to build and operate a family recreational facility that would accommodate youth baseball, fastpitch softball, and adult slowpitch softball. The brothers' dream became a reality in January of 1998; the Odekirks opened the first Big League Dreams Sports Park in Cathedral City, California, near Palm Springs, with scaled-down replicas of famous ballparks such as Chicago's Wrigley Field, Boston's Fenway Park, and New York's Yankee Stadium. This complex of five fields is home to the Mary Nutter Collegiate Classic, the nation's largest and most prestigious preseason college softball tournament, held over two weekends in February.

Nothing against Fenway, Wrigley, or Yankee Stadium, but the play there doesn't match the speed of the game here. If you've never seen a women's softball game, or only watched on television, the speed is hard to comprehend. Fast and powerful athletes play on a Little League sized field—the distance between bases is sixty feet in women's softball—and everything from game strategies to what kind of players take the field reflect this sixty-foot distance.

In 2015, the fastest baseball player from home to first, ninety feet in the major leagues and college and high school baseball, was Billy Burns at 3.85 seconds. But if you count a drag bunt attempt, the closest thing to a slap in softball, the fastest run down to first base in 2015 was Billy Hamilton, the speedster of the Cincinnati Reds. Hamilton burned to first in just 3.52 seconds to beat out a drag bunt against the Minnesota Twins in late June. Infielders have to play in when batters such as Burns or Hamilton come to bat, and speed causes miscues in fielding and throwing when infielders rush. But how is Hamilton's time compared to women getting down the line in softball? Very, very slow.

Caitlin Lowe, former star at the University of Arizona and leadoff hitter for the national team, is considered by many experts to be the fastest softball player in the world. Lowe, a left-handed slap hitter, has been clocked at 2.55 seconds from home to first. (Numerous players have run in the 2.6 second range.) An infielder who can field a ball off Lowe's bat and throw her out at first would, in the same amount of time, have thrown Hamilton out on that drag bunt attempt by 25 feet! It's hard to believe if you've never watched a women's softball game in person. Believe it.

When I go to a baseball game, I'm always struck by how far back the infielders play, the shortstop and second baseman often parked on the outfield grass, the corner infielders well behind the base paths. Balls hit up the middle or in the holes can be caught, and the infielders typically have time to set their feet and make a strong throw in time to first base. On a routine two-hopper, a baseball shortstop looks like he's dawdling, as he slowly takes the ball out of his glove, sometimes adjusts his feet to get momentum toward first, and then fires over to the bag. In softball, infielders don't play back. And when a fast slapper is up, or someone bunting, the corners are often no more than thirty feet from home plate. No one, even when the batter isn't fast, can be casual.

Women's fastpitch softball debuted in 1933 at the Chicago World's Fair, and for the next forty years was played seriously and competitively by thousands of company and city teams. Only in the 1980s did slapping become part of the women's game, when Gayle Blevins, who took Indiana University to three Women's College World Series and the University of Iowa to four, began her Hall of Fame career by crafting teams around speed. "I always loved working with the speed game," she recalled. "Stealing, slapping, running plays, pressuring the defense, making things happen … this was always a part of our offense. As we well know, speed never slumps."

In the 1980s at Indiana, Blevins took average righty hitters who were fast runners and converted them to lefty slappers. "I remember working on convincing them how much better they would be offensively and what an addition to our program this would be. The very best early slapper I trained was Karleen Moore from Boulder, Colorado. In 1986 she led the nation in hits and was integral to our third place finish at the Women's College World Series." To slap, the hitter doesn't anchor her back foot and swing through the pitch the way a typical hitter would. Instead, she slides her front foot back slightly to time the pitcher's motion and to open up space for the back foot, which she then brings forward and plants, aimed at the left side of the infield. She chokes up on the bat, wanting more control, and keeps the barrel of the bat behind her hands. As she contacts the ball, her front foot is moving forward, so that she's beginning to run. She's also only fifty-seven feet at that point from first base, three feet closer that can make the difference between safe or out.

Slapping has multiple forms. For the slap-bunt, the slapper moves through the box and drops a quick bunt down; unlike baseball, a five-foot bunt by a slapper is a sure base hit. A common form of slapping is the infield slap: a soft roller in a hole or a high bouncer that she can beat out. The final addition to the slapping repertoire is the power-slap, something hit hard and intended to make it through the infield. Occasionally the power-slap turns into a line drive, which, if the outfield is playing in, can go for a triple.

Being a good slapper is taking advantage of opportunities. Right before slappers enter the box, they quickly assess the defensive strategy against them. Slappers might bunt or soft slap if the infield is at normal depth. If the infield is in and the outfield back, slappers might choose to push a soft fly to the edge of the outfield grass or hit a high chop, depending on the pitch location. If all the fielders are up close, slappers might power-slap, a scary prospect for infielders close to home plate when the ball comes off the bat. Reading defenses, and then pitches, is key for a slapper.

A few lefty slappers also become gifted at hitting away. Such athletes are difficult to defend and difficult to pitch to, because pitching coaches don't know when they're giving the sign for pitch and location what the batter will do. When Haylie McCleney was young, she watched older players slap and tried to mimic them, but her coaches at Alabama,

The shorter base paths for softball make speed much more important than it is in baseball. Former University of Arizona great Caitlin Lowe is shown here slapping while playing for the USA national team. Lowe gets down to first base in 2.55 seconds, a full second faster than the speediest major league baseball player. Courtesy USA Softball.

Patrick Murphy and Alyson Habetz, broke down her swing and worked with her in the batting cages, teaching her to hit away as well as to slap. McCleney became a three-time First Team All-American, and ended her career in 2016 not only as the storied program's all-time leader in batting average at .447, but third in slugging percentage at .690. Her power numbers went up each year, and she finished her career with an incredible on-base + slugging percentage of 1.259 (remember, baseball's major league leader is often under 1.0). How did she choose whether to slap or hit away? "It came down to reading defenses," she said. "If I felt like a particular team was weak on the left side or if the shortstop was respecting my power and playing deep, I would more than likely slap. If the shortstop was in, not respecting my power, I would more than likely swing away and try to hit something hard past her. If the pitcher was throwing a lot of drop balls, I always felt more comfortable hitting away. Even if I missed the down pitch, I still had the speed to leg out an infield single." Softball, McCleney said, "is definitely a constant chess match. That's what makes it amazing!" McCleney, by the way, owned a 4.0 cumulative grade-point average in exercise science throughout her college career, and was twice the *Academic* All-American player of the year.

If Blevins' Indiana teams demonstrated that lefty slapping could contribute to an effective speed attack, the University of Arizona teams under Mike Candrea in the 1990s showed that a mix of speed and power could be devastating. With Tucson's desert air and altitude, deep fly balls carried for home runs; the desert heat also baked the infield so that slappers could chop grounders that would bounce high and make it near-impossible to be thrown out at first. Larry Ray, an assistant under Candrea, became renowned as an instructor of slapping, and the Wildcats won five national championships in the 1990s. Despite changes in the last decade that have favored power hitting, slapping has remained prominent. The bat manufacturer Demarini has even designed a bat specifically for slappers, the DeMarini CFX Slapper, with a long barrel weighted more to the hands to give optimal control and manipulation.

In those early years, slappers were usually transformed during their college careers; now, you'll have young players in travel ball who are refining their skills in the short game. Emily Allard, who played shortstop for Northwestern University from 2011–14, is such an example. She used her speed and slapping expertise to set the school's all-time record for most stolen bases as well as to produce a career batting average of .402 that included a single-season record-breaking .491 average during her sophomore season. Growing up, Allard was a right-handed power hitter and pitcher. She began the switch to a lefty slapper at fifteen years of age, when her legendary travel ball coach, Phil Mumma of northern California's Sorcerer Gold, foresaw that Allard had a higher ceiling by changing pretty much everything, from position to the side of the plate she hit on. It wasn't easy for Allard to make the conversion to the speed game, but she grew to love it, and she's carried her talents and dedication to two post-college careers, playing professionally for the Chicago Bandits and starting her own company, the softball academy Be the Momentum, which focuses on speed and slapping. One of Emily Allard's favorite lines? "I love slapping because if I do it right, the infielders have to be perfect to get me out."

Slapping techniques and the short base paths make speed crucial in softball. Oklahoma State's head coach Kenny Gajewski, a former baseball player and baseball coach, said to me, "Coming from men's baseball, I spent my entire first year of coaching trying to figure out how everything had to be adjusted to this speed." And, he went on, he meant everything, from teaching fundamentals of fielding to who to include in his lineup to game strategies.

At Indiana in the 1980s, Hall of Fame coach Gayle Blevins introduced slapping and the speed game to women's college softball. She is shown here coaching Iowa, who she took to four WCWS appearances, including three straight from 1995 to 1997. The player is Mindy Heidgerken. Courtesy hawkeyesports.com.

* * *

What athletes wear has long been a cultural, as well as sports, issue. Female volleyball players, for example, wear short, tight spandex shorts, or a bikini for beach volleyball, while male players wear looser shorts that end just above the knee. Male golfers typically wear long pants—and such pants are required on the PGA tour—while female golfers are encouraged to wear skirts or shorts unless the weather is too cold. Decades ago, female softball players wore shorts and a loose top while playing. By 2000, some women's college softball teams were wearing full uniforms, in part as a way to distinguish collegiate ball from travel ball. The uniforms, however, were slightly re-worked men's baseball uniforms, baggy and saggy, and did not fit properly, particularly the pants. Once manufacturers began designing with the female athlete in mind, the full-length uniform quickly became the norm. But the emphasis is on athlete more than gender, as function triumphs over fashion. All players want to look sharp in their uniforms, but softball games are, in a sense, a celebration of what the body can do, not what the body looks like. Softball uniforms are revealing, but they reveal muscles and suggest power.

The same weekend I was watching athletic women play softball at the Mary Nutter Classic, *Sports Illustrated* was publishing their issue that makes the distinction between function and fashion all the more meaningful. The potential good news for women's sports fans? *Sports Illustrated* had a woman on the cover. The definite bad news? She was Danielle Herrington, a model not an athlete. Arguments about what photos of scantily clad women "mean" to viewers have been seemingly endless, with some people saying that such photos are demeaning to women, and others saying that a woman who chooses to reveal her body proudly has agency and asserts a woman's control of her sexuality. I certainly understand when many women say that sexy and empowered can go together, but wherever we might come down on the appropriateness of bikini photos, what gets lost each year when the swimsuit issue appears is the sexism of *Sports Illustrated* in general.

Though proclaiming on their website that they delve into "sports and the human spirit that makes us who we are," and that they are "committed to providing sports fans with a deeper, richer understanding," *Sports Illustrated* doesn't report well on women *playing* sports. The fifty-six covers of *Sports Illustrated* in 2017 demonstrate this (fifty-six covers because two weeks had three different covers). Women adorn the cover in only four of those weeks: in one, the "Gatorade High School Athletes of the Year" cover, Sydney McLaughlin shares the cover as she smiles while "hurdling" a non-existent hurdle; in a second, the "protest" cover, Candace Parker from the WNBA is one of ten sports figures and is not prominently placed; in a third, Sloane Stevens has the entire cover to herself, a rarity, but the photo is not an action shot of her playing tennis, showing instead Stevens holding her U.S. Open trophy and smiling broadly, looking composed and serene. Women (or a woman) are most prominent in the three covers devoted to the supermodel Kate Upton, shown basically naked in the Swimsuit Issue. Stud female athletes competing aggressively? Non-existent.

Many pieces on female athletes, and not just by *Sports Illustrated*, are feel-good stories that discuss, for example, how a WNBA star balances raising kids with playing the game. The media sometimes seems less interested in powerful female athletes performing than in what female athletes look like and do off the field. In the late 1990s, women's sports fans thought the times might be a-changin.' At the 1996 Summer Olympic Games in Atlanta, United States women's teams won gold medals in basketball, soccer, softball, and gymnastics. Dot Richardson, the former UCLA star who was the 1980s NCAA Player of the Decade, left her orthopedic residency to play shortstop for the inaugural Olympics softball team and she became a poster child for women's sports. This "Year of the Woman," as it became known, helped launch a new magazine, *Sports Illustrated Women/Sport*, which appeared in spring of 1997, a magazine aimed at women and written predominantly by women.

The first few issues were offered as trial runs; in March of 2000, the magazine now calling itself *Sports Illustrated for Women* began appearing every two months, covering women's sports primarily and targeting an audience of women eighteen to thirty-four years old who had a passion for sports. By 2002 *Sports Illustrated for Women* had a website, a circulation of 400,000, and a jump in ad pages of more than 25 percent—its revenues had increased in two years by nearly 75 percent. In 2002, the magazine received a nomination for General Excellence from the *National Magazine Awards*. December of that year marked its last print run. The mass media corporation that owns *Sports Illustrated*, Time, Inc., said publicly that the women's version was not proving economically viable.

* * *

Away from Palm Springs, a story was unfolding to determine which of the Power-Five conferences looked to be number four and which number five—or, less politely, the Atlantic Coast Conference and the Big Ten were playing to see who might sit at the bottom of the Power-Five conferences this year. The ACC–Big Ten Challenge (or Big Ten–ACC Challenge as it is called in alternating years) began in 1999 as an ESPN made-for-television men's basketball series between the two conferences that consider themselves tops in the country in that sport. Each year half the games are played at Big Ten sites and half at ACC sites. In 2016 the two conferences decided to extend this series to softball, though ESPN doesn't televise the games and weather restrictions make it that no Big Ten team ever hosts. The two conferences are also behind the SEC, Pac-12, and Big 12 when it comes to softball.

In 2017, ACC powerhouse Florida State went 21–2 in the conference but no other ACC team was ranked in the top thirty of the RPI. FSU graduated off that team one of their all-time great pitchers, Jessica Burroughs, the ACC Pitcher of the Year in 2016 and 2017, but she had been replaced by Florida Atlantic transfer Kylee Hanson, a redshirt senior whose knee injury cost her the 2017 year, but who was Second Team All-American in 2016. Beyond FSU, the league for 2018 had expectations of more balance, with traditionally strong programs such as Louisville and Notre Dame returning to form. The Big Ten has been, in recent years, primarily a two-team conference, with Minnesota and Michigan perennial top-fifteen teams but no one else. Both programs were graduating First Team All-American pitchers in Sara Groenewegen and

Megan Betsa, and so it appeared in the off-season as if the conference might take a further dip. But the first weekend of action had given fans of the Big Ten cause for optimism.

Former great programs appeared headed in the right direction: Northwestern went 4–1 at the Kajikawa Classic, losing only to #7 ranked Arizona; Nebraska went 5–1 at the same tournament, beating two ranked teams in BYU and Utah, with a loss only to a ranked Arizona State team. Ohio State went 5–0 at the Florida Atlantic "First Pitch" Classic with pitcher Shelby Mc-Combs posting a 3–0 record with a 0.34 earned-run average. All looked better than their 2017 teams. Michigan and Minnesota likewise looked strong. Behind sophomore hurler Amber Fiser, who went 14–0 as a freshman, and catcher Kendyl Lindaman, off a campaign that notched her Big 10 Player of the Year and Freshman of the Year, the Gophers went 5–0 in the SportCo Kickoff Classic in Las Vegas. Though Michigan only went 3–2 on their opening weekend, they looked to have a replacement for Betsa in their touted freshman pitcher Meghan Beaubien. Growing up near Ann Arbor in Newport, Michigan, Beaubien made known her desire to play for her hometown team when she was still a pre-teen. A three-time Gatorade Player of the Year

Highly-touted freshman pitcher Meghan Beaubien grew up dreaming about playing for her local University of Michigan program. In her first game, she no-hit Georgia State. She went on to lead the nation in victories with thirty-three and was a top-three finalist for Freshman Player of the Year. Courtesy Daryl Marshke/ Michigan Photography.

for the state of Michigan, a three-time High School All-American, Beaubien made her college debut with a six-inning no-hitter against Georgia State. Few programs hand the ball to a freshman pitcher when facing a powerhouse, but Michigan's legendary head coach Carol Hutchins did just that the next day when she threw Beaubien against #2 Florida. Though she lost, Beaubien pitched well, giving up only two runs on four hits.

National attention to the ACC–Big Ten Challenge was focused on the action in Tallahassee, where Florida State and Notre Dame were taking on Minnesota and Michigan. Beaubien continued her solid work, posting a 2–0 record with a 0.48 ERA and 12 strikeouts in 14.2 innings pitched. She threw a complete-game two-hit shutout at #8 Florida State, taking a perfect game into the seventh inning, and she beat Notre Dame. Michigan split their four games, but Minnesota lost all four of theirs, exceeding their three regular season losses from all of last year. Was this one weekend where their bats went a bit quiet and the pitchers were just a little off, or did this signify that there might be a changing of the guard in the Big Ten?

The results of the Challenge certainly suggested that the ACC was the stronger league, borne out in the overall results where the ACC teams went 26–14 in their match-ups. Louisville and North Carolina split their games 2–2 against Ohio State and Northwestern, and ACC teams Boston College, North Carolina State, Georgia Tech, and Pittsburgh all likewise split their series. What surprised many occurred at the lowest profile site. One of the big stories in the ACC for 2018 was that Duke University, a new program, would be playing their first games. With financial resources, a high academic reputation, and name clout, Duke would be looking to emerge in future years under Head Coach Marissa Young, when their very young team would have gained some experience. But Duke went 4–0 against Penn State and Purdue in Durham, North Carolina, as did their fellow ACC team Virginia Tech. Duke will likely need many years to become a powerhouse, but on this second weekend of the softball year, they were celebrating not only the opening of softball at their new facility, but celebrating some wins.

* * *

I followed opening weekend of the softball season by keeping track of games on my computer; on the second weekend I watched games in person at the Mary Nutter Collegiate Classic. An attraction of attending is that between innings you get to look out to the west and view the rugged beauty of the San Jacinto Mountains looming ten thousand feet high. Unlike being at a university site, where you plop down in a seat to watch an entire game, at this event, with its multiple fields, you can catch a few innings of a game here, a few innings there. Teams were everywhere, changing fields, warming up behind the fences, all in their colorful uniforms identifying their school.

The Mary Nutter Classic succeeds in part because it rarely rains in Palm Springs in February, particularly compared to Florida or the South. Rain can mean game cancellations as well as delays in the schedule. This weekend was warm during the days and cool in the evenings, pretty ideal both for viewing and playing. In Minnesota, early in April, I've watched games dressed in my warmest winter jacket, gloves, and a knit hat. Fans in the South or desert Southwest are sometimes sweating buckets in their shorts and t-shirts during May. But this weekend's weather passed the Goldilocks test.

Arkansas softball, in particular, was grateful for the weather. Arkansas came to the Mary Nutter Classic having had all their games the previous weekend washed out by rain, so they were opening against teams that had already played. Arkansas had a breakthrough year in 2017, Courtney Deifel's second year as head coach, winning thirty-one games, reaching the SEC tournament, and then getting a berth in the NCAA tournament. Deifel was seeing a steady progression. "In our first year here," Deifel said, "the players sometimes didn't think they could do it. But they came out of that year hungry, ready to work hard and wanting to take the next step. Last year, they saw they can compete with the best. We're no longer the program that SEC teams think they have a breather with. That's our new standard. I'm excited for this year, to see the players compete and to come into their own."

Arkansas returned nearly all of its roster, though Nicole Schroeder and her seventeen home runs graduated. But power was no issue this weekend; they hit seven dingers. The talent level had risen, as they started four freshmen in their opening game, including outfielder Hannah McEwen, designated player Linnie Malkin, who homered twice, and the all-freshmen battery of winning pitcher Mary Haff and catcher Kayla Green. Haff and sophomore Autumn Storms made up a strong pitching duo in the desert, as Arkansas swept its five games.

Two Pac-12 teams playing in the Mary Nutter Classic this weekend continued their unbeaten starts to the season. The Cal Bears extended their record to 10–0. By the end of the weekend, Cal had five players hitting above .400: Kobie Pettis, Lindsay Rood, Sabrina Nunez, Mikayla Coelho, and Bradie Fillmore. They showed increased pitching depth, as last year's ace, Zoe Conley, had been joined by Fresno State transfer Kamalani Dung—both pitchers were 5–0 with ERAs under 1.00 so far this season. UCLA and its freshmen continued their hot start, likewise extending their record to 10–0.

Kirk Walker, currently an assistant coach at UCLA, was the head softball coach for Oregon State University when he began to consider creating his own tournament, which became the Mary Nutter Classic. "At Oregon State," Walker said, "we were traveling all the time during the early part of the year, and I thought 'wouldn't it be great to host a tournament.' When I was thinking about a location, I thought of this facility, which was pretty new at the time, and this valley [the Coachella Valley], which had been a supporter of other sports and events. There was no better place in terms of the weather in February. My first priority was to have UCLA and Arizona; the national team preparing for the 2004 Olympics was doing a tour, so I invited them; when I had those three teams locked in, I went after other strong teams, particularly when the coaches were friends of mine. Everyone bought in to the concept of the event and was excited to come. The planning for that first tournament took two years."

The tournament began in February of 2004 with sixteen teams from across the country. Walker soon had a waiting list. The universities who came wanted to come back, not just because the weather meant they could get all their games in but because they enjoyed the fan support. Palm Springs is a destination location in February, and so teams' fan bases, not just parents, would come to make a vacation out of watching softball. And the Big League Dreams Complex lies in between a hub of metropolitan areas that have strongly supported women's softball over the years: Los Angeles, Phoenix, and Las Vegas.

In his eighteen years at Oregon State, Walker became the winningest coach in program history, leading the team in 2005 to its first league title, the first for any OSU women's sports program, and in 2006 to their first and only appearance in the Women's College World Series. When Walker left Oregon State in 2012 to return to UCLA, he wanted to keep the Mary Nutter Classic. Oregon State, who had benefited financially but had not been involved with managing the event, was fine with that. Walker has had tempting offers from other locations to move the event. He has turned them all down. No new location, he said, has those beautiful mountains to look at. He became the most animated when he talked about the tournament's impact on the area. "The coolest thing for me," Walker said, with strong emotion in his voice, "is that the whole Coachella Valley has taken great pride in this and the city of Cathedral City has become a major backer of the event. We surpass most of the events done in the valley. The Chamber of Commerce is a big backer because of the revenue we bring in for the local businesses." Before the first pitch of the first game, the Cathedral City city council stood in front of home plate with Walker. The mayor praised the event, thanked the fans for coming out, and thanked Walker for his vision of creating such a tournament.

THREE

California Dreamin'

In an interview, the baseball legend Ted Williams, considered by many the best hitter who ever played, made a point that has been repeated millions of times: hitting a baseball is the hardest thing to do in sports. As Williams said, "a round ball, round bat, curves, sliders, knuckleballs, and a ball coming in at 90 miles to 100 miles an hour, it's a pretty lethal thing." Williams' own experience should have taught him something different: hitting a softball is even harder. At least for a baseball player.

On two separate occasions in the 1960s, in exhibition games in Waterbury, Connecticut, Williams batted against the softball icon Joan Joyce. In a game situation, Joyce struck out Williams; in a batting practice session, he didn't hit the ball solidly once. Great baseball hitters facing great softball pitchers has become the stuff of softball lore, mostly because the hitters don't even get a sniff of the ball. After the championship softball game at the U.S. Olympic Festival in 1981, the festival organizers arranged for Kathy Arendsen, who pitched for the top amateur team in the country, the Raybestos Brakettes, to face off against Reggie Jackson, Mr. October. She blew fifteen straight pitches by him. There are more such stories.

Not only baseball players in that era had trouble hitting softball pitchers; the softball hitters couldn't do much, either. The epitome of dominant pitching at the college level occurred in 1991, when two very good teams, Creighton and Utah, went thirty-one innings until Creighton scored to win 1–0. Older coaches and fans comment frequently about "the old days" when so many games—particularly between strong teams in league play or in the NCAA tournament—ended 1–0 or 2–1. It often took a walk, an error, and a ground ball out to get the game's only run across home plate. In 1984 UCLA's aptly named Debbie Doom threw 102 straight scoreless innings.

Beginning in 1987, when the pitching rubber was moved from forty to forty-three feet away from the plate, the NCAA has adopted various rules that have lessened pitching's dominance. A yellow ball with raised red seams and a harder core was introduced, which hitters could see better and hit farther. A rule was initiated to prohibit pitchers from leaping in the air and to prohibit them from doing a "crowhop"—a step, re-plant, and throw, in effect reducing the forty-three foot distance. The NCAA established a two-foot wide pitching lane which the pitcher must step in, as a way of discouraging pitchers from using angles to gain advantages when delivering pitches.

NCAA rule changes lessened pitching's dominance, and so did improvements in bat technology. Alloy bats, typically made all or mostly out of aluminum, have been around since the 1970s; these one piece bats have thin and responsive barrel walls that don't break because of aluminum's strength. Beginning in 2000, composite bats became popular, bats that have, in essence, two barrels: an aluminum wall surrounding an inner core typically made with a mixture of graphite, carbon fiber, and titanium. A composite bat is lighter and therefore can be lengthened without adding additional weight to the bat, the longer length allowing for a bigger sweet spot. Because power hitters generally preferred the one-barrel alloy bats with their greater mass and weight, manufacturers then began creating a hybrid bat, a two-piece design that incorporated an alloy barrel and a composite handle in an attempt to gain the benefits of each. The lighter handle allowed for a longer barrel than a traditionally manufactured alloy bat with no added weight. Hybrid bats, like composite bats, have a large sweet spot and reduce the vibration on a mishit.

To further assist the hitter, bat manufacturers began producing bats weighted differently throughout its length. A balanced bat has the weight evenly distributed throughout the bat and leads to a smoother, faster swing. End loaded bats have extra weight in the barrel of the bat, which will generate more power if the batter hits the sweet spot. Occasionally a bat has been introduced that is too "hot"—creates too much speed coming off the bat's barrel—as happened in 1993 with the introduction of titanium bats. But these were quickly banned by all the softball associations. A team's bats are now tested routinely during the season, and a list of banned bats is posted and updated regularly.

Even after the pitching rubber had been moved back to forty-three feet, Louisiana Tech led the country in 1989 by hitting eighteen home runs as a team. In 2015, Louisiana Lafayette hit 116 home runs, and many of those were at fields who had moved their fences back by ten or twenty feet from the earlier era. Slightly hotter bats were not the main reason for the power surge. The big shift came from two developments: one, through better strength-and-conditioning work at the college level—these athletes train year round and have explosion that was not wide-spread in earlier decades; and two, through technological changes that allowed coaches to better teach hitters.

When pitching dominated the game, coaches emphasized what was called the pure linear swing, in which the hitter takes the knob of the bat straight to the ball, without any hip/back elbow connection. She was taught to get her weight forward, to keep her shoulders level, to extend her arms at

Oklahoma's Jocelyn Alo demonstrates a classic power-hitter's swing, here crushing one of her thirty home runs, which led the nation. She also hit .420. Evoking comparisons to Lauren Chamberlain, an all-time great hitter who likewise played at Oklahoma, Alo was named USA Softball Freshman of the Year. Courtesy Caitlyn Epes.

contact, and to roll her wrists. Power was generated primarily through the arms and wrists.

Most softball pitches go down, either because they are drops, curveballs, or change-ups, or they are just slow enough fastballs that drop because of gravity. You have to be throwing real heat and spinning the ball to rise to actually have it go up. And so with nearly all pitches, a perfectly flat swing means you're actually hitting down on the ball. You might get a line drive or a sharp ground ball single through a hole, but you won't get much home run power. To hit a dropping ball with force, you need an upwards launch angle to your swing.

A swing is fast, the blink of an eye. It's hard to see what really happens when an elite player swings, which makes it difficult to prove or disprove an opinion. Freeze frame video made its way into baseball well over a decade ago, and then followed into softball, revolutionizing hitting instruction because it could demonstrate exactly what the power hitters did. It turned out that almost all did more or less the same thing. They didn't have a linear swing. They had what has come to be called a rotational swing, in which you don't extend your arms or roll your wrists. You keep your hands back, your weight back. Your back elbow is bent and tucked to your side, in connection with your hips. You rotate your shoulders on an axis, generating tremendous power with your entire body. These hitters create a swing path on plane with the pitch, and then swing up through the ball.

College players at every level are now video recorded when hitting, and they've been aided tremendously in understanding their swings by slow motion or freeze frame video. The new technologies for hitting instruction take this one step farther. Hitters can attach to their bat knob a sensor that does real-time swing analytics by measuring speed, power, quickness, and control. RightView Pro, Diamond Kinetics, Zepp, Rapsodo, HitTrax—all have technologies that track a hitter's swing path: her body movements, the bat arc. Each swing, furthermore, can be shared immediately on a tablet, so that the hitter herself or a coach can watch and analyze. The hitter can then go back in the batting cage and make adjustments.

While a swing happens all at the same time, a hitting coach can use the technology to focus on one part of the swing, hand cast angle, let's say, the term for how the hands move during the swing. The bat sensor measures how far the hands move in a lateral direction away from the player's load position at the start of the swing to the point where the hands are at impact. A larger hand cast distance is usually inefficient and suggests that the back elbow and hip connection isn't being maintained, which lessens power. Focusing on this one element can help the batter keep the bat over the back shoulder, stay inside the ball with her hands, and uncoil body and hands together. When she gets the feel of doing that properly, she can go on to address other elements of the swing, such as her launch angle or trigger-to-impact time.

Sales reps for the technology companies tell me that softball adoptions have been happening more quickly than in baseball, where coaches tend to say, "Here's how we've always done it...." Many softball programs have been eager to embrace sophisticated technologies for instructional use, including two-time defending champion Oklahoma, who uses Diamond Kinetic Sensors, the Rapsodo Hitting monitor, and Dartfish Video Analysis Tools. JT Gasso, the hitting coach for Oklahoma, stressed that these new technologies empower the player, in that during the off-season, for example, players can still be using video individually. Between fall ball and the beginning of January practices this year, Oklahoma players could go to batting cages, get video shot, analyze it, and work on their swings. It's a changing world for hitting instruction, and therefore pitchers.

*   *   *

Only the Women's College World Series itself exceeds the hoopla around the second weekend of the Mary Nutter Collegiate Classic. The sheer number of teams, thirty-two, and the number of ranked teams from across the country—including six of last season's eight participants in the WCWS—make this a softball junkie's dream. If you were there, you witnessed plenty of offensive fireworks. Batters smoked line drives into the outfield gaps as well as hammered pitches over the fences. Eleven games were decided by run-rule, which is invoked if one team is ahead by at least eight runs after the opposing team has had five at bats.

Kirk Walker's original vision for the Mary Nutter Classic was to get team match-ups that might happen again three months later in the NCAA tournament. The Mary Nutter would preview where those teams were early in the season. As general interest in women's college softball has boomed with all the television and streaming exposure, these early season regional match-ups have become even more exciting. Softball fans who might not follow a particular team have still watched those players on TV, and now they get to see them in person. Fans live for early out-of-conference games such as LSU-Oregon or Oklahoma-Arizona.

For the top teams, playing strong programs from elsewhere in the country primes them for league play. Not all the teams playing here were ranked, of course, but even for those programs down a tier or two from the top-25, their Mary Nutter experience can be beneficial. First, they get games in because of the weather. Second, when they compete against the stronger programs, they raise their RPI ranking. Third, when they recruit, they can tell players that the program goes to the Mary Nutter Classic and plays against programs such as Oklahoma or UCLA. All teams can test themselves and measure how they're progressing.

The big national story from the previous week was that Oklahoma, Florida, and Oregon all lost their first game, which paved the way for undefeated Washington to jump to #1 in the week's rankings. The best game I saw at the Mary Nutter pitted those Huskies against #6 ranked Texas A&M. Both teams have strong fan bases that travel, and when the game began, the stands behind the plate and down the lines were filled, and fans were sitting in outfield bleachers and on the grass. The father of Heather Tarr, Washington's head coach, led the Huskies fans in a "Gimme an H—H, Gimme a U—U" chant, the program's customary opening cheer, which was followed by the players standing in front of the dugout and saying "Go," with the fans then screaming out "Huskies," which they did about six times. And then it was A&M's turn for their customary pre-game ritual. The starting players lined up down the third base line, crouched down, and did the "Farmers Fight" cheer, which was likewise done in the stands by their fans, though the close quarters make it a bit more difficult to fully do all the actions.

Washington started their freshman from Australia, Gabbie Plain, who had difficulties early with her control, consistently getting behind the hitters. In the bottom of the first, A&M loaded the bases on two infield singles and a walk, and then a sharp single to right plated two. Washington answered in the top of the second to even up the game, and then this became a pitchers' duel, even though the strike zone was being called tight. For years, umpires routinely called a strike on pitches that ended up in the "river," the name for the six-inch space between the edge of home plate and the batter's box line. It was believed that any ball that ended up in the river had clipped an edge of the plate with an edge of the ball. The NCAA then showed with diagrams how this wasn't really true. The softball is 3.8 inches in diameter, and though a ball thrown by a right handed pitcher to a right handed batter that is caught outside in the river might have clipped the front part of the plate, one thrown inside in the river could be several inches off the plate. In 2012 the NCAA made it a point of emphasis for the umpires to no longer call the river automatically, thereby narrowing the strike zone. Once this happened, batters had more opportunity to get a ball they could drive, rather than having to swing at something in on their hands or off the end of the bat. The number of walks went up until pitchers realized that they had to throw strikes.

Washington had several subsequent scoring chances, aided in part by errors, but A&M's Samantha Show came up with the big pitches when she needed them. A&M, likewise, had numerous scoring opportunities, including in the bottom of the fourth when a single, a walk, and a hit by pitch loaded up the bases for Texas A&M with one out. Kaitlyn Alderink hit a slow grounder down the first base line, which Kirstyn Thomas bobbled and then dropped out in foul territory, which caused Thomas and Alderink to collide. But a run for A&M was negated when the home plate umpire called Alderink out for stepping out of the box prior to making contact with the pitch.

The year 2018 marked a big change for slappers—the out-of-the-box rule was changed from the batter being called out if her entire foot is beyond the line to being called out if any part of her foot crosses the line. Umpires say that this is not a difficult call because it happens right in front of them, and every game I saw seemed to have one or more such calls made. Rules adjustments take some time, particularly for slappers who had practiced for years stepping onto the line. Adjustments are also difficult for fans, many of whom don't yet know new rules. The Texas A&M fans erupted after Alderink was called out, telling the umpire that he was horrible, because they thought Alderink had been called out for interference. I was sitting at the media table and behind me a fan was screaming that there had been no interference; I decided to inform him that because of the new rule she was called out for being out of the box. About a minute later, I felt a tap on my shoulder. "Excuse me, what's the new rule?" I explained and about a minute later, another tap. "She wasn't called out for interference with the first baseman?" No, I said, she was called out earlier, at home plate. "Could you explain that rule to me again?"

Gabbie Plain got out of the bases-loaded jam for Washington, but that wasn't the end of the baserunners, for either side. The pitchers—Show for

A&M, Plain and then Samantha Manti, who relieved her in the fifth, for Washington—came up with the big pitch when needed. Or their defense bailed them out. In the top of the seventh, with a runner on, Washington's Thomas launched a deep fly ball to right that Sarah Hudek went back on, reached over the fence, and caught. In the bottom of the seventh, with a runner on third and two out, Washington's speedy center fielder Kelly Burdick caught up with Kristen Cuyos' long fly ball in deep center to send the game to extra innings.

In tournaments, where teams are on time schedules and other games will follow, the International Tie Breaker rule is put into place from the eighth inning on, as a way to end the game more quickly. The hitting team places the person who would be the ninth hitter of the inning on second, which often means that a sacrifice bunt and a grounder or fly ball can score a run. Earlier this season, under the International Rule, North Dakota State's Jacquelyn Sertic lost a no-hitter and the game simultaneously in the ninth inning when she gave up a single that plated the winning run.

In this game, Show was still pitching for A&M, and when the Huskies' batter pulled back on a bunt attempt, the runner was caught trying to steal. The Huskies didn't score. In the bottom of the eighth, A&M's runner placed on second was advanced to third on a perfect sacrifice bunt by Show; an infield error allowed a baserunner but the runner didn't advance home; two ground ball outs later, the Huskies were out of the inning. The game finally ended in the ninth, when Washington scored two and A&M could only answer with one. The tie-breaker rule did create drama, though having a game manipulated in this way, when results matter for the RPI index, seemed unfortunate.

*   *   *

A few minutes after Washington defeated Texas A&M, two games that could also preview WCWS match-ups concluded. Arizona's Taylor McQuillin outdueled Oklahoma's ace, Paige Parker, with a two-run homer by Louisiana Lafayette transfer Aleah Craighton making the difference. Immediately following Arizona's 2–0 win, another pitchers' duel ended when Tennessee behind Matty Moss and Caylan Arnold bested Oregon 1–0. Five games in the tournament ended 1–0 or 2–0, and there were numerous other low-scoring games.

When the hitting explosion overtook college softball in the 2000s, coaches realized that they would have to make adjustments with their pitching, particularly in how they prepared a game plan for their hurlers and how they created a multi-person staff. Very good pitchers often get hitters out the first few times through the line-up, but good batters have become accomplished at making in-game adjustments, so that by the third time through, let's say, they begin hitting the pitches that got them out before. Even the top programs, with the best pitchers in the country, now rely on two or even three pitchers to get through a season, and sometimes even a game. A starter may go through the line-up twice, and even if the team is ahead and the pitcher is going well, the coach may send in a new pitcher just to give the opposing lineup a new look.

Mike White, Oregon's head coach, was born in New Zealand and grew up playing men's fastpitch. A dual citizen of New Zealand and the United States, White was one of the game's premier international pitchers for twenty-five years, until he began devoting most of his time to coaching. As a head coach who is also a pitching guru, White says that one of the things he's come to enjoy the most in his nine years of coaching is how to use an entire staff and not just rely on one pitcher. "The new style," he said, "when you look at teams like Florida or Oklahoma, is that teams are going to multiple pitchers rather than just one. With multiple pitchers you can try to get the match-up you want. You throw a certain pitcher against a rise-ball hitting team because they'll have trouble hitting her drop, or you throw your rise-ball pitcher against a team because they have trouble with that." Rather than having one pitching ace who shoulders most of the season's innings, White alternates starts between three superb pitchers: Megan Kleist, Miranda Elish, and Maggie Balint.

In 2017, the University of Washington had a great year, making it to the semifinals of the Women's College World Series before their ace, Taran Al-

In past decades, teams often relied on one pitcher. With changes in hitting technologies and instruction, coaches have come to rely on pitching staffs, rather than aces. This publicity photograph from University of Oregon symbolizes the change, as Miranda Elish (left) and Megan Kleist were both All-Americans and named to the Top Twenty-Five list for Player of the Year. Courtesy Eric Evans.

velo, ran out of gas against Florida after pitching nearly all the team's innings through the post-season. Washington's head coach, Heather Tarr, recognized this year that she wanted a better-rested Alvelo going into the post-season, as well as a back-up or two she could rely on in crucial moments. "We are committing this year," Tarr said to me, "to maintaining a rotation. Where this gal gets this game, and this one gets this next game, and this one the next. How long we do that, if we do it through the conference season, I don't know. But we're committed to developing a staff." The risk, of course, is that the team loses games it might not have, which hurts its RPI, which hurts its seeding for the NCAA tournament. Tarr knows the risk but doesn't care. "We have to do it," she said. "The pitchers need that development to see what they can do when the stakes are high." True to her word that she was trying to develop a pitching staff, Tarr had her freshman, Gabbie Plain, starting in the circle against Texas A&M, and she relieved Plain with her sophomore, Sam Manti, in the fifth. Both pitchers got to throw on a big stage, and Washington still won.

*　*　*

The Big League Dreams Complex is laid out to maximize a fan's viewing pleasure. Five fields were in use for the second weekend of the Mary Nutter Classic, and so there were always several games occurring at once. Three of the fields extend out from a central point, making it very easy to keep track of multiple games. At one point on Thursday, watching at Fenway, I saw Oklahoma State come from behind in the bottom of the seventh inning to edge Wisconsin, 3–2, on two bunt singles, a walk, a sac fly, and an error. I walked about thirty yards to Wrigley to check out the Missouri-Arizona game, where a few minutes later Cayla Kessinger hit Missouri's third home run of the game to go up 4–2 and excite the Missouri contingent hoping for an upset (though not to be, as Arizona would score six runs in the seventh inning to come from behind). From my viewing spot at Wrigley, I could see Yankee Stadium simply by turning my head, and less than a minute after Kessinger's home run, Texas A&M's Sarah Hudek hit a sixth-inning blast to break a tie with Notre Dame and go up 5–3, a score that held for the Aggies.

The crowds roar for game-changing home runs, but having so many games to watch can give a fan smaller moments of pleasure, where you see an accomplishment less noticeable but equally dependent on years of practice. In a different Texas A&M game, I watched Keeli Milligan, who has elite speed and is a superb base stealer, facing off against Zoe Conley, the Cal Bears right-handed pitcher. Hitting the ball in the 5–6 gap is ideal for a slapper, because a fast runner is hard to throw out from the left side of the infield. But Cal's infield was in tight, and the low and away pitch, which in some ways is the easiest to hit into that gap, can be difficult to handle because a slapper often is pulling away as she moves through the box. Slappers are often looking, therefore, for an outside pitch, so pitchers will challenge them inside. But if you put a pitch on the inside and a slapper recognizes that pitch and turns on it, they're often hitting at a first baseman perhaps thirty feet away. Numerous possibilities. What would Conley throw?

Conley's first pitch was a backdoor curve that just missed the outside edge of the plate. The backdoor curve is really hard to hit for a slapper, and if you're swinging at balls just off the plate you won't be successful. Milligan rightly let it go for ball one. Conley came back with an inside curve ball that Milligan fouled off. Pitch three was low and away that Milligan took for a ball. Conley had gotten behind in the count, which made it less likely she would throw a change-up, which is the hardest to throw for a strike but is an effective pitch against a slapper as she can end up out of the box in front. Pitch four was another fastball outside and up. 3–1 count. The Cal pitching coach might have believed that Milligan would take on this 3–1 count pitch, and Conley threw a chest high fastball down the middle, taken for strike two. On 3–2, Milligan saw a pitch she liked, a fastball on the outside part of the plate but above the waist, one difficult to hit down on. Instead of slapping it toward the 5–6 hole, she reached out and poked a soft fly over the drawn-in third baseman's head, in front of the left fielder playing medium-deep. Milligan didn't come around to score; the at bat had no noticeable effect on the game. But as a battle within the battle, it was well-played.

* * *

Scan the sports page of *USA Today* and you might not know that women's sports exist. Scan the sports page of a big-city newspaper and you see primarily coverage of professional sports and the most popular college sports, men's football and basketball. If you like to read your print coverage on-line, the most popular sites such as ESPN.com or CBSSports.com certainly relegate women to the margins; the tabs they provide on their "home" pages almost exclusively take you to men's sports. Equity advocates who study what drives or lessens interest in something will point out that if sports fans see numerous articles about a team, have easy access to that team's games on television, and read numerous profiles and stories about the team's players, then certainly they will have interest in that team. If media actually covered women's sports more proportionally, equity advocates argue, then interest in these sports would rise.

The blogosphere interested in gender and sports regularly excoriates ESPN and the media in general. A typical view is that of Kiley Kroh, writer for *ThinkProgress*, a news website that advocates for a progressive public policy. "Women's sports have never been more popular—everywhere except on television, that is," Kroh wrote on June 12, 2015. Kroh and the authors of the study she was responding to are certainly not wrong when it comes to media coverage on SportsCenter, in big-city newspapers, or on national websites. But passionate fans have plenty of outlets for coverage. The universities themselves write frequently about their women's teams and have social media that keep fans up to date. A handful of websites cover fastpitch softball. Perhaps the most important non-television outlet is FloSoftball, because not only do they report on games and programs with articles and video, they live-stream over a thousand games each year, from travel ball tournaments to all levels of college softball.

Brentt Eads has worked for several decades as a media industry executive with expertise in integrating digital media and marketing. His career has always had a sports focus, though it took some years and daughters who played softball for him to specialize in the sport. After working for companies such as ESPN and Student Sports, Inc., Eads struck out on his own in 2014 with the creation of Full Count Softball, a fastpitch softball media company focusing on the travel ball and high school softball world. He worked incredibly hard to put up content daily, writing hundreds of articles a year and posting photos and some videos. In 2015 Full Count Softball was acquired by FloSports, a company that began in 2006. FloSports focused first on wrestling and track, posting video online or streaming live events to these niche sports communities who had little to nothing on regular television to watch. Eads' company became FloSoftball, with a three-pronged platform: live streaming of games; a web site that has written content added daily; and a video training series and video documentary series which delves into the personalities of people in the game.

Beginning in 2016, the Mary Nutter Classic began partnering with FloSoftball to live stream and archive the games. Fans from around the country could now watch the tournament for a FloSoftball subscription fee. "If you're a softball fan—particularly college softball—and you want to see the highest level of play, the Mary Nutter Collegiate Classic is the ideal event," said Eads, the General Manager of FloSoftball at the time the partnership was announced. "It's a privilege for us to show these games live and on demand, and to be associated with such talented players, coaches, and teams."

His new partner was equally enthusiastic. "I am ecstatic to partner the Mary Nutter Collegiate Classic with FloSoftball to bring a whole new audience and exposure to the best collegiate softball tourney in the nation," said Kirk Walker. "I look forward to working with a media company that is a leader in our sport and passionate about advancing the sport of fastpitch softball across the country."

FloSoftball attempted from the beginning to be all-inclusive, to cover travel ball, college teams, the professional league, and international tournaments. Chez Sievers is their Senior Editor, a position that seems ready-made for her. Sievers played travel ball for the California Cruisers, helping her teams to two national titles. She went on to star at the University of Texas, where she was All-Big 12 three times. She graduated with a degree in communications, which she put to use even when she was coaching as an assistant at the University of California, Riverside. "I launched my own website, my own podcast, and started recording my own videos," Sievers said. "I taught myself how to do multiple things, including shooting and editing video, and interviewing coaches who were my colleagues." She moved back to Austin, where coincidentally FloSports is located, and in 2015 helped coach the first-year Texas Charge, a professional women's softball team. Sievers can bridge all the communities FloSoftball wants to serve.

Sievers praises FloSoftball for allowing her to be as creative as she would like to be. The challenge of her job is keeping up with the game's growth. "Everyone wants coverage," she said, "and it's close to impossible to meet everyone's needs. When I look at my content calendar and the months, I try to identify themes and to balance breaking news, exclusive content, player-written features, shows, funny videos. Part of what we do is meant to be entertaining to the fans. I want this all to be fun. I want the FloSoftball site to be a place where people see and read cool things about people in the sport."

A softball game at the Mary Nutter Classic in February has three reasons to watch: match-ups of ranked teams, great California weather, and views of beautiful mountains. #22 Long Beach State's Jessica Flores pitches to #1 Washington's Taylor Van Zee. Courtesy Kirk Walker.

FloSoftball covers all levels of fastpitch softball and does so year round on the internet, continuing the model that FloSports began with for wrestling and running. But women's college softball, unlike those sports, also has a sizable mainstream audience and is one of ESPN's most lucrative sports to telecast. In 2018 ESPN continued its commitment to NCAA Division I Softball by showing live more than 650 games across its portfolio of networks: ESPN, ESPN2, ESPNU, ESPN3, SEC Network, Longhorn Network, SEC Network +, ACC Network Extra, and the ESPN App. While many sports fans might watch events through their cable packages and therefore pick up only the occasional conference fastpitch game and the NCAA tournament, they won't realize the less-visible but large audience that softball has, one tied to contemporary technology and games streamed digitally. And it's not just ESPN that shows women's softball. In 2018 Oklahoma had regular season games televised on the ESPN family of networks, on regional Fox Sports networks, and on Sooner Sports TV. The Pac-12 Networks televised more than ninety games in 2018; the Big Ten Network televised games on its own channel and, for a subscription price, aired each university's softball games via its BTN2Go programming; the Fox Sports regional networks broadcasted Big 12 games. If you're a softball fan, you can watch hundreds of games a year, or far more. If you're not a fan, you probably have no idea of softball's popularity.

ESPN was at the Mary Nutter Classic, though not to televise. Under a large tent at the Big League Dreams Complex, in a space that serves usually as an all-weather turf soccer field, ESPN had set up to do photoshoots of players and coaches that the network would use for its coverage of the SEC tournament, the NCAA tournament's regionals and super-regionals, and the Women's College World Series. During the weekend, I was under the tent doing the occasional interview, and so I got to watch the ESPN video and photography crews work. Teams that ESPN anticipated would be in the tournament came into the area for their hour: Auburn, Oklahoma State, Oregon, Texas A&M, and the like. In one area set up for filming, each player did something fun to be taped for personality video intros. In another area, a photographer took head shots. Another photographer captured a still photo that was less glamour than attitude, with the players posing with their gloves or bats. The filming that got the most whoops came in yet a fourth area: power hitters from a team entered one by one to be tossed a "softball" that they hit. The crackable ball was filled with chalk that matched the team's colors—blue for UCLA, purple for Washington, and so on—and when the batter smashed it, the chalk in the ball settled around like smoke. The college softball players were getting some unexpected star treatment, and they laughed and whooped their way through their hour.

* * *

The big college sports story of the week concerned the scandals of college basketball, scandals that we began hearing about back in September when an FBI investigation into fraud and bribery in college basketball led to ten arrests and the seizing of computers at ASM Sports in New York, a leading sports agency for the NBA. Yahoo Sports published a report detailing names of players and amounts paid to them or family members. Payoffs of six-figures to high school recruits to get them to a particular school, the coming indictments or firings of big-name coaches, the heavy sanctions potentially coming to glamorous programs—all this had the general sports world in an uproar, and the most typical response was "College sports is broken."

Such claims, of course, are always only about sports such as men's football and basketball. Perhaps the collegiate model for the big revenue sports *is* broken; entire books have been written that critique that model and offer suggestions to fix it, suggestions that no one believes will be enacted. But talking to coaches, parents, players, and fans at the Mary Nutter Classic, watching the games and the sportsmanship exhibited, learning about how after the games the players go study, I certainly was made aware that not all college sports are broken.

FOUR

Icons and Culture

Judi Garman was born in the United States but grew up in Canada. She graduated from the University of Saskatchewan in 1966 and played for two years on the Canadian women's national softball team. After moving to California, Garman got the head coaching job at Golden West College in Huntington Beach, a junior college, where she won four consecutive national junior college championships from 1975 to 1978. In July 1979, Garman was hired as the first softball coach at California State University, Fullerton, and she built one of the best programs in the country. Between 1981 and 1988, she led Fullerton to eight consecutive 50-win seasons. After four trips to the College World Series resulted in two second-place and two third-place finishes, Fullerton won the championship in 1986. Garman retired after the 1999 season, with a career record at Fullerton of 913 wins and 374 losses. In 2006, the university began honoring her legacy with an event, the Judi Garman Classic, that has grown over the years into a premier tournament.

Until the passage of Title IX in 1972 and the subsequent granting of athletic scholarships to women, college softball had a club team atmosphere. *Competitive* women's softball in the United States, however, has a longer history, one told in Erica Westly's book *Fastpitch: The Untold History of Softball and the Women Who Made the Game*. Westly focuses her story on the company and city teams that competed through the 1940s, 50s, and 60s. The country's best teams, professional ones such as the SoCal Orange Lionettes or Connecticut's Raybestos Brakettes, competed for national championships and occasionally toured overseas. The game had its stars: Bertha Ragan Tickey, Joan Joyce, Margie Law, Billie Harris, and Shirley Topley, among others. But compared to athletic trailblazers such as Babe Didrikson Zaharias or Billie Jean King, those softball stars never became generally known, and no group has successfully promoted their accomplishments.

Women's college softball, however, has been good in honoring its foremothers. Many Hall of Fame coaches, such as Garman, were pioneers in the college game, were coaches who led their programs to league or national titles in the decades after Title IX was passed: Sharon Backus, Linda Wells,

Sharon Drysdale, Margie Wright, Gayle Blevins, Dianne Baker, Yvette Girouard, JoAnne Graf, and Sue Enquist, among others. Some coaches have been inducted into the Hall of Fame and are still piling up the wins and honors, such as Patty Gasso, Rhonda Revelle, Mike Candrea, Patrick Murphy, Lori Meyer, Donna Papa, and Jo Evans. One Hall of Famer, Carol Hutchins, the winningest coach in college softball history, was at the Judi Garman Classic this weekend with her University of Michigan team.

Albert Hammond famously sang "It never rains in Southern California" and there had been little precipitation in SoCal the past twelve months, but the softball was played in fits and starts because of the rain. Opening day of the tournament saw #2 ranked Florida and #25 Michigan each win a pair of games. Michigan wasn't impressive but beat Loyola Marymount 3–2 and UNC-Charlotte 5–0. Florida's results were more imposing. The Gators' Aleshia Ocasio was a Third Team NFCA All-American as a freshman and First Team All-American as a sophomore. She dominated teams in the circle. But such was the pitching depth last year, with Delanie Gourley and Kelly Barnhill, that Ocasio became an everyday player in the outfield and only occasionally pitched. As a senior she had returned to the circle in style, posting an 8–1 record with a minuscule 0.80 ERA. Ocasio and Florida beat Loyola Marymount in the opener, 13–0. Barnhill followed with a one-hit gem against Cal St. Fullerton, the Gators cruising to a 10–0 win.

Through the first month of the season, Michigan had played a difficult schedule, accounting for some of their losses, but Hutchins wasn't happy with her team's play if the constant tinkering of her line-up was any indication. On day two of the Judi Garman Classic, against #8 Baylor, Hutchins inserted two new freshmen into the starting lineup, Lou Allan and Taylor Bump, to go with fellow freshmen Natalia Rodriguez and Meghan Beaubien. It was senior Tera Blanco with a first-inning three-run home run, however, who got Michigan on the board, and then an inning later junior Faith Canfield homered. When the rains came causing a delay, Michigan was up 6–0 and Beaubien was throwing a no-hitter; when the game started up again, Baylor's Shelby Friudenberg singled to break up the no-hitter. Baylor mounted a mild comeback when Goose McGlaun hit a 3-run home run in the sixth (McGlaun is from Humble, Texas, and by all accounts her character matches her town). But Michigan held on, and then in their second game of the day, they stretched their winning streak to six with a 3–1 win over #18 Louisiana Lafayette.

Hutch, as she's known in the softball world, has the best combination of scowl and smile you can imagine: her scowl can make the most resolute quiver; her smile brings sunshine to the world. Every weekend she was adding to her record number of wins. Hutch has led the Wolverines to the Women's College World Series in twelve of the last twenty-three seasons, and in 2016 was the inaugural winner of the espnW Pat Summitt Coaching Award.

She is a fierce proponent of the value of women's sports and a fierce opponent to the sexism that seems never to end.

In his illuminating 2017 espnW article "How a verbal jab from a men's basketball coach lit the Title IX fire in Carol Hutchins," Andrew Kahn relates how the young Hutchins, a two-sport athlete at Michigan State, became angry enough about gender inequities that she and her basketball teammates sued the university: "In 1978, Hutchins was the captain of the Michigan State basketball team and a star on the softball squad. But while the Spartans' men's team—including Magic Johnson—traveled to games via chartered buses or planes, ate at real restaurants and slept two to a room, the women's teams were driving themselves in station wagons, eating McDonald's every meal and sleeping four to a room. 'The inequities were stark in every way,' says Kathy DeBoer, Hutchins' basketball teammate who was also a volleyball player and is now the executive director of the American Volleyball Coaches Association. The basketball players' attitude? We're done with this. We're going to fight because we can win. They hired Jean L. King, a lawyer who took on the case pro bono. 'The law only works if you use it,' Hutchins remembers King, who became a Title IX advocacy legend, telling them. 'If you stick it out, you will win.'"

The all-time winningest college softball coach, Carol Hutchins of University of Michigan, can scowl or smile with the best of them. She is shown here in a light-hearted moment with Sierra Romero (2013–16), four-time All-American and 2016 Player of the Year. Courtesy Daryl Marshke/Michigan Photography.

As captain of the basketball team, Hutch got her name on the lawsuit: *Hutchins v. Board of Trustees of Michigan State University*. Perhaps because of the lawsuit, conditions improved for the team; the case was settled favorably in the 1980s. Unlike many female sports pioneers, Hutch has not had to sue again under Title IX rules. But that battle would be only the first of many against gender inequity that she has fought.

The victories and championships aren't what people reference when they talk about Hutchins. The legendary Hutch has arisen because of the devotion she has from her former players and from fellow coaches who know her. Hutch wants to win softball games—no one would dispute that—but she wants even more to mold girls who enter the Michigan program into confident, powerful, principled young women. When Hutch got her 1,458th win to pass fellow Hall of Famer Margie Wright, Michigan's athletic department assembled a twenty-minute video tribute. Plentiful amid all the congratulations were the thanks from former players to Hutch for being a mentor and inspiring leader. Players from fifteen and twenty years earlier quoted her sayings that have shaped them.

The devotion that Hutch inspires doesn't extend only to her players—her assistant coaches have been crucial to the program's success. Bonnie Tholl, a former Michigan player who became the first player in Big Ten history to earn first team all-league honors four times, is in her twenty-fifth season as a member of the Michigan coaching staff and her sixteenth as associate head coach. Assistant coach Jennifer Brundage is in her twentieth season as the pitching coach, though she also works with Michigan's hitters, which is no surprise as Brundage held all of UCLA's hitting records when she graduated from there in 1995. Tholl and Brundage are accomplished enough to have gone on to head coaching positions elsewhere. Schools have inquired and offered. In the glamour men's sports, proven assistants move frequently, trying to rise up "the chain," trading one program for another in order to get a salary raise, or more responsibility. In a typical career path, an excellent assistant in a powerful DI program takes a head coaching job at a lower-level or mid-major DI school, and if they have success there, they jump to a weak team in a Power-5 conference, and if they have success there, move to a different school. But not at Michigan, for Tholl and Brundage. And not for numerous accomplished female assistant coaches across the country.

Retired UCLA head coach, Hall of Famer Sue Enquist, says that female coaches tend to "nest," which she describes as looking to build or contribute to a program and keep it going. "Successful female coaches," Enquist said, "aren't always looking around, looking at this position or that new opening, hoping for a bit more money or a school seen as more prestigious. It's not that female coaches aren't ambitious—they are—but not as we commonly measure ambition." Enquist described how gratifying it is to establish a multi-generational coaching sequence. Ralph Raymond, the "grand old man" of softball who led the professional Raybestos Brakettes for decades, coached Sharon Backus in the 1970s, who after her playing career ended became the UCLA coach. Backus coached All-American Enquist, who went out to Connecticut and also was coached by Raymond. When her playing career ended, Enquist became an assistant at UCLA, then co-head coach with Backus, and succeeded her as sole head coach in 1997. Enquist handed the reins of the program to her long-time assistant who was also a star at UCLA, Kelly Inouye-Perez.

Bonnie Tholl made it clear that she can't speak for everyone, but her story and beliefs are pretty typical for women's softball coaches in general. "I want to judge my own happiness by my own emotion and measures and not by societal expectation," Tholl said. "It's not most important to me to have my name on the marquee as the head coach. Coaches are in the business of empowering people, and I see that the resources and leadership at Michigan provide those opportunities. I am more interested in helping student athletes create their own powerful and lasting experiences than in my climbing the ladder. Now, that doesn't dismiss my competitiveness and commitment to win championships. But fulfillment in life is really about connections. Our former student athletes come back to campus and rarely talk about the RBI double that won them a Big Ten title, rather they share the bus discussions or the conditioning workout that stretched them outside of their comfort zone."

If a coach's personal goals align with what society generally deems success, then the coach will most likely jump from program to program to try and move up. If the goal is personal happiness that comes from relationships, then it's more difficult to leave a program and community that you've helped build. "I am incredibly fortunate to coach at Michigan," Tholl said, "and to help young women develop into leaders in their professions, communities, and families. I am charged with the responsibility to enhance their lives yet I feel that they have given me so much more."

*   *   *

On Friday at the Judi Garman Classic, Florida had two games cancelled due to rain, but they came back Saturday to play Baylor in the marquee game of the tourney. Barnhill got the start in the circle for the Gators, and it was my first time to see her live after watching her so many times on television. In 2017 Barnhill had a year for the ages. She won numerous awards, including USA Softball's Collegiate National Player of the Year and the 2017 ESPY Award for Best Female Collegiate Athlete. She compiled a 26–4 record and 0.51 ERA. Doing a modern version of UCLA's Debbie Doom, Barnhill had two separate streaks of more than forty-five scoreless innings. In SEC play she really ramped up, holding batters to a .114 opposing batting average and allowing only one earned run in eighty-two innings. This year was looking like more of the same, as she came into the Baylor game 9–0 with an ERA of 0.25.

I watched from right behind home plate, so my angle was pretty much what the batters saw. While some pitchers spin the ball considerably, moving it from right to left and often down, and others are power pitchers, with speed and a rise ball—Barnhill spins the ball and throws the heat. Television obscures just how much spin Barnhill creates on all her pitches, and how similar that spin looks right after the ball leaves her hand. I saw one pitch coming chest high, spinning hard, looking like a rise ball that would move up out of the zone; when the ball flattened and curved away, the batter froze. Strike three called. About all you can do is shake your head and say "nice pitch," or "that's simply not fair." Barnhill did struggle a bit with her control, walking five batters, but she also no-hit Baylor through six, striking out thirteen. Ocasio entered in the seventh to close out the game, striking out the side. Florida won 4–0, behind their pitching and home runs from Nicole Dewitt and Kayli Kvistad.

New head coach Gerry Glasco brought his Louisiana Lafayette team to the Judi Garman Classic ranked eighteenth and looking to continue their

Kelly Barnhill seen doing the Gator chomp, Florida's ritual after a win. As a highly decorated pitcher, Barnhill has made possible many such celebratory chomps. Sophia Reynoso is at left and Haven Sampson is behind. Courtesy Tim Casey and Florida Athletic Department.

solid play. Glasco had an unexpected off-season. After having been an assistant at Georgia from 2009–2014 and at Texas A&M from 2015–2017, he took a job on Mickey Dean's Auburn staff in September. Two months later, when Louisiana fired its long-time and successful head coach Michael Lotief, Glasco was hired to run the program that has reached elite status despite being in a mid-major conference. Louisiana captured the Sun Belt season championship twelve times in fourteen years, advancing to three Women's College World Series (2003, 2008, 2014), seven NCAA super-regionals, and fourteen NCAA regionals. Glasco had the Louisiana job because of Lotief's firing, of course, and he was having to come in and make the best of what he had, because Louisiana had offered unconditional releases to any player who wanted to transfer. Three did, including the All-American shortstop D.J. Sanders, two-time All-American outfielder Aleah Craighton, and reigning Sun Belt Freshman of the Year Alyssa Denham, a pitcher.

Assessing his team in the winter, Glasco decided that they had lost a lot of power but still had a lot of speed, so he emphasized small ball and base stealing. So far in 2018 he was getting solid pitching from an unexpected source—Summer Ellyson had taken a big jump up from her previous year and become the ace of the staff. Casey Dixon and Kylee Jo Trahan were throwing quality innings. The hitters were inconsistent but were doing enough. Louisiana's breakthrough had come in a three-game set with Florida, where after losing the first two games, they won the third 4–3 when Casidy Chaumont hit a walk-off home run in the eleventh inning. Despite the transfers of three stars, Glasco had the Ragin' Cajuns playing well when they came to the Judi Garman Classic. Unfortunately for the team, two games were cancelled because of the rain. Louisiana easily beat Fresno State, 7–2, behind Dixon and a lot of offense. They lost 3–1 to Michigan and lost a close game 1–0 to Baylor, when they got eight hits off Gia Rodoni but couldn't score a run, and Baylor's Goose McGlaun hit a solo shot that stood up. Confronting adversity and playing strong teams, however, was setting up Louisiana Lafayette for their league play to come.

* * *

One form of sexism in our society concerns the lack of equal opportunity for women in leadership paths or career paths such as high-level sales where a person needs to be strong and aggressive. Another form of sexism, and one difficult for softball to respond to, concerns the appropriate emotional climate for women's teams. Should there be different expectations for how girls or young women are motivated or disciplined than there are for boys and young men? Words, particularly these days, mean much. The culture of a men's football team is simply different than the culture of a women's softball team, so that football players being "motivated" by a coach cursing would seem like emotional abuse to some female softball players. That reality may be sexist, but it is a reality.

All college softball coaches I've talked to or read interviews by have stressed that they emphasize building a positive team culture, one that will help empower the female athlete. Perhaps because softball's iconic college coaches were strong and skilled female athletes, who then became articulate and passionate proponents of gender rights, the culture has its roots in a hybrid of male sports aggression and female desires for relationality. An influential adage tells us that much can be accomplished when no one cares who gets the credit. The adage is rarely true in prominent men's sports, where fame and huge salaries are linked to who gets the credit, but the message is baked into the culture of most high-achieving softball programs.

In his award-winning book *The Boys in the Boat: Nine Americans and Their Epic Quest for Gold at the 1936 Berlin Olympics*, Daniel James Brown describes those moments in rowing where every boat member gets in perfect rhythm, propelling the shell with the greatest velocity for expended effort. There's no room for individual heroics, because if one oar pulls harder than the others, the boat will actually slow. What's needed is for all to work as one, for individual ego to be pushed down for group success. The task for the crew coach, Brown writes, was "to find which few of them had the potential for raw power, the nearly superhuman stamina, the indomitable willpower, and the intellectual capacity necessary to master the details of technique. And which of them, coupled improbably with all those other qualities, had the most important one: the ability to disregard his own ambitions, to throw his ego over the gunwales, to leave it swirling in the wake of his shell, and to pull, not just for himself, not just for glory, but for the other boys in the boat."

While softball players pitching, hitting, and fielding is not an exact analogy to a crew rowing, the most successful teams come together in such a way that individual egos are subsumed to team goals. It's become almost humorous to me when I'm watching the star of a game interviewed—perhaps she's pitched a no-hitter—and she praises her teammates' defense and how her offense got her some runs, and never mentions her own command of her pitches. I'm struck by how deferential and modest these female athletes are, particularly compared to the cockiness of many male athletes. Female athletes have plenty of ego and competitiveness. They want to excel and they need to be confident; when a hitter is up in a clutch situation or a pitcher needs to go out and shut down the opposing team, she needs to believe in her own abilities. But the desire to play hero-ball is stronger in men's athletics because society uses concepts such as individuality and glory to construct masculinity, while women are socially instructed to work together and to downplay personal success.

In softball, players absolutely believe in themselves and the best players know that they are stars, but their behavior rarely undermines a team. Tim Walton, who played and coached minor-league baseball before moving to softball and becoming the head coach at the University of Florida, suggests that the difference lies in the variety of activities that women admire: "With the female dynamic there really isn't one pecking order. A great male athlete can get away with a lot more with his teammates. The players on a softball team hold each other more accountable than in baseball for what they do. In baseball, the best players may not pick up the trash in the dugout, or do some job, because they are the star. But in softball, there's respect from the team for those who are strong in and devoted to academics, and those who are interested in service work in the community, or who are great teammates because they encourage and challenge each other, and so there are multiple pecking orders, which means there really isn't one clearly established one." If we accept Walton's insights, then a coach who promotes the value of activities off the field reinforces cultural gender norms, which together can help create a team-first attitude. And perhaps this is one reason why college softball culture stresses academics and community service, as well as athletic prowess.

An obsession with winning and the accompanying drive and attempt to control leads, perhaps, to the off-field problems that run rampant through men's college sports. "Winning is the only thing" heightens the possibilities that those involved will cut corners ethically, or even do something directly against NCAA rules. If you have to win a championship to have your season be a success, you doom yourself generally to failure. If winning individual games though not a championship is the measure, even then, half the participants in an event will be losers. Softball culture doesn't want half its women to feel like losers after a game, nor 99.7 percent of its participants to feel like losers after the season is over. How then can a sport produce players who feel that they have won? Or, to put it another way, that winning is contextual and metaphorical, not literal?

Social constructions of gender make women, not men, primary communicators and caretakers. Boys are taught to be stoical and uncommunicative, taught to hide pain or emotion. Boys are taught that self-worth comes as an individual. Girls witness women taking care of others and talking about feelings and relationships. Such generalizations aren't true for *all* girls and boys in all families or social situations, of course, but the overall social construction falls along such lines, which makes more possible the creation of the particular culture found in women's softball.

Amy Hogue, head coach at the University of Utah, says that softball is a vehicle to teach players about the need for compassion, humility, kindness, patience, forgiveness, and love. Her role as a coach, she believes, is to assist her players in developing great character, which will allow them to do great things with their life beyond the game. Rather than trying to win to create the desired culture, Hogue suggests a re-ordering of priorities. Think first, she suggests to new coaches, about what culture you want—what you represent—and then figure out how to implement that culture. Be patient. "Winning games shouldn't be our number one priority," Hogue said. "Create a culture you are proud of."

In her inspirational book *Finished It: A Team's Journey to Winning It All,* about the University of Alabama team that won its first and only softball national championship in 2012, Cassie Reilly-Boccia, the starting first baseman, describes the culture-building that she believes got the team to that championship. Reilly-Boccia makes a distinction that was stressed within the program between hating to fail, which puts the emphasis on the individual, and hating to lose, which places it on the team. That 2012 Alabama team didn't care who had the clutch hit or fielding play, didn't care if they got pinch-hit for—they were all in it together, she says. Reilly-Boccia praises Head Coach Patrick Murphy and his Associate Head Coach Alyson Habetz for their numerous strategies, mottos, and team-building exercises that created this camaraderie. In one such exercise, the team gathered in a circle. A player had to turn to her teammate next to her and tell her one aspect of her game that she needed to improve, and the player then, in response, had to say one thing that her teammate was really good at. Learning to take criticism and then return a compliment breaks down defensiveness and promotes communication.

Rhonda Revelle, a Hall of Fame coach who has spent nearly her entire career at her alma mater, the University of Nebraska, bases her coaching philosophy around love: "We are a team-first program," she has said. "From the administrators, support staff, and coaches to the players and fans, we believe that love is the greatest source of motivation. By that, I mean love for the game, love for one another, and the will to do the hard work it takes to be a champion." If you are going to preach character and love, as Hogue, Revelle, and countless other coaches do, then you're going to have to recruit girls who can stand up to not only on-field expectations but off-field expectations, as well. Describing the kind of player she goes after, Revelle says—on the Nebraska website, no less—that a potential Husker softball player should be "students and then athletes. They are honest, hard-working people who conduct themselves with class. We want student-athletes to join our family who have the values of diligence, take responsibility for their actions and respect themselves and others. We believe these are some of the qualities of high-level performers, and we want to protect our family by bringing in only athletes of high moral character."

When the best coaches at the best programs say that a softball player needs to be great on the field, conduct herself with class off the field, and be excellent in the classroom, the message comes through loud and clear. You don't coast through school. You don't run afoul of the law. You treat everyone with respect, including your parents, which can be difficult sometimes for teenagers. I have had more than one coach tell me that when they are recruiting a girl, they watch intently, after a game, how the girl responds to her family. "If the player doesn't want to listen to her parents, or acts as if they don't matter," the coaches have said, "she's eventually going to treat me the same way." All these principles preached by college coaches filter down. On first encountering the idealism in women's softball, I believed it to be isolated, unusual, exemplified by only a few coaches. But in talking more to coaches and players, I've realized that accepted practices and expected behaviors we might call idealistic are simply bedrock for softball culture.

A coaching vision that stresses improvement and the building of character, not just winning, means that teams who don't win a championship or who even have a losing record can be metaphorical on-field winners and literal off-field winners. The players are not trying to make millions with a pro career; they are playing a game they love and learning further lessons about hard work, overcoming minor setbacks or injuries, and coping with failure. They are graduating and moving on to lead good lives, whatever a good life will mean for them. The culture of college women's softball reinforces the desires for a well-rounded life.

Part of such a life is recognizing your blessings and giving back to the community that supports you. I asked Kris Ganeff, long-time associate coach at Notre Dame, why Notre Dame softball emphasizes community service and what in particular such service does for the players. "How we represent ourselves," Ganeff replied, "also represents our families and our university. One of our program's guiding principles is Be Selfless. What better way to be selfless than when you are giving of your time and resources to help someone or something else?" Like so many of her coaching peers, Ganeff is idealistic: "Our players learn through our community service initiatives a perspective on what is going on outside of themselves and the team. We are extremely proud of how our players are able to use their status as a Division I athlete at a highly exposed university to do good. Our job is not to create great softball players, but rather to cultivate great human beings to go out into the world and continue to do good."

Florida State's Lonni Alameda is another coach who demands off-field effort beyond academics in the classroom. "Sometimes when we say community service," she asserted, "it's like we're serving the community, but in reality I think the community is serving us." FSU softball is measurably the most service-oriented athletic group on campus, with each player averaging thirty-six hours of community work during the year. Every Monday one set of players picks up trash on streets and in neighborhoods, and another set visits Tallahassee Memorial Cancer Center. "We're on the ballfield and it can be amazing fun," Alameda said, "but sometimes it does begin to feel like a hard grind. But the true grind is people working all day and then going and getting chemo at night. Visiting these patients while they sit for long hours getting their chemo treatments is important to show players what tough is." Sometimes the team will do more than just sit with patients in a hospital.

Florida State softball has befriended several young people battling cancer, including Taylor Foster, who they "adopted" in 2013. Alameda says of Foster and the other girls, "To see where they're at in their fight, and then they think we're the superstars? I mean, that's just completely backwards. They're the ones that are teaching us the lessons about life." Foster was a young softball player who in middle school was diagnosed with a bone cancer, osteosarcoma. In a blog for espnW, Lacey Waldrop, star pitcher from those years, explained what Foster meant to the Florida State players. Here are some excerpts: "Taylor is one of those people who lights up a room, who can make any one smile and laugh. She has changed our team for the better. Although she is fighting a tough battle every day, you would never know it. She carries herself with extreme optimism, with hope for the best in life and excitement for better days to come…. When we lose a tough game or she knows the team is struggling, Taylor is the first to text or call us and tell us to get ready for the next game, and there is no one else we'd rather hear it from. Taylor is fighting a battle for her life every day, and we are lucky enough to play softball each and every one of those days, so when Taylor gives us encouragement and tells us to kick it into high gear, we do it…. Taylor is a big part of our family, so we try and brighten her day whenever possible. Each week during meetings we write letters to her, and we even had the opportunity to send her little gifts. We also have a Taylor Foster practice day every other week, and on those days we Skype with Taylor while wearing our special Taylor Foster tie-dye T-shirts…. Taylor has been a great influence on what we call 'The Gate.' Each day we start our practice at the gate, where we take everything that has gone on that day and leave it outside of the field. Whether one of us has had a bad day or not done well on a test, when we get to the gate we know it's time to get to work and make our family better. At the gate we also remember to appreciate our abilities and play for those who can't, like Taylor. We are living the dream, and if we don't make the most out of it, then we are taking our abilities for granted. Coach Alameda and Taylor help remind us of that every day."

* * *

Florida's head coach Tim Walton passed a milestone in February, when he got his 800th career win. Walton surely looks like he's on his way to the NFCA Hall of Fame, as he's averaging over 50 wins a year in his thirteen years as head coach at Florida, and he has led the Gators to eight Women's College World Series appearances and two national championships. In conversation, Walton talks often of the Florida *program*, by which he means all the softball teams down the years, the legacy, a reputation formed on and off the field. When he discusses the importance of building a program, he references playing Michigan and having former players fill rows in the stands. "We played Michigan for the national championship," Walton said, "and they had more alumni in the first three rows of the stadium than any team I've ever seen. Coach Hutchins has created a long-standing history with all those people, and those kids aren't coming back to watch unless they're really connected to that program."

Speaking to my question about how softball honors its pioneers, such as Judi Garman or Margie Wright, Walton replied that "obviously there's a male and female category." But he went on to say that he doesn't believe a divide exists between male and female coaches: "I think that divide has probably washed over now because there's a lot of talented female and male coaches in this sport who genuinely do it the right way and take care of the young people and graduate them and win along the way." Perhaps because prominent male coaches such as Mike Candrea of Arizona, Patrick Murphy of Alabama, or Walton have accepted whole-heartedly the values and culture that were established in women's softball before they began, their success has been accepted, in return. The norm for women's softball coaches is definitely not win at all costs, or that minor cheating is necessary—no, the culture says teach the players that success comes from within, and involves much more than game results. Candrea is just behind Carol Hutchins in career wins, and he has led Arizona to eight national championships. His style might be different than Hutch's, but his concern for the player and her life, not just winning games, is similar. "You don't coach players for four years," goes one of his oft-repeated mottos, that has two layers to it, "you coach softball players for a lifetime."

Five

Spring Break Adventures

I went to Florida in mid–March to attend the Clearwater Spring Break Classic, and I witnessed softball's version of Girls Gone Wild: players stealing second, sliding in head first, popping up and clapping their hands; shortstops ranging into the 5–6 hole, gloving hard grounders and making strong throws to first to nip batters; pitchers spinning curves and bringing the heat from the circle. Saturday was both hot and March 17, St. Patrick's Day, and the green Gatorade was flowing.

The women's college softball season can be divided into three parts: weeks of non-league play at sites where a variety of teams gather, followed by conference games, and then the NCAA tournament for teams who qualify. Mid-March is a transition time for the DI calendar. Schools whose leagues have numerous members and warm weather, such as the SEC and Sunbelt Conference, begin league play early, the weekend of March 9–11 this year. The Big South and the Pac-12, with good weather but fewer teams, were opening this weekend. The Spring Break Classic is the fourth in a series of events hosted by the University of South Florida (USF), 2018 marking the sixteenth year of college softball teams coming to Clearwater to play at the Eddie C. Moore Complex. While the first two events of the series had teams from across the country, the next two, including the Spring Break Classic, primarily had drawn northern teams who still had weeks before beginning league play. The seven-member America East Conference, for example, doesn't begin their conference schedule until the end of March, when the cold and the snow have exited the region—the teams hope—and their fields become playable.

Unlike the Mary Nutter tournament, where sixteen ranked teams played, the Spring Break Classic had no team ranked in the top twenty-five. While fans across the country tend to focus on programs such as UCLA, Florida, and Oklahoma, only about 550 women in DI play for ranked teams, while more than 5500 play for teams that focus on conference play to make the NCAA tournament. That these teams won't likely be playing late into May doesn't dim the players' enthusiasm—they seemed quite ecstatic, actually, to be outside and playing a sport they love.

Jill Karwoski played two years of basketball and four years of softball for Lewis University, in Romeoville, Illinois. Named to the 2001 NFCA All-Region Team, Karwoski, like many softball players, also achieved highly in the classroom, where she was a four-time NFCA Academic All-American. With her measured speech and modish glasses, she reminded me of a partner in a law firm, but she's the coach of Quinnipiac's softball team and well aware of the difficulties that northern teams—Quinnipiac is in Connecticut—face playing a spring sport that begins its season in early February. The difficulties are increased, she pointed out, if your program's budget is on the small side.

While a northern team from a Power Five conference, Notre Dame for example, did play its first twenty-seven games on the road, the team flew out-of-state on four weekends *before* embarking on its spring break trip that included ACC match-ups with North Carolina State and Louisville, as well as mid-week games in Jacksonville, Florida. Quinnipiac, on the other hand, can only budget money for two flights each year. The team waits until the season's second weekend to begin play, typically flying to Florida, where it's often competing against southern schools who have been practicing outdoors and have already played five or more games. The Quinnipiac players' warm-ups are the first time in months that they have seen dirt or fielded fly balls with sun and wind. The team then sits out the next weekend, practicing indoors under less-than-ideal conditions, before bussing south to get in some games, if the weather cooperates. This year, two of their five games in Maryland were cancelled. In their first two weekends of play, mostly against southern schools who had practiced outdoors and played more games, the team went 1–8.

Early in the season Quinnipiac always travels to play, and even if all goes well and they get in their games, the team returns to their indoor facilities. The team hopes to be on their outdoor field in March, and sometimes they get out for a few days, but then they can have snow fall and make their field unplayable. Over the past three years, Quinnipiac's Connecticut campus has been hit with snowstorms over spring break, which puts their home opener, typically in late March, in jeopardy. Surprisingly to me, Karwoski takes this pretty much in stride, as do coaches of other northern teams that I've been talking to. "It's part of our softball culture," she said, "to have these built-in issues. We know that we're going to have problems with the weather, and we have to minimize the rollercoaster effect that can create. We know that we're going to be on the road, and we prepare them for this as students and players. I don't restrict their choice of major, for example, but they'll have to figure out how to make up lost work. I preach to my players that they have to become advocates for themselves, going to professors ahead of time and making arrangements for how to minimize their absences. That's part of our culture, playing softball at Quinnipiac."

Like other coaches at northern schools, Karwoski tries to turn a disadvantage into an advantage. "We use the terms work-life balance a lot," she said, "because the more quickly they're able to figure that out, the more successful they'll be after they leave here. And one of the advantages from a recruiting standpoint is that we do travel and we can experience different parts of the country. We're emphasizing the experience of what we do, as compared to winning." At the Spring Break Classic, Quinnipiac did a bit of both, going 3–2. They got three wins in the circle from senior Casey Herzog, who gave up only one run, and outfielder Erin Larsen went 8–14 on the weekend, with seven RBI. Quinnipiac got run-ruled, however, in their two losses.

The University of Maine softball team was set to play its first thirty-two games on the road and not open at home until April 11. Maine, like Quinnipiac and Lehigh, came and played in two USF events—the university was on its spring break—and also picked up a few games midweek. Maine's head coach, Mike Coutts, is no newcomer to the difficulties that arise from coaching a spring sport at one of the most northern universities in the country. The differences in schedule for Maine and other northern schools actually begin in fall ball. Warm-weather colleges might begin their year with conditioning drills and individual skill lessons, then begin formal practices in mid to late September and play their fall ball games in late October or, like Florida, even later in mid–November. But in the north, the days begin getting quite short and so fall season runs from the beginning of September to mid–October. When players return to school following the Christmas break, they won't play on their field for months. Maine has a dome for practices, but they can only put fences out at 150 feet—outfielders don't really see fly balls like they will see outdoors—and they have no dirt for infielders. But Coutts does not use the weather as an excuse. "Everyone who comes here," he said, "knows what we face, and we try to use that to our advantage, to build character and see what we can accomplish in difficult situations." He acknowledged the difficulty in recruiting girls who have opportunity to play in warmer places, who say they're sick of practicing indoors or playing in the cold when spring comes. "But sometimes it works the other way," he said. "I have two girls from California and one from Florida who are coming to our program next year. They each said they wanted four seasons, wanted to be in a place where it snows."

Coutts expects his team to struggle early in the year, when they are traveling and playing against teams in higher-tier conferences, or against teams who have been fielding and hitting outdoors. It's particularly eye-opening to his newcomers, he said, who have to adjust to college competition, to the travel, to doing their academic work on the road. "We slowly get the ball rolling," Coutts said, "so we're reaching a peak when we get to our league season—early on, we're as interested in teaching the players how to compete, or how to be a good teammate. If those things are in place, then the winning will follow." He has adapted his expectations to the reality of the situation.

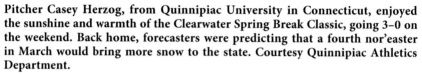

Pitcher Casey Herzog, from Quinnipiac University in Connecticut, enjoyed the sunshine and warmth of the Clearwater Spring Break Classic, going 3–0 on the weekend. Back home, forecasters were predicting that a fourth nor'easter in March would bring more snow to the state. Courtesy Quinnipiac Athletics Department.

The northern teams playing in the Spring Break Classic were happy to be in Clearwater, playing softball outdoors in the sunshine, but reports from back home were of blizzards and nor'easters. Coaches I talked to were contemplating how many of their upcoming games would be cancelled. One northern team looking ready for conference play was Maine, who went 3–1 on the weekend, including a big win against ASUN member Florida Gulf Coast University, who at that point was 22–4 with a nine game win streak. Maine was not picked to win the America East Conference—Binghamton was—but the Black Bears looked ready to contend. Perhaps the most impressive northern team at the Spring Break Classic was Long Island University-Brooklyn, who won four games. Their next game would be their opener in the Northeast Conference. For these northern teams beginning conference play against opponents with similar weather conditions, the playing field would at last be level, and (they hoped) literally free of snow.

Southern hospitality is legendary, but the University of South Florida, the event host, treated badly the visitors they played. The Bulls went 5–0, shutting out four of the teams and run-ruling three. They came into the tournament with considerable advantages, and not just the ones that come from staying home and playing on your home field. Quinnipiac had played sixteen games before beginning the tournament, Princeton only ten. USF had played twenty-nine games, all in South Florida and most of them on their home field. The computer crunching the numbers for the RPI didn't know that, of course.

* * *

Now, imagine you're the coach of a northern school that about 80 percent of high school students don't qualify for because of standards for height-weight, general fitness, ADHD, asthma, mental health issues, current medications, or location of tattoos. Now add in that you're looking to recruit only women who can play DI softball and who are qualified to get into an academically rigorous school. That small pool is made even smaller because you're asking them as teens to make a twelve-year commitment. And if you do get players on campus, they will almost always be sleep-deprived.

You've entered the world of Michelle DePolo, who in 2009 was named the head coach for Army's softball program, the first female coach for the program since it moved from DII to DI in 1991. In her first season, 2010, Army won the Patriot League title after being picked next to last in the pre-season poll. In 2012 the team went 37–21. DePolo had an incredible 2016 season where the team narrowly lost the league but won thirty-nine games, the winningest season in program history. How does Army softball do this? While her pool of recruits is tiny, DePolo feels strongly that if they can get the recruit on campus, Army has a good chance of enrolling them. "A lot of our roster had never heard of West Point before I talked to them," DePolo said, "but there are some players who have wanted to come forever, or who have military in the family. We get a wide demographic."

The year 1972 marked the passage of Title IX, which declared that women should have equal opportunities in universities receiving federal aid. In 1976, 119 women became the first female cadets at West Point when they joined the Class of 1980. DePolo's father was a naval commander, and Michelle grew up wanting to be a female cadet, to go to West Point to play softball. "One of the pillars that is most cherished at West Point," she said, "is the 'selfless service' aspect—you're not here to serve yourself, but to serve your team, or your institution, or the greater good. 'Me' ahead of 'you' is not part of this. I hold that as a personal value which aligns with the values of West Point, which is part of why I had always wanted to go there." DePolo didn't qualify for West Point, however, not because of the usual things, but because she had two heart surgeries when she was a newborn, which turned out to be disqualifying. DePolo landed instead at nearby Georgian Court University, an all-women's college in New Jersey whose sports teams compete in DII. As a pitcher for the softball team, she led Georgian Court to four league titles and, in 2001, compiled a 0.50 ERA. She starred in soccer and basketball as well as softball, and somehow still managed to excel in the classroom, graduating magna cum laude in English.

West Point has a values-based sports program in which all students must participate for the physical development and for the mental development that comes from being part of a team. Some cadets play competitive intramural programs, while others join a competitive club sports program. Then there are the athletes who add participation on DI intercollegiate teams to their academic load and military training. DI athletes balance what are in essence two nearly full-time jobs, playing softball and being a student, and Army players add a third: military training.

When I heard about the daily schedule of an Army player, I said to De-Polo, "To me, it's kind of a miracle that you win any games."

"Yeah, to me, too," she replied.

In 2018 Army softball had a twenty-six-player roster, most of whom De-Polo recruited, and a few who walked on. DePolo needs a large roster. Military training not only physically and mentally taxes the players but has the potential to end seasons. At the Spring Break Classic, Army had three players out with season-ending injuries, none softball related. "We're going to have people injured," DePolo said, "and injuries have to be taken care of immediately. At another school players might wait to have surgery, but we can't do that because they will have summer training and the students have Physical Education classes that are required in order to graduate." All cadets take lifetime sports classes and have to pass a swimming test, but these aren't the kind of classes that Army softball need worry about. Graduation requirements also include combatives, military movement (a difficult obstacle course), and boxing, in which athletes have been known, not infrequently, to suffer concussions. West Point takes its concussion protocol seriously; a concussion in the required boxing class can put an athlete on the shelf for a month.

Observing the landscape of American young people, cultural commentators coined the term Snowflake Generation, a label that has caught on to describe how young adults of the 2010s are more prone to take offense and are less resilient than previous generations in coping with views that challenge their own. "Snowflake" has become a label for children raised by their parents in ways that give them an inflated sense of their own uniqueness. The culture of a sports team—a women's softball team, let's say—can combat the impulse to offer excuses or to not accept consequences. The culture at West Point reinforces this in spades.

"West Point does a good job of keeping young people humble," DePolo said. "This even comes down to the way we travel. We wear our army uniforms on the plane. Identity comes mostly from being a cadet, not from being an athlete. If you're waiting in an airport, you have to sit up straight and have your uniform looking good. You can't do anything that wouldn't represent West Point well." Cadets—Army softball players—don't get plush new athletic dormitories or apartments. They sleep on a twin-size bed in barracks. Cadets are told what time to get up every day, what they will wear every day. A compensation? "My players are low maintenance," DePolo said. "If we're having sandwiches for dinner, they don't complain."

One thing Army softball players would definitely like more of is sleep. During a game at the Spring Break Classic, I was sitting behind home plate at the media table, and next to me were three injured players responsible for the team's video cameras. I was interviewing only one of them, Mae Wadyka, but when I asked, "How many hours do you sleep at night?" there was general laughter by all three players. "We have formation every day at 7:00," Wadyka said, "and plebes [first year cadets] have to be on The Wall counting down the minutes before that. Our first class starts at 7:30 [more general hooting when I told them that my students complain about having a 9:00 class], and classes go until 4:00. We usually start practice between 4:30 and 5:30, but on alternate days the team doesn't have late classes, so we can practice earlier in the afternoon. When we have later practices, we can't make it to the mess hall, and so the coaches put in for rations and food is provided."

I asked Wadyka when the players typically get back to their barracks. "After showering and eating," she said, "on a normal day it's 7:30 or 8:00. And then we have to study at night."

"So you're locked into a schedule for an entire day."

Wadyka: "Yes, sir."

Win Muffett is from La Center, Washington, but he was in Florida for the Spring Break Classic. His daughter, Megan, is a freshman catcher for Army, and he can attest from a parent's viewpoint about the demands of being an athlete at Army: "They're often up by 5:30 in the morning. If I text Megan in the morning, I don't hear from her until perhaps late at night, after she's returned to the barracks. Sometimes I get a text that I know was written at 11:00 at night, saying that she still has a couple hours of homework to do, and you know that she's going to have to be up very early the next morning." Michelle DePolo had commented that one of her biggest challenges is working with players who are almost always sleep-deprived, and I asked Muffett if he worries about his daughter in this regard. "I mostly just try to wrap my head around the fact that she does everything that West Point asks these cadets to do." With a laugh, he added, "I'm glad it's not me. My college experience was a lot easier than that."

I asked him if he knew a term that college administrators and faculty have been talking about constantly for the last decade: helicopter parent. "I'm very familiar with the term and that is something that we can't be," Muffett said. "I don't even have weekly calls. I have texts a few times a week. And that's it. The cadets have made their choice and if they're going to develop into the leaders that West Point wants them to be, they don't need parents to be weighing in about what to do. My job was done before she left. I trust her to make good decisions. I come to softball games to see her face to face."

As a freshman, Wadyka had been one of Army's best players on perhaps their all-time best team. She hit .314 while starting 58 games, but she's out injured for a second straight year. She's a junior, which at West Point means she is a "cow" (this is not gender-specific; men are also cows). She played travel ball in Houston and started getting recruited by Army before her sophomore year in high school. Though she knew nothing at first about West Point or service academies, something about the school struck a deep chord. "At first I was resistant to the idea of going there but then I started getting into it," she said, and added with the utmost sincerity, "how do you say no to this kind of opportunity."

Attending West Point is at least a twelve-year commitment: four years of school; five years as a commissioned officer; and if you leave at that point, three years in the reserves. I said, " So you knew the commitment, and you were only 15 years old at the time, but you thought 'this is for me.' "

"Yes, sir," Wadyka replied.

I had not been called "sir" in my entire lifetime as much as I was called "sir" during the interviews I had with Army players.

Ashley Yoo was another of those juniors out with a season-ending injury. Yoo attended high school in Yorba Linda, California, and played on an elite SoCal travel ball team. Some West Coast schools were interested in her, but

In addition to playing a DI sport and succeeding at an academically rigorous school, Army softball players include military training in their schedules. It's an understatement to say that their days are demanding. Courtesy of West Point Athletics.

she knew she wanted to go back east for school. Turning down various offers, including one from a Big Ten school, Yoo went to Army, started fifty-seven games as a freshman, and blossomed last year into an all-league player who was named NFCA Third Team All-Northeast Region. Izzy Gates, from Minnesota, the third junior who would have played significant innings this year without her injury, had actually committed to a Big Ten school before changing her mind in fall of her senior year and signing with Army.

Ally Snelling *was* playing, starting at shortstop as a freshman. She was not a hard sell for DePolo. Snelling said that she always liked the idea of service, and she was patriotic, and she knew she wanted to do something big with her life. "Softball is, for four years, a big part of our lives here, but at the same time we do have a chance to make the world better. To be at West Point has been so great—to be a part of history, to be a part of all these great people who went to the academy. You gain a team for life. You gain a great amount of humility by going to West Point." Some humility, and satisfaction, comes from simply managing to do everything that is asked of you. "West Point," Snelling says, "preaches 'be the standard.' With your uniform, or how you act, or accomplishing your duties, you just try to be the standard."

While West Point culture instills teamwork and self-sacrifice, the school also excels in leadership training. All cadets have to be ready to lead under any circumstances, even as they have to be team players, ready to obey orders within a larger group. Wadyka was a squad leader, a position she didn't get out of when she was injured. Her squad consisted of three yearlings (sophomores), who were each responsible for a plebe—making sure that the freshmen were accomplishing their military duties, succeeding in the classroom, obeying the rules, and so forth. These relations are not gender-based. "We don't really think about gender," Wadyka said, "when it comes to how we organize." Wadyka sees her leadership training and experiences as invaluable for her future, and was part of what interested her in attending West Point.

Snelling echoed this desire to lead. Perhaps the understanding as teenage girls that a leadership role will be not only possible for them but will definitely happen creates a similarity of character in teammates. Asked about being a commissioned officer upon graduation, Snelling said that it's nerve-wracking to think about, but also a challenge. "I'll be twenty-one years old, leading about thirty-five people, who could be both younger and older than me, both men and women. There's some pressure in thinking about that, but more excitement than anything. I know that by the time I get there [ready to lead] I will have been prepared to do that job. That's what West Point is for, to prepare me to be a future leader."

The West Point military culture, with its emphasis on hierarchies, with leading and following, can make for some tricky relations on the softball field. "When players get on the field," DePolo said, "a plebe might be the heart and soul of the team, but there is a pecking order. A plebe can't fraternize with upperclassmen. A senior team captain can't go out and have dinner with the young players. And so if you have a freshman shortstop or catcher, they have some difficulty in telling the upperclassmen what to do." DePolo had humorous stories about the intertwining of softball roles and West Point hierarchies. One concerned a freshman who was a fantastic defensive center fielder, but kept letting balls drop in front of her in left and right center. "One day it was happening again," DePolo related, "and I'm wondering what's happening out there. I confronted her directly. It turned out that she was waiting for the right fielder to call her off, because the right fielder was a senior. And she had a junior in left, who she was treating the same way. I had to convince my freshman that she was the centerfielder and had to take charge and take all the fly balls she could get to." The Army at large is a team, and so is the softball program, and players have to figure out how to mesh the two.

Army's softball team so far this year was a work in progress, given the injuries, the changes in the line-up that those injuries entailed, and the more ambitious schedule that DePolo created this year. It's unlikely that they would win thirty or more games, particularly given that five games had already been cancelled due to weather issues, and more cancellations were likely. They almost had an excellent weekend in Florida, but ended with a 3–2 record when they gave up a five-run lead to the University of Tennessee at Chattanooga in the final inning. But as much as DePolo and the team want to win, and she wants to win badly, there are other perspectives. "Every player on our team," she said, "is just a fantastic individual. When we find that small fraction of people who *can* come here and then who *want* to come here, they are just something special. If you ask me what is the number one thing I love about my job, it's working with these young women."

*   *   *

While the unranked teams at the Spring Break Classic, including Army, were trying to improve and be conference-ready, the powerhouse SEC and Pac-12 conferences were showing just how many contenders for the national crown they each might have. Washington was undefeated and ranked #1 heading into their weekend series at Arizona State, but the Sun Devils took the series 2–1 behind ace pitcher G Juarez, who threw two shutouts against the high-scoring Washington line-up. Arizona State was one of those teams under the radar and underrated coming into the season; of their four season losses, three were to Oklahoma, Washington, and Tennessee, all teams ranked in the top five. Third-ranked UCLA also fell from the ranks of the unbeaten, going down twice to sixth-ranked Oregon in Eugene. In the series opener, the Bruins' Rachel Garcia homered and went the distance in the circle, beating Megan Kleist, but Kleist and the Ducks turned the tables in the series closer, when Oregon's Shannon Rhodes hit a walk-off three-run homer to beat UCLA and Garcia 3–0.

The weekend's biggest news came from the SEC, when Georgia won a series from Florida. That Florida lost two games was a bit surprising; the way they lost had implications that could affect their season. In the first inning of the first game, with two outs and two strikes on Georgia's Alyssa DiCarlo, Florida's All-American pitcher Kelly Barnhill got DiCarlo to pop up but was called for an illegal pitch. With another chance, DiCarlo homered, as did the next two batters for Georgia, Alysen Febrey and Mahlena O'Neal. At issue is whether Barnhill re-plants when she throws—a call she seldom had go against her in previous years, perhaps because the penalty, a ball on the batter and an advancement of one base for all runners on, seemed severe. But with the rule change that an illegal pitch only results in a ball and not an advancement (though the offensive team can take the results of the play), umpires may be calling illegal pitches more often this year. In the second game of the series, Barnhill got another illegal pitch called in a crucial situation, and DiCarlo hit another homer not long after. Georgia was expected to be good this season, but no one anticipated this much improvement after they went 6–18 last year in conference play. Also improved and another early-season surprise in the SEC was Tennessee, expected to be good but looking great. The #4 ranked team in the country, Tennessee swept through the Rainbow Wahine Classic in Hawaii on their spring break trip, winning six games to up their record to 30–1.

Like Tennessee, Williams College was ranked fourth nationally, #4 in their division, DIII. But they had not yet won, or lost, a game. On Sunday, March 18, they opened their season with two wins at the Spring Games in Clermont, Florida—their ranking was based primarily on their having reached the DIII World Series in 2017 and returning most of their line-up, including some superb pitchers. Williams, one of the best liberal arts colleges in the country, makes academics *the* priority. The team won't fly south during a week that classes are in session, because the players would have to be gone on a Thursday and Friday, missing classes, perhaps even labs or exams. The team can't schedule home games before April because the campus is located in western Massachusetts. So they wait until their two-week spring break before traveling to Florida, and then they play a lot of softball: doubleheaders many days; half of their season schedule.

From February 22 until March 30, teams from northern climates whose fields aren't playable descend on Clermont to participate in the Spring Games, which caters to programs who play at the DII, DIII, and junior college levels, as well as colleges that play in the National Association of Intercollegiate Athletics (NAIA). The 340 college teams playing this year owed a large debt to Dot Richardson, the event's founder and initial organizer, who is now the head softball coach at Liberty University. In her college softball career, Richardson was a standout shortstop at UCLA, receiving All-American honors every year and helping the Bruins in 1982 win their first of eleven national championships. She was named the 1980s NCAA Player of the Decade, but her accomplishments didn't end there. She graduated from UCLA with a degree in kinesiology, received a Masters Degree in Exercise Physiology from Adelphi University in 1988, and an M.D. from Louisville in 1993. Midway through a post-doctoral residency in orthopedic surgery, Richardson joined the national softball team preparing for the Atlanta Olympics in 1996, and she helped Team USA win the gold medal that year and again in Sydney in 2000.

Medicine and softball became intertwined for Richardson in a new way when she retired after the Olympics. She got married in 2001, began a private practice in Clermont, and became an executive with South Lake Hospital, in part because of their connection to the National Training Center, a state-of-the-art sports and fitness facility that the hospital opened as a way to embed sports, health, and fitness activities within an education and wellness campus. "When I was hired by the hospital," Richardson recalled, "I was hired as the executive director of the National Training Center: pool, track, multipurpose fields. I said let's get some team sports here, and we raised three million dollars and created a partnership between Lake Sumter Community College [now Lake Sumter State College], Lake County, and the hospital. We put the fields on Lake Sumter's property, because they could get matching funds from the state. Then the CEO of the hospital told me that the new facilities would have to make some money to pay for their upkeep."

Dot Richardson tags out a runner during the 2000 Sydney Olympics. The enthusiasm and charisma she shows here extends to everything she has done: starring at UCLA in the 1980s, playing for Olympic teams in 1996 and 2000, practicing medicine in Florida, and founding the Spring Games in Clermont, Florida. She brings her energy to her position as head softball coach of Liberty University. Photograph by Nick Wilson.

"The year before the Legends Way Ballfields were completed was the year that my former coach, Marge Ricker, had sold The Rebel Games [a long-standing Florida tournament] to another individual. So I decided to begin my own tournament aimed at teams in DIII, who didn't really have a good place to go at that time. I got on the phone and called colleges, talking about our fields, and DIII coaches started saying 'I'm coming' because they weren't getting all that they wanted at other tournaments. I asked them what they needed, and it wasn't a lot: great fields, a drag between games, good umpires, water in the dugout, and medical help if there were injuries. Our first year in 2008 we had forty-eight teams. We started with DIII, then went to DII, then we heard from NAIA. We had about 340 teams last year."

The Spring Games: during their spring breaks, 340 teams from DII, DIII, JUCO, and NAIA levels descended on Clermont, Florida. The players from DIII Williams College, a school in Massachusetts, are shown here on a March day with warm sunshine, watching the action on Field Five of Legends Way Ballfields at the National Training Center. Williams plays half their season schedule over these two weeks. Courtesy Kris Herman.

The Spring Games is one of many activities promoted by PFX Athletics, the organization that Richardson founded with a mission to open the doors of opportunity for women and girls through sport. To this end, PFX Athletics does outreach throughout central Florida for softball teams of all ages, though the Spring Games for college teams are its biggest event, which at its height has games played at three venues in addition to Legends Way Ballfields. As president and executive director of PFX Athletics, Alison Strange is responsible for scheduling all these teams and managing these sites.

The Spring Games serves well these non–DI schools located in cold weather climates who have small budgets and can't afford to travel multiple times; games are scheduled to play a large role in team development. For purposes of scheduling, Strange asks each coach to indicate if there are teams they'd like to play (teams coached by a former player, for example) or teams they don't want to play. She also asks coaches to rank themselves along an A-E scale, which goes like this—A: We expect to go to regionals; B: We expect to go to conference; C: We hope to win more games than we lose, but we're average; D: We're probably going to struggle; E: We hope to survive the season. (Strange mentioned that the number of Es she gets surprises her.) A coach who ranks her team a B will play mostly against other teams similarly ranked, but might play a game up one level or down. Over the course of their stay at the Spring Games, a team will get to challenge itself at its desired level. Computer software helps Strange with this complex scheduling, but listening and hard work matter equally.

Alison Strange is Dot Richardson's niece, but when you come to know her sports journey, you understand that no nepotism was at work with the hire. Strange played college softball at Stetson, and then toured in a pro league. In addition to her undergraduate degree, she has an MBA and is a practicing attorney. She wrote her undergrad thesis and her law school thesis on Title IX, both its history and legislative administration. She's a mother of two, with a ten-year-old daughter and a five-year-old son, who often accompany her to her work. Strange is an articulate advocate for girls' and women's softball at all levels, and a passionate proponent generally of women's rights.

One of her goals with the Spring Games is to consider the needs of all women. As one example of change she's enacted, female umpires and male umpires each have their own rooms where they undress to put on their gear, rather than having, as many facilities do, one changing room for everyone. For coaches, Strange wants to make the experience family-friendly: "I want this event to have a culture such that a coach can have a family in tow and that's okay. With the Spring Games, I see pregnant coaches, coaches with babies in papooses, and I know that coaches who are on maternity leave are watching the live stream so that they can keep up with their team. My experience is that our society is transitioning so that you can be a mother and a breadwinner and not have to choose between these roles. How can I be an advocate for women in business or women in sport and not support the women who are trying to balance work and families? We try to be very women-focused, women-friendly."

Strange knows, from personal experience, how exciting softball can be at all levels. "I want people to see softball," she said, "and not with the prejudice that I had when I came out here. To be honest, DI was what I knew, and this was DII, or DIII. In my first day out here, standing up on the mezzanine overlooking all the fields, I watched a triple play, a collision at the plate, and a diving catch in the outfield within five minutes. I went, 'oh my gosh, you don't see ball like that every day.' When we match teams that are of equal caliber, it doesn't matter what division they are, or where they are ranked, you can end up watching a great game. We need to get corporate America to see it for what it is, because I've never had someone watch a college softball game and not be impressed by the female athletes."

Media coverage of most sports, focusing on the highest level that is played either nationally or locally, leaves out the vast majority of teams. In softball last year, 1382 teams and about 26,000 college players participated at a level that is not DI. All those players are dedicated and skilled, even if most don't have the elite speed or powerful bodies of the players we watch on ESPN telecasts. Strange has worked hard in recent years to livestream the Spring Games, and she's proud that she's made relationships and partnerships that have allowed her to do that. More than 1500 games were livestreamed this year, so that fans anywhere could watch their teams or just watch good softball.

Perhaps because of her background as a player and as an executive, Strange understands the many ways that sexism exists in softball. She's adamant that the sport needs to livestream its games because she believes that women's softball has, to some extent, lost its visual history—current fans have no video to see former legends. One of my favorite stories that Strange related was about a female announcer, a former DI softball player who was calling a televised playoff game for the Sun Conference championships, which PFX Athletics hosts at Legends Way Ballfields. After a great play by a shortstop, the announcer called it a "Derek Jeteresque" play, referring to the Yankees' legend. The press box and the offices are in the same area, and when Strange heard this reference, she quickly got up from her desk, went over to where the production was happening, and during a timeout between innings told the announcer that she had two choices, she could reference Dot Richardson or Natasha Watley but not a baseball player. "She looked at me," Strange recalled, "and said, 'I would be happy to do that but I've never seen them play.'" Watley, one of the all-time greats of the game, who starred at UCLA, starred for the 2004 and 2008 Olympics teams, and holds career batting marks in the pro leagues, retired only in 2017. There's considerable awareness raising to do.

Six

You've Come
a Long Way, Baby

Most Americans regard the eleven "titles" of 1964's Civil Rights Act as race legislation that ended segregation and unfair voting practices, but its landmark status eventually extended to other areas. Two particular titles paved the way for later gender rights opportunities. Title VI ("Nondiscrimination In Federally Assisted Programs, Section 601") states, *"No person in the United States shall, on the ground of race, color, or national origin, be excluded from participation in, be denied the benefits of, or be subjected to discrimination under any program or activity receiving Federal financial assistance;* and Title VII, the "job discrimination" law, states *It shall be an unlawful employment practice for an employer ... to discriminate against any individual with respect to his compensation, terms, conditions, or privileges of employment, because of such individual's race, color, religion, sex, or national origin."*

Numerous women, in and out of politics, were instrumental in pushing forward women's rights in those years, including Martha Griffiths, a Congresswoman from Michigan whose efforts succeeded in getting the Equal Rights Amendment to the House Floor for discussion. But it was Shirley Chisholm who on that day, August 10, 1970, got up on the House Floor, spoke in favor of the Equal Rights Amendment, and shaped the contours of the debate.

Shirley Chisholm is an important but largely forgotten American, who few in today's softball world would know as a pioneer who influenced the passage of Title IX in 1972. She graduated from Brooklyn College, got her M.A. in 1952 from Teachers College at Columbia University, and after years of local public service was elected as a Democratic member to the New York State Assembly in 1965. There, she was instrumental in getting unemployment benefits extended to domestic workers and was known for her sponsorship of a SEEK program (Search for Education, Elevation and Knowledge), which provided disadvantaged students the chance to enter college while receiving intensive remedial education. In 1968, Chisholm became the first black woman elected to the United States Congress, where she served for seven terms. In 1972, she became the first black presidential candidate for a major party's nomination, as well as the first woman to run for the Democratic Party's presidential nomination. In 2015, she was posthumously awarded the Presidential Medal of Freedom. Chisholm is a foremother of women's college softball not because of her personal example, or her years of hard work on behalf of underrepresented groups, but for one electrifying speech that she gave on the House Floor in support of women's rights.

Reminding the House of Representatives that legislators had been discussing gender rights for forty years without doing anything, Chisholm argued that the push for civil rights on the basis of race had to extend to gender. "As a black person," she said, "I am no stranger to race prejudice. But the truth is that in the political world I have been far oftener discriminated against because I am a woman than because I am black." She argued against the commonly held view that women are already protected under the law: "Existing laws are not adequate to secure equal rights for women. Sufficient proof of this is the concentration of women in lower paying, menial, unrewarding jobs and their incredible scarcity in the upper level jobs. If women are already equal, why is it such an event whenever one happens to be elected to Congress? It is obvious that discrimination exists. Women do not have the opportunities that men do. And women that do not conform to the system, who try to break with the accepted patterns, are stigmatized as 'odd' and 'unfeminine.' The fact is that a woman who aspires to be chairman of the board, or a Member of the House, does so for exactly the same reasons as any man. Basically, these are that she thinks she can do the job and she wants to try."

She thinks she can do the job. She wants to try. She aspires to whatever men can do. She should be given an opportunity. Younger Americans who have grown up in the 1980s or after might have difficulty understanding the doors that were once closed to women. For just one example in sports, when Bobbi Gibb made history by competing in the Boston Marathon in 1966, she had to begin the race dressed as a man, because women were banned from competing—women's races were limited to 1.5 miles by the Amateur Athletic Union (AAU), the national ruling body on amateur sports at the time, who publicly stated that if a woman ran farther her uterus might burst!

The Equal Rights Amendment passed the House, passed the Senate, and over the next few years was passed by thirty-five state legislatures, though it ultimately failed to become the law of the land when it fell short of the thirty-eight states needed for ratification. But if the ERA failed to become a constitutional amendment, the debates about women's rights partially succeeded. Congress extended 1964's Title VI (*"Nondiscrimination In Federally Assisted Programs, Section 601"*) to women in schools, with the passage in 1972 of Title IX of the Education Amendment of 1972, which states in Section 1681: *"No person in the United States shall, on the basis of sex, be excluded from partici-*

pation in, be denied the benefits of, or be subjected to discrimination under any education program or activity receiving Federal financial assistance."

The author of Title IX and its chief Senate sponsor, Birch Bayh of Indiana, argued on the Senate floor that this amendment was "an important first step in the effort to provide for the women of America something that is rightfully theirs—an equal chance to attend the schools of their choice, to develop the skills they want, and to apply those skills with the knowledge that they will have a fair chance to secure the jobs of their choice with equal pay for equal work." Discussions of Title IX, which has largely made possible women's sports as we know them, never referred directly to sports. Its proponents were trying to open doors of medical schools, law schools, business schools, and the like to female students.

Women did not begin playing college sports only after passage of Title IX. For decades, colleges and universities had fielded women's teams, and before that, reaching back into the 1920s, the Women's Division of the National Amateur Athletic Foundation and the Committee on Women's Athletics of the American Physical Education Association had overseen opportunities for girls and women to play sports. Their emphasis, however, was on participation and sportsmanship. Until passage of Title IX, women's sports were part of a recreational model that primarily encouraged women to try new activities; the sports were taught by Physical Education instructors, who were responsible for a large number of classes as well as out-of-class sports teams.

A women's equality march in Washington, D.C., in 1970. The push for gender rights didn't get the Equal Rights Amendment to the U.S. Constitution ratified, but the drive succeeded with legislation such as Title IX that had far-reaching consequences, and not just in the sports arena. Photograph by Warren K. Leffler.

The Association for Intercollegiate Athletics for Women (AIAW), founded in 1971 to govern collegiate women's athletics in the United States, grew in membership and influence throughout the late 1970s. The AIAW wanted a model different from the NCAA's model, one focused less on money, scholarships, and competing. Their 1974 policy statement on character states that "inner satisfactions are the fundamental motivation for participation in sports." The AIAW forbade programs, for example, from offering scholarships or having coaches recruit off-campus, until they were sued by players and coaches from two colleges in Florida. When the NCAA in the late 1970s got interested in administering women's sports, a battle ensued. The NCAA was a powerful adversary for the AIAW because of its wealth and history. When it offered to pay all expenses for teams competing in a national championship and to create financial aid, recruitment, and eligibility rules that were the same for women as for men, the NCAA won the day. Representatives from Divisions II and III voted in 1980 to join the NCAA; in 1981, Division I members followed.

While the goals of amateur athletics and the AIAW were admirable, far fewer girls and women than boys and men were participating in sports. But the possibility of landing a college athletic scholarship created a boom in the number of female participants. In 1974 Ann Meyers became the first woman to receive a full college sports scholarship when she accepted an offer from UCLA to play basketball; by 2015, women were receiving more than a billion dollars per year in scholarship money. The year before Title IX was enacted, about 310,000 girls and women in America played high school and college sports; forty years later, in 2012, more than 3.3 million girls and women participated. Though some observers now look back fondly at the AIAW, in hindsight we can see that the AIAW model was likely to become a version of segregation: separate and decidedly unequal. Compared to men's programs, women's teams in the 1970s were vastly underfunded, and this applied to coaching salaries, equipment, travel expenses, and facilities.

Because the number of women's college teams was rising rapidly in the 1970s, as were the expectations for those sports to go beyond recreational play, the colleges were looking for coaches. So began a heady decade for female coaches, when anything seemed possible and everything seemed like an improvement. Linda Wells was one of those groundbreaking coaches. A five-sport athlete at Southeast Missouri State, she enrolled after graduation in the exercise physiology graduate program at the University of Minnesota, and by the age of twenty-four, in 1974, she became the first full-time female head coach at the University of Minnesota. She was hired, on a small salary, to coach three sports: women's volleyball, basketball, and softball. "I also was teaching classes in physical education," she recalled, "and taking graduate courses and working in the physiology lab. In addition, I continued to play field hockey, intramural basketball, volleyball, and softball, and participated in a few amateur tennis tourneys." It's difficult to imagine that she ever slept, but her life did get easier a few years later when her head coaching duties for basketball and volleyball were dropped, though she had to sue the university to make this happen.

Wells has been inducted into ten Halls of Fame, by organizations which she helped develop such as the National Fastpitch Coaches Association, or at universities where she played or coached, including the University of Minnesota and Arizona State University. "Those years of women's rights and advancements of women in education and professions were exciting," Wells told me. "I am proud of my many accomplishments as a player and coach and realize the mix of hard work and passion that contributed to my success." Her story is unique in its particulars but not unusual in those early days of expanding opportunities.

Softball icon Margie Wright, a long-time coach who made her greatest mark guiding the Fresno State program into a perennial national power, remembers those years with great fondness, though her responsibilities might now shock a young coach. "When I first started," Wright recalled about her beginnings in the late 1970s, "a head coach was responsible for everything. We did all of the administrative duties like academics and eligibility, we ordered and took care of the small amount of equipment we were allowed to purchase, we had one set of uniforms and the head coach was responsible for washing them, we did our own fields to prepare them for practices and games, we drove station wagons, vans, and mini buses to transport our teams, we secured our own umpires, and we generally had a graduate assistant as our assistant coach who also had classes that sometimes conflicted with practice. If we wanted any equipment other than what we had in our budget, we would go to other departments and have them make it for us as independent study projects (like protective screens). The head coach was ultimately responsible for everything, including recruiting, and we all loved it because it was an opportunity of a lifetime in our view."

*   *   *

Rather than attending a specific event or league series, this weekend I was following game results on my computer—712 college softball games across all levels were played alone on Saturday, March 24—and I was watching softball games on television from the comfort of my living room. I am not a subscriber to FloSoftball, who was streaming a handful of Big Ten games as well as the Spring Games from Clermont, Florida, but I can access some Big Ten and Pac-12 games, as well as everything showing on Watch ESPN, which in itself had scores of games over the weekend. At one point, I was flipping between a handful of marquee match ups, staying in touch with the pulse of each game. It wasn't exciting the way attending a game and sitting close to the action is exciting, but in a different way I was in couch potato softball heaven.

The weekend was marked by the number of 3–0 series. Against a good Texas Tech team that came into the weekend 20–10, two-time defending champion Oklahoma pushed their win streak to nineteen when they swept the Red Raiders, including a 19–1 beatdown in the series finale. While top-five teams Washington, UCLA, and Florida all lost two of three games to strong opponents last weekend, this weekend they all got back on track: #1 ranked Washington beat #9 Arizona in three close games in Seattle; #4 UCLA swept Oregon State, who sat at #17 in the RPI; #6 Florida continued their surprising domination of a perennial power when they beat #8 Texas A&M three times, pushing their recent record to 13–1 against the Aggies.

For many fans, dominant performances by dominant programs create excitement, as fans anticipate potential match-ups in late May in the Women's College World Series. But other fans like surprise teams, teams that were underrated when the year began. A big story out of the SEC, which seemed to have a different big story each week, was South Carolina's home sweep of #2 ranked Tennessee. South Carolina was picked to finish twelfth in the pre-season SEC coaches' poll, largely because they had graduated their two best pitchers, Nikkie Blue and Jessica Elliott. But Cayla Drotar, the third pitcher last year as a freshman, had stepped up with ace-like numbers, posting a 13–1

In 2018, Giselle "G" Juarez, starting her windup here, got healthy, got more confident, and became an All-American pitching ace for Arizona State, helping launch them into the top ten of the rankings by mid-season. Courtesy Sun Devil Athletics.

record with a 1.49 ERA. Not far behind were Kelsey Oh, a freshman from New Jersey, who had a 1.64 ERA to go with her 7–2 record, and Dixie Raley, who was 8–1 with a 1.90 ERA. Raley, a junior pitcher in her first year with the Gamecocks, had transferred in from Georgia Southern, where she was a 2017 All-Sun Belt second-team selection. With the sweep of Tennessee, South Carolina improved their record to 28–4 and climbed to #9 in the rankings.

Arizona State was ranked #23 in the pre-season NFCA Coaches Poll, so they were on the radar, unlike South Carolina. But the Sun Devils, at 27–4 on the season, were still a surprise story out of the Pac-12. While they had announced themselves nationally last weekend by taking two of three from Washington, Arizona State showed that they were no fluke as they went to Berkeley and swept #20 California, putting them atop the Pac-12 standings with a 5–1 league record. The team's fine play added one milestone to the weekend, as Head Coach Trisha Ford got career win #200. After four years at Fresno State, Ford is in her second year at ASU. One can only believe that her next 200 wins will come considerably faster.

Arizona State had a good 2017 campaign, finishing 31–22 and #26 in the final RPI rankings. How do you make the jump from being good to being a contender for Oklahoma City in late May? Three ways. First, you improve your pitching. Three capable starters were returning, but in 2018 G Juarez was performing like an All-American, carrying a 0.71 ERA to go with her 13–1 record, and returnees Breanna Macha and Dale Ryndak were throwing consistently and could be counted on to keep ASU in any game. Second, you bring in a freshman stud to anchor your batting order. First baseman Danielle Gibson, through the weekend, was hitting .413 with ten homers and twenty-eight RBI. Third, you get some top-notch transfers, and Ford had gotten four of those who had become fixtures in the starting line-up. I asked Ford if she had believed the team would be this good. Pause. "I didn't," she said, laughing pretty hard. "As a coach you get caught up in the process and working on specific things. I knew we had some special pieces, but you don't ever really know until it comes together."

*   *   *

Watching dazzling performances in the circle or in the box, I had to remind myself that passage of Title IX in 1972 didn't preordain what women's sports has become. Title IX's status as law in the decade following passage was often not upheld, and in the 1980s its existence was threatened by the U.S. President and struck down, for the most part, by the U.S. Supreme Court. It took hundreds of court cases and more legislation to get women's sports on something even resembling an equal playing field.

In the early 1970s the average university spent less than 1 percent of its athletics budget on women's sports. Following passage of Title IX, proponents weren't looking to have money spent equally, which would have been impossible given the number of men's teams in relation to women's teams, but proponents were looking to have their opportunities expanded as their right of law. By the end of July 1978, the Department of Health, Education, and Welfare had received nearly one hundred complaints alleging discrimination in athletics against more than fifty institutions of higher education. The Department determined that it should provide further guidance on what constituted compliance with Title IX, and thereby issued a clarifying policy statement. Schools could show compliance with Title IX, the Department said, simply by making progress in *one* of three ways: (1) having the percentages of male and female athletes substantially proportionate to the percentage of male and female students enrolled at the college; (2) having a history and continuing practice of expanding participation opportunities for the underrepresented sex; (3) "fully and effectively" accommodating the interests and abilities of the underrepresented sex.

Looking back, we can see how modest the "three-pronged test" was, seven years after Title IX had passed. To fulfill the second prong, for example, universities simply could slowly increase the number of women's teams it fielded. But opportunity for female athletes was only part of what could factor into discrimination—treatment also mattered, because it is discriminatory if, let's say, the men's and women's basketball teams have substantially unequal facilities, practice times, travel arrangements, and so forth. Under Title IX, budgets for men's and women's teams do not have to be equal, but the benefits provided must be relatively equal. Travel expenses, for one example, must be equitable for men's and women's teams, which includes such things as the transportation used, the quality of hotels, and the types of restaurants and services provided to teams when they travel. By 1980, the average university's expenditures on women's sports had climbed to 16 percent, but that was too much for many men and many universities. Female athletes began learning that their only recourse was suing their universities. Many people believe that when a law is passed the problem that law addresses gets solved. But the law of the land isn't necessarily followed, which is why we have a judicial system that can find on behalf of plaintiffs and nudge enforcement forward.

A judicial system can also undercut the intent of legislation, which is what happened in the early 1980s. Within months of Ronald Reagan assuming the presidency, his administration announced that it would review Title IX's guidelines. While Title IX is a legislative act and could only be changed directly with passage of a different law, the Reagan administration on behalf of social conservatives was putting pressure on legislative acts that challenged gender norms. The Supreme Court's February 1984 decision in *Grove City College v. Bell*, which was not directly about sports, effectively undercut the enforcement of Title IX. Grove City College had sued the federal government because it did not want to comply generally with Title IX principles and federal oversight, and it claimed that as a private college, it received no federal funds. The defendants in the lawsuit, the federal government, argued in response that although the college received no direct federal funding, its students did in the form of federal Pell Grants, scholarships that were being used to pay tuition at the college. The Supreme Court ruled in favor of Grove City College, saying that the sanctions of Title IX—the cutoff of federal funds—were limited to the discriminatory program and could not be applied to any other programs at the school. Under the Court's ruling, for example, a school that discriminated in its athletic programs could continue to receive federal funding if that funding was not used specifically in that program.

The decision in *Grove City College v. Bell* set back women's sports. Scholarships for women plunged immediately; women's teams were cut; pending lawsuits of discrimination were dropped. But the genie had gotten out of the bottle, and so it was hard to get it back in fully. The norm of pre–Title IX days had shifted over the subsequent decade. Some schools continued to fund women's sports, or even increase the opportunities for female athletes. Moreover, the Supreme Court's decision against the ability of the federal government to uphold Title IX's enforcement extended to race, age, and handicap discrimination, not just sports. Groups of all kinds began lobbying passionately to reverse *Grove City College v. Bell.*

It took four years, but in January of 1988 the Senate and House passed the Civil Rights Restoration Act (or the Grove City Bill, as it came to be known), which overturned the Supreme Court's decision and declared that Title IX, as well as the 1973 Rehabilitation Act, Title VI of the Civil Rights Act of 1964, and the Age Discrimination in Employment Act, were to be enforced by the federal government. President Reagan vetoed the bill, but Congress overrode his veto. Once again, the athletic departments of universities, colleges, and high schools were being asked to fund their male and female athletes somewhat equitably. The directive was still met with general resistance, but with passage of the Equity in Athletics Disclosure Act of 1994, resistance became more difficult. The new measure required schools to disclose information on roster sizes, scholarships, coaching salaries, budgets for recruiting, and other expenses.

For anyone interested in the relation between social movements and our judiciary system, Title IX lawsuits concerning women's sports team make for fascinating reading. Year by year, court case by court case, with two steps forward and one step back, female athletes slowly progressed in their attempts for equal opportunity and equal treatment. In *Haffer et al. v. Temple University*, a case that was settled out of court by the University in 1988, a group of female athletes sued not only under Title IX considerations, but charged that Temple was violating their rights as citizens under the Fourteenth Amendment (the "equal protection under the laws" amendment). The athletes also had the case successfully designated as a class action suit, which can trigger larger penalties as the results get spread more broadly. In *Cohen et al. v. Brown University*, a complex case that took years of litigation before it was resolved in 1997, female athletes from Brown successfully argued that the university was out of compliance with Title IX because it was counting all available slots on women's teams, not the actual number of athletes; furthermore, while the university was claiming compliance because it had surveyed the student body and believed there wasn't further interest in starting women's teams, the athletes said the university had created an environment that diminished interest in women's sports. A landmark Title IX case in 2005 involved neither females nor athletes—Roderick Jackson, girls' basketball coach at Ensley High School in Birmingham, was fired after informing the school's administration of numerous Title IX violations; Jackson sued, and in *Jackson v. Birmingham Board of Education*, a decision asserted that retaliation for reporting discrimination is also discrimination, and that guarding against retaliation is essential for ensuring the effectiveness of Title IX.

New Title IX lawsuits still emerge every year, at both the high school and college level. In many cases, the plaintiffs are suing about inadequate treatment or facilities; in other cases the lawsuits, related to *Jackson v. Birmingham Board of Education*, come from a whistleblower who has been fired or harassed. Women's college softball has had a number of the latter, including a high-profile case in 2017. Mike Lotief, one of the most successful head coaches in the country, was given a performance bonus by Louisiana Lafayette in September; on October 6, after a run-in a few days earlier with an athletic administrator, he was put on leave; Lotief was fired November 1 for creating, the university contended, a hostile learning and working environment—subjecting student-athletes and coworkers to violent, vulgar language and verbal and physical assault.

When Lotief was placed on administrative leave in October, the softball players spoke out in a letter released to the general public that claimed the university's athletic department was "conducting an unjust and uncorroborated investigation of our softball head coach." The players went on to say they believed the athletic department was "intentionally trying to destroy our program" by targeting Coach Lotief with "slander and untrue comments." In the run-in with the athletic administrator, Lotief had lost his temper because his continual complaints about the way the university was treating its female athletes were not getting addressed. He believed that the athletic department was in violation of Title IX. His players, in their letter, also claimed that they were being discriminated against because of gender and reported that they had sought out legal counsel.

*   *   *

Margie Wright articulated what many of those early pioneers felt in the years after Title IX, when she called it "the opportunity of a lifetime." Those were heady days for female coaches, even if the headwinds of change blew hard. When women's sports grew, when lawsuits about equal facilities and equal pay began to make a dent in the unequal treatment of women's programs, a new kind of headwind blew—male coaches began applying to coach women's teams, and many university administrations and their male athletic directors felt more comfortable hiring men. Title IX, while helping female athletes, said nothing about who was to coach them.

Linda Flanagan, in a 2017 article in *The Atlantic*, notes how few women coach at the youth levels. "According to a 2015 survey conducted by the Sports and Fitness Industry Association, one of the few national organizations that carries out research on youth sports," Flanagan writes, "only 27 percent of the more than 6.5 million adults who coach youth teams up to age 14 are women." Flanagan profiles Maggie Moriarty, a women's lacrosse player at Holy Cross College who played numerous sports growing up. Like so many female athletes, sports shaped Moriarty's life and identity. Her coaches were hugely influential, providing guidance, leadership, and comfort when needed. She estimated that she had twenty coaches before college. "What united all her head coaches, across sports," writes Flanagan, "was gender: All were male."

Our social constructions of gender normalize positions such as "team mom" or "coach dad." Many women don't coach youth sports because of the unequal sharing in the home of housework and childcare. A male coach can travel to a tournament and leave behind his wife to take care of other children in the family, but a female coach expecting the same thing would be transgressing social norms. A more subtle but related transgression concerns confrontation and leadership; coaches need to lead and need to be willing to confront players, parents, umpires, and fans if necessary, and social constructions of gender give messages that those are masculine, not feminine, qualities. When it comes to careers, Title IX and equal opportunity for women in the workplace has probably been more successful off the playing fields than on—while the numbers of women in law, medicine, and government or serving as Fortune 500 CEOs have risen dramatically, the number of female coaches has actually gone down.

Nicole LaVoi teaches in the School of Kinesiology at the University of Minnesota, and she is also the Associate Director of the Tucker Center for Research on Girls & Women in Sport. The Tucker Center, established in 1993 and the first interdisciplinary research center of its kind, has pioneered efforts to examine how sport and physical activity affect the lives of girls and women, their families, and their communities. Much of LaVoi's work a decade ago focused on youth programs, on how girls might best be served; she then shifted her scholarly interests toward media matters, toward the representations of female athletes; her current focus is on female college coaches. In the mid–1970s, 90 percent of women's teams were coached by women; by the late 1980s, that number had dropped to about 50 percent; for the last decade, LaVoi's research shows, the percentage has stayed consistent at 43 percent of women's teams having female coaches.

LaVoi says that many of her colleagues who study gender and sports believe that college athletics has "gone to war" against female coaches. But why does it matter, one might ask, which sex is doing the coaching? Shouldn't we care exclusively about whether it's done well? If skill at teaching and communicating counted for more than gender, then women would be coaching men's teams. They aren't. What, after all, is so different about male athletes that women can't instruct them or lead them, if men can do those activities for female athletes? And what messages about teaching and leading are you giving to girls when they grow up with male coaches in youth sports, in high school, on travel ball teams, and then in college? Many girls go through their entire athletic careers and never see a female role model. Statistics show that women become coaches more often if they themselves had a female coach. As Carol Hutchins, head softball coach at Michigan put it: "If you play only for male coaches, you tend to not view yourself as a coach. I played for strong women and I always wanted to be them." Or, as LaVoi often says, female role models matter, because who and what you see demonstrates what is relevant or not relevant, what is valued and important, and who or what is not. An argument that girls shouldn't be coached only or mostly by men—so that girls will have the opportunity to have a female role model or to see a female decision maker—has a parallel angle on the boys' side. Many people who work with boys believe that it would serve those boys well to have female coaches, to see women as a role model for leadership, to have female cultural values infuse boys' sports.

For LaVoi, Hutchins, and many others who think hard about gender and sports, the legacy of Title IX is mixed. Decisions about who is the best person for a coaching job intertwines with who the person is making that determination. If it's a male athletic director who knows little about women's softball (though he may know baseball), as many of the decision makers are, then it's no wonder that so many former baseball coaches are hired to coach softball teams. Research has proven again and again that people hire those who are most like them, in looks and values. The looks can exclude women or people of color, if the athletic director is a white man. Male athletic directors might feel less comfortable with a woman, particularly if she is perceived as a feminist, a label that few coaches are willing to claim, even though their work demonstrates that they are challenging gender norms at multiple levels.

If you are an outspokenly avowed feminist, and a lesbian, you might become a target. On March 15, 2018, a federal jury in Duluth Minnesota awarded Shannon Miller $3.7 million for her wrongful firing. In December 2014 Miller, head coach of the University of Minnesota Duluth women's hockey team, had been asked to retire or resign by the athletic director, in a meeting attended also by the UMD Chancellor. She refused, and the university declined to renew her contract, saying publicly that the decision was "financially driven." Miller claimed otherwise, saying that her outspokenness about her program receiving far less resources than the men's hockey team, as well as her sexual orientation, had gotten her fired. In her years at UMD, Miller's teams had won five national championships and made an additional six Frozen Four tournament appearances. She was and still is the most successful women's hockey coach in NCAA history, and she was paid $93,241 less than the men's hockey coach in her final year. The jury agreed with Miller.

Shannon Miller's firing was an egregious example at the University of Minnesota, Duluth, but one whose reverberations spread, chilling the atmosphere in which coaches of women's teams might complain about Title IX equity issues. If you want to get in-depth on what can happen in a particular department, try reading Annie Brown's long article, "A Man's Game: Inside the Inequality That Plagues Women's College Sports," printed on May 5, 2016, in *Reveal: The Center for Investigative Reporting*. Brown dug into allegations that the University of Iowa, once a model of a university moving toward gender equity, had become a difficult place to work if you were an outspoken female coach. The athletic director who was hired in 2006, Gary Barta, had forced out five female coaches in six years, Brown writes, and had "replaced two of the five female coaches he ousted with men—and paid those men 25 percent more than their female predecessors. For the three he replaced with other women, he paid those women 13 percent less, according to public salary data. By comparison, when Barta replaced male coaches with other men, he paid the new male coaches 10 percent more." The most public firing involved the female coach most likely to stand up to Barta, as well as the winningest: field hockey coach Tracey Griesbaum, who in her fourteen years as Iowa head coach had led the team to four Big Ten titles and twelve winning seasons. In spring of 2014, she was accused of verbally abusing players; the university investigated and uncovered "insufficient evidence ... to substantiate a violation of university policy." She was fired without cause three days later. "The claims," Brown writes, "didn't match her spotless reputation. This was a woman, after all, who had earned the nickname 'Tidy' because of her PG-rated language and sobriety." Barta and the University of Iowa responded to her subsequent lawsuit with the familiar attacks, a university spokesman even claiming on Iowa Public Radio that Barta fired Griesbaum to protect the students. In May of 2017, Iowa agreed to pay Griesbaum $1.5 million to end the lawsuit. The law firm representing her got a million dollars more.

*   *   *

A sports truism asserts that if you haven't played the game you shouldn't coach the game. The message behind the belief is that one can't learn a sport well enough to coach it without having been on the "inside" as a player. An outstanding basketball coach, for example, can't take his skills and knowledge of coaching and turn into an outstanding football coach. This truism isn't really true for all individuals, in that a superb communicator can learn specifics of a sport and be an effective coach, but the truism is generally maintained.

In softball, the situation is complex because there are men's fastpitch leagues, though at the town level across the United States, men's fastpitch has been replaced in popularity over past decades by slowpitch softball. Men's fastpitch thrives still at the international level, both in number of participants and fans. The World Baseball Softball Confederation (WBSC) ranks teams, and in the men's game, New Zealand, Canada, and Australia lead the list. A number of outstanding college softball coaches have roots in the game via men's fastpitch, such as Mike White of Oregon, one of the international game's superstar pitchers who grew up playing in New Zealand. Glenn Moore, Head Coach at Baylor, talks about how fastpitch softball was a family sport when he was growing up: "My dad was a pitcher and I grew up watching him. I had four brothers play. In fact, when I was growing up, in rural Mississippi most of the churches had a men's fastpitch league and so it was not uncommon to see men play fastpitch and women to play slowpitch. I was seventeen before I saw a female play fastpitch, in Baton Rouge, Louisiana, at a state tournament. I was mesmerized by it." Moore started playing men's fastpitch softball when he was twelve. "I played with Eddie Feigner and the King and His Court," Moore recalled. "Football put me through school [Moore played football at Northwestern State in Louisiana], and I played some baseball in college, but softball was my passion."

John Tschida coaches at DIII St. Thomas University in St. Paul, Minnesota, and he's in the NFCA Hall of Fame, in part because he's the only coach who has won national titles at two different schools, at St. Thomas and also at Saint Mary's University in Winona, Minnesota. Like Moore, Tschida had connections to men's fastpitch through his family. His father played on a team that was ranked as high as third in the world, and his brothers also played for a high-level men's team. When he was in college and playing baseball, the family asked him to play; he did and continued into his 40s. He began coaching softball as an assistant at his alma mater, St. Mary's; he became the head coach five years later and ended up turning down the baseball job when it became available.

The male coaches who grew up playing fastpitch, such as Moore, White, Tschida or Ken Ericksen at the University of South Florida, have played the game and at a high level. But if it's a sports truism that if you haven't played the game you shouldn't coach the game, it's also a truism that you need to understand the lives of your players, which suggests that women's teams should be coached by women. This truism, again, is not really true for all individuals, in that empathy and listening can help you understand people who have had or are having experiences very different from your own. But when the majority of male college coaches not only haven't played the game and don't know what it's like to grow up female, some people become rankled, particularly when deserving female coaches are passed over.

Gerry Glasco, hired this past year for his first head collegiate coaching job at Louisiana Lafayette, played baseball in high school, had daughters who played softball, and turned to coaching softball at the high school and travel ball levels. When he was hired as an assistant at the University of Georgia in 2008, Glasco had been an assistant coach at Johnston City High School for six years, as well as coach of a junior high school program that finished 29–0 while winning the state championship in 2007. But high schools aren't where coaches make their mark—travel ball is, and nearly all elite travel ball organizations are run by men. Glasco founded the Illinois Southern Force Softball organization and served as head coach of the nationally successful Southern Force Gold from 2001–08. Glasco and the Southern Force coaching staff were honored as the "National Travel Team Coaching Staff of the Year" in 2004 by the National Fastpitch Coaching Association. Head coaches of DI softball teams, in particular, often dip into the travel ball world for their assistants, much as basketball coaches do in the AAU circuit, when a powerful AAU coach might bring some of his best players into that college's program.

Many male coaches have their roots in playing and coaching baseball or even other men's sports. NFCA Hall of Famer Bill Edwards coached college hockey and high school football and baseball in New York state before turning to softball. After twenty-five years and 928 victories, Edwards retired from Hofstra University, where he had built a regional power. George Wares of Central College in Iowa, the winningest softball coach in NCAA Division III history, began as a boys' high school basketball coach. Arizona's Hall of Fame coach Mike Candrea played and coached high school baseball before breaking into the collegiate softball ranks in 1981, and Alabama's Hall of Famer Patrick Murphy did the same in 1992. Mike Smith, head coach at Mississippi, was a two-time all-district pitcher on his college baseball team and went on to play in the St. Louis Cardinals organization; he served as a baseball pitching coach before deciding to focus on women's softball. Florida's Tim Walton has a similar background. Walton played baseball at the University of Oklahoma, even earning a win in the 1994 College World Series championship game, before going on to play several years of minor league ball. Patty Gasso hired him at Oklahoma as a softball assistant in 1999, where he stayed for four seasons before getting the head coaching position at Wichita State University. From there, he was hired at Florida.

The men I've mentioned are just some of those coaching women's softball teams, and in general they have done excellent work. All the coaches I've ever talked to have stressed that they want to build character in their players, to create well-rounded women who value off-the-field success. These male coaches want to teach the young women to compete and to respond positively to adversity. All coaches say, and I believe them, that they want society's sexism to end. And yet a tension does exist for many in the softball world about which gender is teaching these messages, a tension that arises because the sexism in our society gives men the opportunity to coach women's sports but does not give women the same opportunity to coach men's sports. Because nearly 100 percent of college men's teams are coached by men and only 43 percent of women's college teams are coached by women, if you're a woman thinking of college coaching as a career path, you might want to consider that over three quarters of those jobs will be taken by men. And, if we extend leadership jobs to administrative positions, 80 percent of college athletic directors are men, a number that balloons to 90 percent at DI.

Women's college softball has done better than most college sports in having coaching opportunities for women. Nearly 70 percent of head coaches are female. And it's certainly true that women's college softball has profited from its male coaches, many of whom have used their clout to further the women's game. Are male coaches of women's softball teams helping move their players and society to a more egalitarian plane? The answer is most assuredly yes *and* no, which is often the case for questions involving complex social issues— even if our society has neither appetite for complexity nor tolerance of gray areas. No easy solutions ensure that female softball players who want to coach will have opportunity; there is usually no easy answer to the question about who is the best coach for a particular job.

In the same era as Title IX, the makers of Virginia Slims cigarettes began marketing their product with the slogan that came to have resonance for feminism and women's liberation: "You've Come a Long Way, Baby." Virginia Slims sponsored the Women's Tennis Association Tour from 1971 to 1978, a sponsorship credited in part for women's tennis growing during the 1970s and early 1980s. Bonnie Tholl, associate Head Coach to Carol Hutchins at Michigan, articulated how she has gotten to the position she now holds, and it isn't due to a corporation's marketing campaign: "I am the beneficiary of women who battled to create equal opportunities in schools and in the workplace. My salary is the result of individuals who demanded equity for work relative to male counterparts. My role as a coach was prioritized by women who recognized the relationship between competition and empowerment. My holistic viewpoint is that young women need to experience strong female leaders and mentors to envision their own futures or possibilities." A female assistant in a prominent program has come a long way, indeed, particularly in regards to salary and extra-curricular duties that are now handled by staff.

When we look at the growth of women's college softball, "You've come a long way, baby" is certainly true, but many would also reply, "And look how far we still have to go." The social fabric of unequal pay for women manifests itself everywhere, including with female coaches in softball. Softball coaches are underpaid compared to their counterparts in baseball. Softball facilities, while improving, still don't match the baseball facilities, whose fields often look like minor league stadiums. Budgets for men's and women's sports are not comparable. Some of softball's improvements have actually been driven by the negotiating strategies of successful male coaches; many female coaches would be well served by hiring an agent and approaching salary and job negotiations as coaches do in men's sports. "Improvements" do bring, of course, new challenges. "The danger," Margie Wright suggested, and she is one of those who had to fight for appropriate facilities and money, "is that the high salaries will make it tempting to win at all costs. And that is not good." More money can bring corruption of principles, can change what is most admirable about women's softball culture.

I asked Carol Bruggeman, the Executive Director of the National Fast-pitch Coaches Association, what the struggles with Title IX look like from her vantage point. "We still hear a lot about Title IX, for sure," she said. "We hear about success stories, we hear about concerns, and we hear a lot of fear. We now give, as part of our coach's membership, free access to legal counsel. Members can use our legal counsel to review a contract, to review team policies, or if a coach has an issue with an administrator. But we see that Title IX issues come to our legal counsel, too. If a situation might be heading to a lawsuit, she will connect the coach to a lawyer in the respective state." While Bruggeman said that Title IX compliance still arises, mainly with facilities and sometimes with personnel, colleges are getting better. "Nearly all have Title IX administrators who you can now go to. And when you begin as a coach at a university, you will sit down and have Title IX education. People do have a safe place to go, for the most part. But at the end of the day, the coach will still be that person who says 'this just isn't fair.' And many coaches are afraid that protesting will end up getting them blackballed or cause some retaliatory move against them."

In the United States, social change toward equality happens with some combination of legislation, court rulings, and shifts of public opinion. Title IX and gender rights are only part of this larger story. Depending on a person's values, Title IX can be viewed negatively as the federal government's over-reach into mandating public policy and as a threat to established gender roles that maintain the fabric of families; or Title IX can be viewed positively as necessary legislation that was only a first step toward gender equality. In any case, Title IX did engineer significant social change, largely in how it has helped parents to have similar expectations for their daughters and their sons. In medical schools. As public officials. On ball fields.

Seven

Female Athletes Performing Gender

The glamour teams of men's college sports receive a great amount of national media coverage—from websites, newspapers, 24/7 sports stations, tv and radio telecasts. Attention drops off considerably, however, for teams who don't compete in a Power Five conference, and male athletes in non-revenue sports such as wrestling or golf receive even less coverage. The downward trend continues when we consider teams playing at the DII or DIII levels, who are often covered only by local print media such as a hometown newspaper. To put this all in a different way: 99 percent of the attention on men's college sports is about 1 percent of the action.

Women's college sports begin behind men's sports in media attention, but the drop-off is similar when it comes to the DII and DIII levels. If you have access to cable television or a streaming package for women's softball, you'll mostly see teams from the Power Five Conferences. You may have watched Paige Parker over her first three years win big game after big game for the Oklahoma Sooners. But you are unlikely to have watched or even heard about Hanna Hull, who in 2017 was a dominant freshman pitcher and the NFCA Player of the Year for DIII champion Virginia Wesleyan, or Coley Ries, who led Minnesota State (Mankato) to the DII championship, and was named Player of the Year for her thirty-six wins, sixteen shutouts, thirty-one complete games, 1.02 ERA, and 426 strikeouts.

After her great senior season, Ries played for the Texas Charge of the National Pro Fastpitch League, and signed a contract for 2018 with the Chicago Bandits. Many fans of the game have no idea about the quality of softball being played at DII. The better teams in DII have players who were recruited by DI schools. Sometimes a highly athletic girl who plays multiple sports and doesn't play in an elite travel ball program gets missed by the top DI programs; by the time she's a college sophomore and focusing on softball, she's good enough to start on Power Five teams. There are DII schools who would be very competitive with mid-major and low-major DI teams.

Two such schools, Colorado Mesa University and the University of North Georgia, had created by early April a fun narrative for the DII softball season. Colorado Mesa's Mavericks, located in Grand Junction, were ranked #1 with a perfect 34–0 record. They have been very good in recent years; in 2017 they went 48–8 and won their league, the Rocky Mountain Athletic Conference, before being bounced out of the NCAA tournament by perennial power Angelo State, who was runner-up for the national championship. This year, Colorado Mesa upped the level of difficulty for their non-conference play, heading in early February to Rio Rancho, New Mexico, where they defeated #2 ranked Angelo State, #22 ranked St. Mary's of Texas, and a strong Texas A&M-Commerce team. The Mavericks were favorites to sweep through the rest of their schedule, largely because they were a hitting machine.

The Mavericks' AnnMarie Torres had eleven home runs and fifty RBI, second on the team in both categories, but her .404 batting average was only seventh. Maggie Manwarren, Hailey Hinson, Kaila Jacobi, Zoe Pakes, and Alexandria Dufour were all hitting above her in the .400s. Talk about a murderer's row. But those glittering numbers were transcended by Brooke Hodgson, who at this point was one of the frontrunners for DII Player of the Year. As of April 2, she was batting .549, and check out these power numbers: eighteen doubles, twelve home runs, sixty-nine RBI. Her slugging plus on-base percentage was a staggering 1.594—Major League Baseball's leader is usually around 1.00.

The Mavericks weren't simply a one-dimensional hitting team. "The pitching," said head coach Ben Garcia, "has been absolutely great. The team ERA is well below 2.00, and the pitchers [McKenzie Surface, Kimbrie Herring, and Hodgson] have given us an excellent opportunity in every game." Coaches often are reluctant to praise too much, in case the expectations get raised too high, but Garcia wasn't seeing any holes in his team. "The defense has been working hard to get better. We've turned this around in the last three years, from having the highest number of errors in our league to this year having the fewest. We're right now one of the top teams in the nation in fielding percentage. We believe that down the road our defense will win us some games."

Would the Mavericks keep up their phenomenal hitting in the NCAA tournament? That would be a May story, not an April one, but a team who perhaps could cool those bats was #2 ranked University of North Georgia, 40–1 on the season. While Colorado Mesa led all of DII in hitting stats, North Georgia was doing the same in the circle, led by their two ace pitchers, both sophomores. Kylee Smith, a returning DII First Team All-American, was duplicating her freshman season, starting 21–0 with a 0.68 ERA. Amber Johns, 8–3 with a 2.08 ERA as a freshman, had elevated her game to where she was 14–0 with a 0.50 ERA. The Nighthawks team ERA was under a run a game.

Big bats, strong arms: Who wins? In April, Colorado Mesa was ranked #1 in DII softball and leading the country in hitting, led by Brooke Hodgson (above); University of North Georgia was #2 and leading the country in pitching, led by Kylee Smith (below). Photographs courtesy Colorado Mesa University Athletics and University of North Georgia Athletics | Amanda Mazzei.

North Georgia, located in Dahlonega, has a legacy in women's softball. In seventeen seasons as head coach, Mike Davenport has had six fifty-win seasons—he was on his way to a seventh—and a winning percentage above .750. In 2015, he led the softball program to the university's first-ever national championship in any sport. Davenport was loving his pitching, but like Garcia, he didn't believe his team was one-dimensional. "We lost two power hitters from last year," he said. "This year our hitting has been a collective group. We're a bit young through the line-up, but I think our athleticism has given us an opportunity to be successful." With seven players hitting above .300, and Shelby Hammontree and Sydney Sprague supplying the home run power, the team was averaging well over six runs a game. But what Davenport really liked was his defense. "As of late our defense has really stepped up," he said. "Our pitchers have always put us in a position to win, but our defense has kept us out of some tougher situations. They're anticipating the ball very well. We've settled in to who's playing where."

It was fun to imagine such schools meeting in the DII Women's College World Series, but there were a lot of games to play before the tournament even began, and heavy favorites often don't make it out of their regions. Colorado Mesa, for example, was in an extra-tough South Central region, which had five teams ranked in the top twenty of the national poll, any of whom could battle their way to the final weekend.

The NCAA makes the rules on the maximum number of scholarships that can be given out for each sport in each division. DI softball programs have up to twelve scholarships available. DII schools typically spend about half the amount on an athletic program as DI schools, and in softball their maximum scholarship number is 7.2, and so teams rely on a partial-scholarship model. Most players will receive some athletics-based financial aid, but they often supplement the athletic scholarship with academic scholarships, student loans, and employment earnings.

Like the DII softball division, DIII softball teams, which offer no athletic scholarships, exemplify a wide range of play. George Wares, the winningest DIII softball coach in history, has built Central College in Iowa into a program whose expectations of the players are little different than those at many DI schools. He believes that many high school coaches and players, as well as fans, have misconceptions about the level of ball played at DIII. "It's an honest mistake because Division III is so broad," he said in an interview with college staff. "About 390 institutions play softball. There are the upper-level DIIIs that can compete with most DIIs and some DIs. Then you have the middle DIIIs that are solid programs, and some very weak DIIIs. Being in the upper level of our conference, we can offer as competitive an experience as many DII and DI programs in the country."

"As competitive" doesn't mean that the experience is the same for the players. DIII schools play fewer games and travel to fewer early tournaments. Their leagues are much more geographically concentrated—some schools will drive twenty to thirty minutes, or less, for an away game, so they don't have to stay overnight in hotels. Since games airing on television isn't an issue, the teams play doubleheaders on Saturday and Sunday, rather than playing on Fridays or a Monday. Cheryl Milligan, head coach at Tufts University in Boston, enjoys the DIII world because she believes in the model of a true student-athlete. "Soon after I took this head job," she said, "we distinctly decided that there was no reason a very smart kid can't also be a tremendous athlete. There was no reason to let anyone else define us as a high academic school and therefore not as skilled in softball. We embrace both fully. We are not about softball ahead of academics. We are about yes! Yes, you can do both, school and sports. Yes, you can be an engineer, write a dissertation, consult for Apple! There is no limit to what you can accomplish. You need to prioritize and put college partying and some social stuff at the end of the list, but we are not here to limit our players."

"We would not have as successful a program if Tufts University was not the school that it is. Some people unfamiliar with college softball down here at the DIII level are surprised to learn that recruiting is not hard, it's just different. Showing up to a great travel team's first showcase and seeing who we like in the new crop is not really a tactical move for us. But for those players who have the academics for a school like Tufts, we—and schools like us—are very attractive options. You can win, garner awards, and have great expectations at a school like ours. You'll also have some balance in your life. As a school that meets 100 percent of need, we actually can beat financially many schools who offer players a meager athletic scholarship to commit them."

Milligan knows firsthand about the possibilities playing softball at Tufts, having been a four-year starter there at shortstop. She was an assistant coach for six years before being promoted to head coach in 2003. Tufts became the first team in NCAA DIII history to win three consecutive championships, which they did from 2013–2015. (They also lost in the WCWS in 2009 and 2012.) The star player during the championship run was Allyson Fournier, perhaps the greatest pitcher in DIII history, who not only was drafted by the pro league but graduated with a chemical engineering major and performed all kinds of service work while in college. She earned the university's nomination as NCAA Woman of the Year.

Kris Herman is the head coach at Williams College in western Massachusetts, a program that trades off with Tufts and a few other schools for being the top dog in New England DIII softball. Like Milligan, she is a spokesperson for a highly competitive DIII experience. Herman is very exacting with her players within the softball orb, but she believes in limiting the extent of that orb. "I want them to view softball," she said, "as an important part of their college experience, but not even close to the only part that matters. Freshmen come in sometimes and think 'softball is my thing,' because before it has been, but they learn they have many other 'things,' too." Her players have friends outside of the team, in their housing, in their majors, in other activities. They focus on academics. "My personal observation," Herman said, "is that we're doing it right."

Part of doing things right isn't just creating a culture of competing and improving. Herman feels strongly that everyone in the softball world should have fewer formal practices and less travel, as Williams does. "The challenge?" she asked, replying to my question, "honestly, there's not really a challenge. Our conference (New England Small College Athletic Conference, or NES-CAC) doesn't allow a fall season, so these kids work out on their own all fall. We start practice six weeks later than DI, but the players are so committed that they work hard on their own. They love softball and that's the difference. Not all players love what they do."

*   *   *

Some children entering the world of ball sports are told that they "throw like a girl." What does this phrase mean? Does it mean that the grip on the ball, the arm and shoulder rotation back, the forward motion with the arm and the body, are all dictated by a girl's anatomy? Well, of course not, because at seven or eight years old, boys and girls have similar anatomies when it comes to being able to throw. To throw like a girl usually means to throw without skill, to throw like someone who has never been taught. In other words, the phrase is about gender, not sex, about opportunities for and expectations of girls and boys.

Distinguishing between sex and gender can help us understand better how behaviors and values of men and women are often socially, not biologically, constructed. The term *sex* refers to a person's biology: the anatomy of his or her reproductive system, as well as secondary sex characteristics such as enlarged breasts and widened hips for females, or facial hair and an Adam's apple for males. Even this can be complicated, as for an intersex person whose genitalia, chromosomes, or sex hormones are ambiguous or do not fit the typical definitions for male or female bodies. The term *gender* can refer to either social roles based on the sex of the person (gender role) or personal identification of one's own gender based on an internal awareness (gender identity), which again can be complicated, as for transgender persons who believe that their assigned sex does not align with their gender identity. In common usage, we often say "gender" to mean female or male, but if we think of gender as that complex weaving of a biological body and social expectations for that sex, we can better consider how female athletes perform their gender and challenge social constructions of femininity.

My local DI team, the University of Minnesota, had their home opener on a chilly Friday afternoon in late March, after playing their first thirty-one games on the road. In the bottom of the third inning, I watched as Minnesota's catcher Kendyl Lindaman blasted a three-run home run that cleared the left-field wall by at least thirty feet. In 2017 Lindaman was Player of the Year and Freshman of the Year in the Big Ten, as well as First Team All-American, and as the saying goes, she has muscles on top of her muscles. In addition to her home run, I observed her throwing a laser down to second base on a steal attempt. I saw Elle Jensen, Minnesota's freshman left fielder, bunt her way onto first when she motored down the line too quickly for the second baseman to cover the bag, and saw Jensen then score from second on a soft single, turning on the speed as she rounded third. No player I saw that day threw or ran or hit "like a girl." They did, however, cheer a lot.

Before the 1980s and Title IX's mandates had begun to take effect, boys and men were almost always the athletes and girls and women were the cheerleaders. At high school or college games, both sexes were there, but with clearly defined gender roles of who led and who supported. At the professional level, even post–Title IX, the athletes are largely male and the "cheerleaders" are women chosen for their sexiness. Making the squad, if you're a Dallas Cowboys Cheerleader or a Laker Girl, can even provide a living and get you fame. With the giant video boards now in arenas and stadiums, cheerleaders mostly provide close-ups of their bodies to cameras, and therefore fans. Male bodies, of course, get plenty of close-ups in action on the court or the field.

One way to measure how we gender various professions or activities is to see if we need a modifier in front of the noun. We say "male cheerleader" when referring to a boy or man, because the default for "cheerleader" is female. One joy in watching a softball game live is to see how much fun the players create and have—female softball players are both the athletes on the field and the cheerleaders in the dugout. The sport's culture encourages the players to support each other vocally. They feel unembarrassed about yelling for their teammates, or inventing cheers that involve their teammate's nickname, or performing rituals that bring luck. They will even, during rain delays, hold dance competitions in the dugout to pass the time and raise the energy level.

In a baseball game, you may have a fight if a batter thinks a pitcher is throwing at him, or if a shortstop doesn't like how the runner slid into him at the bag. Batters get hit all the time in softball, and they don't start fights. They go down to first base, rub off the bruise, make whatever gesture is the team's latest inside joke, and then root for the following batters to extend the inning. Stepping on someone intentionally or breaking up a double play by sliding into the infielder—these aren't integral to softball, the way they are to baseball. Male athletes, even when they're not playing the most aggressive sports such as football or hockey, have to exhibit macho behavior. Female softball players don't have to continually assert their toughness.

One measure of athletic toughness is aggression or fighting, and another is keeping everything in, not acknowledging that anything hurts, whether from injury or from pride. If a baseball player strikes out for the second time in a game, he will often walk slowly back to the dugout, expressing with every step his disgust with what happened and that he doesn't intend for it to happen again; once in the dugout, a teammate might say, rather quietly, "You'll get it next time," but in general the strikeout victim will exude a "Stay away from me" vibe, an "I've got this" stoicism, even as he angrily slams his bat back into the bat rack. The same is true in the field. There might be chatter behind the pitcher, but every player is invested in the male performance of mastery, which suggests that you are in control and you're primarily an individual. If you're not being serious, the coach and your teammates might think you don't want to win, and winning is everything. Dugouts are rather quiet. Baseball players chew tobacco and spit, or chew sunflower seeds and spit.

Softball players laugh and celebrate, between outs and even between pitches. The third baseman and shortstop will have some ritual they do between every out, and the outfielders will flash the number of outs to each other in some unique way. The pitcher will bounce a change-up ten feet in front of home plate, and she and the catcher will crack up. When players get on base? Well, anything might go. This year, the South Carolina Gamecocks used dance moves from the game Fortnite to celebrate: on first, a player did the "Fresh Dance"; on second, she performed the "L Dance" substituted with the "Spurs Up" sign on the forehead; a triple allowed you to do "Ride the Pony" with the dugout joining in.

Softball players—and this is true of female athletes in general—move quickly, within seconds, from smiling or laughing to being serious. Coaches accept this as part of the culture. Remember the saying "Boys have to win to have fun, but girls have to have fun to win"? The most successful teams model an atmosphere where being serious and having fun are not antithetical, and demonstrating their relation is one way that female athletes perform gender.

As a contrast to the performance of gender on softball fields, imagine a different site of performance, the fashion runway. There, sexily clad female models strut in spike heels between rows of viewers. There's power on the runway, but it's a power that comes from being an object prized by others. What does it take to be such a model? Cameron Russell, herself a model, said in a TEDx talk that it takes 2 percent hard work and 98 percent "gene pool privilege," when what you look like matches up with what society has created as its ideal for beauty. The value of these models lies in how they and their clothes can attract. Now, return imaginatively to the softball field, where female athletes run, throw, and hit within the structure of a sport, and do so in cleats and a uniform that is useful rather than sexual. These athletes are competing, a behavior that counters femininity and helps females in the non-athletic areas of their lives. But the two sites—fashion runway, ball field—are not truly oppositional, nor without connection.Our socially constructed views of female beauty do exist within a range, but generally those views are about what the body looks like on the film screen or in a fashion magazine, not what the body can do. A female body that is superb for accomplishing physical labor or superb for fighting back—a body, that is, that allows the woman to be independent and to feel strong—has not been seen, for the most part, as beautiful. The powerful, muscular female body threatens the gender hierarchy that still underlies social attitudes. Muscular women are described as masculine, rather than admirable or beautiful; such categorizing is, to a large extent, an attempt at control by a patriarchal world. This view is slowly changing; female athletes are helping that change, as are the Victoria's Secret models that now lift weights and show their workouts on their Instagram pages.

The implicit message from a fashion magazine is that life's pleasures come from having a face, body, and clothes that will be attractive to others. The explicit message from sports is that activity and expressions of strength bring pleasure. But think about the power of the phrase "She's so beautiful..." By the time a girl is fifteen, let's say, how many times has she heard that? And what is meant? Not that she's powerlifting heavy weights or displaying athletic prowess on a ball field. The need to have a functional body that performs in sport and to know these social expectations of beauty and femininity has been called the female/athlete paradox. Decades ago, a female could be either beautiful or powerful; more recently, athletes have been seen as beautiful *and* powerful; a true advance will arise when power is seen as an essential component of beauty.

In some sports—tennis, soccer, or ice skating—the disparity between what the body needs to do and social constructions of female beauty is not necessarily all that wide. In others, such as weightlifting or ice hockey, the gap is wide enough that the sports have only a niche fan base, since audiences for women's sports often seem tied to the general sex appeal the athletes demonstrate while performing a particular sport. Softball lies in the middle of this spectrum; as such, softball may allow its participants to resolve, at least to some degree, that female/athlete paradox that suggests a woman can be either powerful or feminine, but not both at once.

Softball culture embraces what often seem like social contradictions. The players are strong women who refer to themselves as girls. They wear softball uniforms which cover the body and are not trying to be physically flattering, but off-field, the players will go out, wear dresses, and pose for glamour shots for each other's social media accounts. Prior to game time, the players put the "warpaint" on their cheeks and eyeliner on their eyes. They sculpt their bodies in the weight room, and then braid their hair and tie a ribbon in it. The on-field performance of power, muscles, and competitiveness suggests the social code of masculinity, but the long hair, ribbons, makeup, expressions of connection, and cheering all suggest the social code of femininity. Softball players create a range for their identity, and as such, help to counter what can be stifling about narrow gender roles.

When a male athlete is intense and aggressive, he reinforces our social construction of masculinity. When a female athlete is intense and aggressive, she counters our social construction of femininity. Individual women and men fall along a broad spectrum of feminine and masculine identity that serves as the poles of such behavior—that is, we aren't either masculine or feminine exclusively, we exhibit various combinations of those traits. When a female athlete veers close to the pole of masculinity, some people will notice and comment, and even if they don't, she's been socialized to know that she's transgressing. At stake for those whose actions counter expected social codes are taunts and insults. The sensitive boy is called a sissy or a girl, or is accused of being gay, as if that's the worst thing one can be. The aggressive female athlete is called a ball-buster or an Amazon, or is accused of being lesbian, as if that's the other worst thing.

*　*　*

Lauren Lappin is the assistant coach at DII University of Missouri–St. Louis, a job she loves. She has been coaching since 2009, staying out of the all-consuming workload of DI in part so that she could continue her professional softball career—she played for five years in the National Pro Fastpitch League before retiring in 2015. In her decorated career at Stanford University from 2002 to 2006, Lappin made two NFCA All-American teams, was twice named Pac-10 Defensive Player of the Year, and garnered a spot on the 2006 Women's College World Series All-Tournament Team. She played on the USA Women's National Team for years, including the Olympic team that won a silver medal at the 2008 Beijing Summer Olympics. She has been one of the game's stars. She is also an out lesbian.

In 2013 the University of Southern California Annenberg School for Communication and Journalism held an event on sports and the LGBT experience. Lappin was a speaker. After reading a quote of hers that addresses the role of sexuality in how female athletes perform gender, I wrote her asking for an interview, which led to a delightful hour last December at the NFCA's annual coaches convention.

Lappin attributes simply to capitalism some of the emphasis on looking feminine. "There's a market," she said, "for super-feminine things in softball. You see sometimes these girls who want to wear make-up and put a bow in

Photograph of LSU outfielder Kirsten Shortridge cheering on her teammates from the dugout. Note the expressions of socially constructed femininity: the bracelets, braids, headband, hairbow, makeup. As an All-American player, who performed with aggressiveness and competitiveness on the field, Shortridge simultaneously challenged socially constructed femininity. Courtesy Chris Parent and LSU Athletics.

their hair and be princesses. But they still love to play softball, and they kick ass at it. That can work, just as I can be feminine and be gay." Role models also influence a particular look. If Sydney Romero, Oklahoma's star third baseman, wears her long thick hair in a tight braid down her back, then all those girls who want to emulate her will sport a braid down their back, even if it's easier for an athlete to have short hair.

If culture in relation to economic markets or role models is part of what shapes softball players' performance of gender, so is culture in relation to society's views of sexuality. "Thirteen- to twenty-two- year-olds," Lappin said, "are still trying to figure out who they are, what they want, who they want to emulate, and at the same time trying not to stray too far from the heterosexual norm. So what's expected of girls because of cultural messages, intentionally or unintentionally, is to follow this norm. If the majority of a team wears bows in their hair, a girl will throw the bow in her hair, even if it's not necessarily something that appeals to her. She doesn't want to stand out. Expressing femininity is in part just going along with what you see, not necessarily countering one's own sexuality."

I asked Lappin if her sexual orientation had negatively affected her coaching career.

"As far as opportunities?" she replied, "No. How I've been treated by colleagues, no. I've never felt like it mattered. But I do think, especially at the Power-5 conference level, that if you have two female candidates that you're deciding between and one is married to a man and has kids, then it can be more challenging for a committee to hire the lesbian candidate." Lappin noted that discussions about beauty and sexuality, or about female coaches and sexuality, are particularly interesting now because of the larger cultural movements, particularly the #MeToo movement. "Women are being empowered and trying to change the meaning of the word feminist, to make it a powerful label, rather than a derogatory one. Everything that is happening politically and socially is helping women to have their voice and to take a stand." Women who speak out against sexism, however, do risk being called a lesbian. In her essay "Lesbophobia as a Barrier to Women in Coaching," Tracy Keats, a former volleyball star at the University of Calgary who now coaches a club team, says that as long as most women are afraid to be called lesbians, then such labeling serves as an effective way to blunt charges of sexism. All women, therefore, are victimized by the use of the lesbian label to control.

While the national social climate around sexual orientation has warmed considerably in recent years, it's still not easy for lesbian coaches to emerge from the closet. The first women's softball coach whose coming out made news, ironically, was Kirk Walker, who in the summer of 2005, when he and his partner had decided to adopt a baby, realized that he'd need to tell his Oregon State team. He came out to the players, who seemed to him to care less about his sexual orientation than how a baby adoption happened. Walker thought that perhaps parents, or prospective players he was recruiting, might be disapproving, but if they were, he didn't hear about it. What's quite remarkable about Walker's personal story is that in 2006 the program had its greatest season, making the Women's College World Series. Walker attributes that success, in part, to the extra trust and connection that he and the players had after his announcement.

Walker has helped form the Equality Coaching Alliance for high school, college, and professional coaches, administrators, and officials to have a network and support group. Walker was the only college coach when it launched in 2011 with a grand total of six members. But now there are over 400 members, with new members joining weekly, and a Facebook page for communication. Walker also helps administer several LGBT athlete groups, and those numbers are also going up.

Emily Lopez, the head coach at Smith College, believes that one way to create a strong team culture is by *acknowledging* differences of all kinds— race, sexual orientation, political views, religious beliefs—not by trying to erase those differences. "At the end of the day," she said, "the softball field is a classroom for life. Student-athletes have to learn to relate to each other, set team and individual goals, push personal limits, interact with authority figures, take care of the facility, and manage their time. It is my job to create a safe space for them to learn all these things."

Masculinity and femininity are social constructs that tell people how in a gendered way they should behave. In theory, there is nothing wrong with taking qualities such as stoicism or expressiveness and saying that one is masculine and one feminine. The problem with doing so, however, can be two-fold. One, if a female, let's say, tends to be stoical, then she is going against the prescribed gender norms for her sex, which can make her feel an outsider. Two, if we take sets of terms—hard and soft, aggressive and passive, rational and emotional—and we use them as either/or opposites, then we also construct power relations. While lists of qualities of masculinity and femininity might seem to be just descriptive, they are also normative: they shape what society comes to prefer, and one side of such a list gets privileged. To think about this more concretely, consider what happens when emotionality is tied to femininity, rationality tied to masculinity, and we decide who will do the best job leading in a corporate boardroom or nursing in a hospital.

We praise masculinity for boys and men, and then describe it as qualities demonstrated by a cowboy or an astronaut, and a heterosexual cowboy at that. Society sees the sports arena as a site for expressions of masculinity, in the way athletes are encouraged to be aggressive and physical. Competent female athletes, by their very existence, shake up such a construct, in that their physical, aggressive, and skilled play counters that the sports arena is a site for only male expressions of masculinity. Performing gender in a way that embraces both feminine and masculine behaviors, female athletes help us see beyond an either/or identity construction. They can both follow and lead. They can cheer and do amazing feats on the field. They can be the nurse or the CEO.

EIGHT

Seeing with Our Hearts

Brilliance can be something flashed or something maintained. We applaud the first for its surprise and the second for its endurance. In the circle in early April, pitchers were showing us both kinds of brilliance.

The University of Oklahoma has had dominant left-handed pitchers for much of the past decade. Keilani Ricketts, an all-time hitting and pitching star who twice was named National Player of the Year, led Oklahoma to three WCWS berths from 2011–13, with the Sooners emerging as national champions in 2013. After a year without a great lefty in 2014—when Kelsey Stevens still led them to the WCWS—Paige Parker arrived in Norman to continue Ricketts' dominating ways. Parker was the 2015 NFCA Freshman of the Year and a Second Team All-American when she helped Oklahoma get to the super-regionals. A First Team All-American in 2016, Parker upped her pitching in the big-stakes games, when Oklahoma won the national championship and she was named Most Outstanding Player at the WCWS. Parker followed that up with a third outstanding season in 2017, when she was Second Team All-American, pitched all the big games to help Oklahoma defend its title, and excelled in the classroom enough to be First Team Academic All-American. What did Parker have in mind for her senior year? To be even better.

After the second weekend of April play, Parker had crafted an 18–1 record with a minuscule 0.30 ERA. Her WHIP (walks plus hits per inning pitched) was an equally minuscule 0.616. Oklahoma has other excellent pitchers, plus a strong defense and very good hitting, but make no mistake, Parker's enduring brilliance had led them every step of the way. The two-time defending champions had won twenty-four games in a row and looked ready to go for a three-peat that would establish them as one of college softball's dynasties.

A different kind of brilliance was flashed over four and a half hours on a Friday night in Baton Rouge, when the LSU Tigers and Ole Miss Rebels took the field and played a game that few could imagine happening in an era when coaches make full use of pitching staffs, not pitching aces. After allowing an unearned run in the first inning on her own throwing error, LSU's Allie Walljasper shut down the Rebels for the next eighteen innings, throwing

Paige Parker elevated her pitching in each year of her career, becoming one of the game's all-time greats. After Parker's gritty performances in the WCWS, Oklahoma's Head Coach Patty Gasso said, "To be honest, right now, Paige Parker is the best pitcher in Oklahoma history." Parker was also a top-ten finalist for the Senior CLASS award and an Academic All-American. Courtesy Caitlyn Epes.

237 pitches, 161 for strikes. Head Coach Beth Torina said afterwards that she considered replacing Walljasper numerous times, but her pitcher made the decision difficult by retiring fourteen straight batters between the thirteenth and seventeenth innings. Ole Miss was 0–17 hitting with a runner on base, and 0–8 with runners in scoring position.

Kaitlin Lee was in the circle for Ole Miss, and like Walljasper, Lee went the distance, throwing 256 pitches. She gave up a run in the fifth inning and then shut out the Tigers until the bottom of the nineteenth. It's hard to say that one pitcher was more impressive than the other, but when you're the home team, you do know that if you give up a run, your batters have a chance to tie it back up or win it for you in the bottom half of the inning. Kaitlin Lee went out to the circle *thirteen* times knowing that LSU could walk off—that's pressure. And until that thirteenth time, she held them scoreless. Lee even no-hit LSU between the eleventh and seventeenth innings.

Neither Lee nor Walljasper dominate with commanding stuff that leads to strike-outs. They keep hitters off balance, keep down the number of walks. Hitters do make contact, and the game was filled with outstanding defensive plays that kept runners off base and runs from scoring. Equally amazing, nearly all the routine plays under pressure got made. I watched this game on my computer until the fifteenth inning, when I finally went to bed, and it was only the next morning when I learned the dramatic outcome.

In the bottom of the nineteenth, the Tigers' Taryn Antoine singled, the first hit for LSU since the tenth inning. She moved to second on a groundout. With two outs and two strikes, Amanda Doyle flared an inside pitch just over the shortstop's head and in front of the left fielder for the game winning hit. Lee was one strike or a few feet away from sending the game to twenty, or more, innings.

Lee and Walljasper are both excellent pitchers: in 2017 Lee won Second Team All-SEC honors and Walljasper was Third Team All-American. But on this one April night, they pitched beyond those high standards, achieving an unexpected brilliance. Two nights later something similar happened, in the Pac-12 this time.

Like LSU and Ole Miss, Arizona State and Oregon State played a game that took four and a half hours, though the length was due in part to a rain delay in the bottom of the seventh inning, when Oregon State was down 1–0. After the delay ended, the Beavers got the tying run home on a two-out, pinch-hit single by Alyssa Pelegrin, but had the potential winning run thrown out at the plate on the play. This game wasn't on television, but we can all imagine the rollercoaster of emotions that took place in a handful of seconds. "We're going to lose" became "We're going to win!" became "We're tied at least"—or vice versa, depending on who you were rooting for. The

Defensive gems such as this one by LSU outfielder Aliyah Andrews kept runs from scoring in the epic 19-inning game between LSU and Ole Miss. Metaphorically, Andrews can fly, referencing both her ultra speed and her ability, shown here, in the air. Courtesy LSU Athletics.

game went on to extra innings, fifteen in this case, and again, the two starting pitchers would throw every pitch.

Arizona State's ace, sophomore G Juarez, threw 208 pitches and struck out fifteen. Oregon State's freshman, Mariah Mazon, threw 261 pitches and struck out eleven. The game featured plenty of baserunners; remarkably, neither team's defense in a long game made an error that could have ended things earlier. Oregon State had nine hits and six walks, but could only push the one run across. Arizona State had ten hits and seven walks, but not until the fifteenth inning, when they scored the winning run on a sacrifice fly, could they score their second run. Two 2–1 games on the weekend, with all four starters throwing over two hundred pitches. Exciting, brilliant.

* * *

Games such as the ones played by LSU and Ole Miss or by Arizona State and Oregon State are fan delights, creating intense and nearly continuous drama because one pitch or play can end it. Just think about watching, however, if you're the parent of a player, particularly one of the pitchers. I decided to find out what the parents go through.

Kelli and Troy Walljasper, the parents of LSU's Allie Walljasper, tag-team seeing their daughter play live, each trying to get out to Baton Rouge every few weeks. Last Friday, Kelli was there for the game, her husband watching on television from their home in California. I asked him what it was like to see her in the circle for that long and with that much pressure on her. "When I'm at home," he said, "I yell at the TV to try to tell her what to throw and where to put it [laughter]. The game was nerve wracking at first, but she was throwing so well, I became a fan, just sitting there rooting her on. When Ole Miss got runners on second and third with no outs [in the tenth inning], that was gut-wrenching, but for the most part, as the game went on I became not a dad, but just a big fan. Lee did a great job for Ole Miss, too. It was a great softball game. I almost didn't want it to end, because I was enjoying the game so much." Troy has been very close to his daughter. They talk on the phone after each game she throws, in part because he coached her growing up and can give her feedback about her performance, though at some point in her LSU career, the feedback became less important than simply the connecting.

I asked Walljasper whether the experience of watching his daughter has changed through the years, and he said that it had: "First, I was her coach. And then, in the first years at LSU, I was a coach to a small extent and mostly a dad who worried and tried to do anything I could to help her. Now, I'm a fan. I just say, 'Go, Allie, go.' And I'm a very proud dad."

Kelli Walljasper was at the game, and her experience was a bit different than her husband's. "That was four and a half hours of complete, total excitement," she said. "When it was getting down to the 15th and 16th innings, I was starting to panic. There was a lot of emotion. If we have a big lead I can sit back and relax, but with this many innings I was really on edge. I chewed off all my finger nails [laughter]. I would text my husband, asking where Allie was missing on some of her pitches. I did get nervous when fans started leaving around the sixteenth inning. I had lost track of time, and then people were leaving, and it dawned on me we were nearly four hours in. Some people who left said they were going to listen to the game on the radio or watch on TV—they couldn't take it any more. It was exhausting to be there and watch it. I don't think any of us could have lasted another hour."

To my surprise, neither Kelli nor Troy were worried about Allie's physical or emotional state, being out in the circle that long. "I knew that she could handle it," Kelli said. "She's been in these situations before, though not nineteen innings of course. She was working so hard. In a game like that you don't want to have another pitcher come in. You want her to be able to finish it after putting in that many innings and so much of herself." Kelli trusted her daughter to let the coaches know if she'd had enough, but said that she could tell that Allie was on a mission and wanted to follow it through.

I asked Kelli whether she wanted to say anything else about her own journey as the parent of a girl who went through competitive travel ball, high school ball, and four years of pressure-cooker SEC and NCAA tournament play. "I'm extremely blessed," she said, "to have Allie represent something so positive. She plays hard and I'm very proud. Not everyone can make it as an athlete at this level, as well as doing the academics. And aside from softball she's just a really good person."

Across the country, Joe and Maryellen Mazon followed the performance of their daughter, Mariah, pitching for Oregon State against Arizona State. The Mazons were not watching in person or on television, but following via LiveStats, which simply posts information on a computer such as who is the batter, how many outs there are, the pitch count, and so forth. Following a game via LiveStats makes it feel as if the game is taking forever. Between updates of a ball or strike, you tend to just stare at the computer.

Maryellen Mazon said that she didn't get nervous following the game, even through the rain delay and into the fifteen innings. "I have been watching our kids play sports for so long," she said, "that when I see Mariah play I know that she will do her best and that is all I can ask of her. I would rather watch in person than follow on Live Stats, but sometimes work doesn't allow us to leave to see her play. My husband, on the other hand, does get nervous sometimes when he follows the game on Live Stats. When he watches her live he doesn't get nervous." What helps Joe be less nervous when he's at the game? Perhaps it's this long-standing ritual: he always tells Mariah before a game that he loves her and to just take care of business. And after the game?

No matter the outcome, he tells her that she did a good job and needs to keep working hard.

As a freshman, Mazon was put right into the spotlight. She started the opening game of the season against Oklahoma State, then ranked #21, and went the distance in an 8–2 win. She has pitched half the team's innings, even though the Beavers had two accomplished starters return in Meehra Nelson and Nerissa Eason. Oregon State played a difficult non-conference schedule, and now they were in their league stretch playing highly ranked Pac-12 teams, but Mazon had continued to pitch well, going 9–10 so far on the season with a 2.39 ERA. I asked the Mazons whether it was difficult to see their daughter lose this many games, when she almost never lost playing travel ball or high school ball. "Well, it is hard," Maryellen replied. "She pitches her heart out and sometimes things don't work out, but that is softball for you. I feel happy that she can play against these teams that are top ten in the country. So we are very happy and excited for her no matter the outcome. We are so proud of her. Of course, we love it when they win."

The Mazons themselves have worked hard to support Mariah's softball career. The competition to play on top travel ball teams is fierce, and parents and their daughters will often make great sacrifices for the opportunity. Mazon grew up in Tulare, California, a town midway between the cities of Fresno and Bakersfield, and she began playing softball when she was five years old. She grew up watching her older sister, Mayleen, play in travel ball and then in college at Sonoma State, a Division II program. She watched her brother, Joe Jr., star in a variety of sports. As a young girl, Mazon excelled, and when she saw the powerhouse Corona Angels in a showcase tournament, and met their longtime and successful coach Marty Tyson, she determined that she wanted to play for the Angels organization. At eleven, she tried out and made the 12U Corona Angels team. That year began the twice weekly car rides of three and a half hours, each way, from Tulare to Corona—so that Mazon could play on the travel ball team of her dreams.

For people unfamiliar with travel ball culture, Mazon's story might seem over the top, but it's not. For top players, even pre-teens, traveling to play on a team that faces the toughest competition is not unusual, though Tulare to Corona might be further than most. Joe and Maryellen Mazon are second-generation Mexican-Americans who are self-employed and own a smog control business; they had no extra money but they did believe in the sports version of the American Dream, whose softball translation is about going to college, not having a pro career. "Our family has made a huge commitment to softball throughout the years," Maryellen said. "Traveling all over has taken a lot of our time and money, but we wanted to do what is best for our kids. Our family knows that all our sacrifices will pay off in the end." The sacrifices began paying off fairly quickly for Mariah, in part because of the exposure you get to college coaches when you play for a team such as the Corona Angels. "When Mariah was thirteen years old," Maryellen recalled, "colleges started showing interest in her." At fourteen, Mariah verbally committed to Oregon State. A free education at a quality university doesn't quite have the same dollar value attached as a multi-million dollar pro contract, but the Mazons were happy. And not just because of the college scholarship. They noted what playing competitive sports has done for their daughter's character and discipline, and they have been grateful for the longtime softball friends they've made, many who have hosted the Mazons over numerous softball tournament weekends.

Most softball parents don't drive their daughters hours each way to practice, but there are numerous ways that parents end up contributing. Sara Moulton had an outstanding career at the University of Minnesota before pitching three years with the professional league Chicago Bandits. She recalled the help that her family gave her, from when she started playing softball at five years old in an In-House Slowpitch K-3 league, to when she was nine and tried out for fastpitch with the Eagan Athletic Association (her Minnesota hometown), and beyond. "My father," Moulton said, "sat for years on a bucket and caught me, and really helped with my pitching development. He was at almost every game, encouraging me. My mom did more with my sister, Emily, who is three years younger and on her own team. My parents split the work up, in a sense, but we always came back together at night and had family dinners. Mom was always the one staying up late on weekends, washing all the uniforms from tournaments. I wouldn't have been half the athlete or half the person I became without my family's support."

Jeffrey Moulton, Sara's father, coached her in the early years, but as Sara moved into travel ball, he preferred a different role. "I remained involved," he said, "but more on the sideline as she developed. We still spent a lot of time practicing. I cannot even guess how many hours I sat on that bucket catching for two pitching daughters."

Moulton had success in travel ball, and she pitched her high school team to a state championship, but then came opening weekend of her college career. "We opened up at New Mexico State," she recalled. "I didn't pitch the first game, but we lost 15–0, which was an eye-opening experience. And then I got the next three games. I lost the first one by giving up a grand slam in an extra inning, and we lost 12–9. That was the most runs I had ever given up. I was disappointed in myself but it lit a fire in me."

Parents can likewise be rather shocked when success turns to failure. Sara's father had flown to New Mexico to watch the games. "I returned from that opening weekend in Las Cruces in a panic," he said. "I had no idea or perspective going in what it would be like. She gave up twenty-seven runs on the weekend. When we talked during the week, I did say that maybe she should contact Coach Tschida at St. Thomas University [a DIII school] and see about next year. I am glad she did not listen to my babble. But two things came out of that first weekend. Sara learned what it means to throw in the 'river' [just off the plate] and I learned to stay far away during games. It was our little deal and served us both well."

As I've talked to scores of parents while researching this book, I have come to understand that post–Title IX opportunities for girls are also opportunities for sports-playing or sports-loving fathers. Many of the biggest proponents of women's softball are men with athletic daughters. Many of these fathers work and play with their daughters in a way that once they would have done only with their sons, creating a bond that wouldn't have happened a generation earlier.

Ryan Ehlen, who lives in Brentwood, California, about fifty miles east of San Francisco, was a multi-sport athlete who played football in college and has spent the last nineteen years coaching youth teams in various sports (baseball, softball, football, wrestling, and basketball). He has also taught and encouraged his three children. His middle child, Riley, will be playing softball next year at Loyola Marymount University, a West Coast Conference school in Los Angeles, on a generous athletic scholarship. Ryan's son, a freshman in high school, plays baseball.

I asked Ryan what it was like to do workouts with his son and daughter, and if he noticed anything different in their approaches to their sports. "I used to try to work the kids together," he said, "but no more. The tone of my son's workouts is completely different than my daughter's workouts. He is not there to listen to music, dance, and treat the day like a beach party. My daughter needs her play list on her phone, her speakers have to be set up, she will bat left handed for kicks, dance, lip sync, and generally find a way to get her work in while working on her performance at the Grammys. He can take me pushing him. She doesn't need to be coddled, but you cannot simply tell her what she is doing is not correct. You need to create a positive feedback, with a bit of advice."

"Me to my son. 'C'mon man, get your hips around and you might at least get the ball to the warning track! I didn't know I had another daughter.' Result: We both laugh and he works a bit harder at getting hips around. Secretly, he wants to hit the ball right back at his father and put me in the hospital. Me to my daughter. 'Nice shot hon, good ball flight, and way to stay inside. You might see that ball fly out of the park if you can get those hips around just a bit more.' Result: She nods, hits the next ball out because the hips led the swing, and she then proceeds to dance in the batter's box while lip syncing to some disco tune. She then asks if we can get a milkshake on the way home. Girls want to please you, but they want to feel secure and that you see value and worth in who they are even if they are not succeeding. And they want to have fun." Ryan noted about his daughter Riley that playing softball had given her a positive identity. "She doesn't need anyone," he said, "to justify who she is or what she is worth. She is strong and independent. She does not need a boy to make her feel important, nor does she need to participate in the poor choices of others." Riley's future career plan is to be a softball coach.

*   *   *

For every set of parents who are jumping up and down when their daughter jacks a ball out of the park in a clutch situation, or shuts down the other team in a crucial game, you have parents of the pitcher who got shelled or the batter who struck out with runners in scoring position. All parents want their child or their child's team to do well, but everyone recognizes that half the teams will lose on any given day, and anyone's child can make an error. Fans also know this. Fan reaction at college softball games is an unusual sports dynamic. Perhaps because these are young women who do not get the media attention of male or professional athletes, which brings heightened expectations, you see commiseration, not criticism. You see encouragement, not booing, after a strike out or an error.

The civil treatment afforded the players is extended less often to particular people who play a necessary but lowly regarded role in softball. If you work, imagine what it would be like to be second-guessed for every single thing you do. If you teach, everything you say will be judged by people who have no interest in being fair. If you have an office job, every decision you make or every email you write to a co-worker will be scrutinized. That's an umpire's world.

I was watching on television the Alabama-Florida game at Rhoads Stadium in Tuscaloosa, Alabama, and you could hear, over the announcers' voices, fans constantly yelling at the home plate umpire, Tom Meyer. Alabama would eventually lose the game 3–2, with Alexis Osorio two-hitting the Gators but also walking eleven, and fans everywhere in the stadium seemed to have a better angle and better eyesight than Meyer, even if they were sitting down the lines and looking sideways. The rivalry between the two schools had the passionate Alabama fans even more animated, if that's the right word for people who jeered if the umpire called something that went against Alabama, and then mock-cheered him if a borderline call went their way. They were protesting vociferously with their voices and arms when an Osorio pitch slid at least six inches outside.

Tom Meyer had been calling high school baseball games before he moved over to softball in 1990. "I fell in love with women's softball right away," he recalled. For two decades he worked games in the northeast, where the season is shorter because the teams are at tournaments during the first six weeks. But when his children graduated from high school in 2011, Meyer went to an SEC tryout in Houston and got offered a contract. He currently works a Power Five conference schedule, calling games for the Big Ten, the ACC, and the SEC. Like the players themselves, Meyer watches a lot of video. "When I'm behind the plate," he said, "I'll re-watch every pitch that I called, and if I missed something I go back and look at it in super slow motion, and try to understand why I might have missed that call." Like the players, he anticipates a big game: "Getting the Alabama-Florida plate game was thrilling. The build-up started about a week out. You have the sense of 'this is the big game.' Every pitch was crucial. Every pitch was one of those 'is it or isn't it.' I had to concentrate that entire game. Those are difficult pitchers [Kelly Barnhill and Osorio] to call. But that's why, to me, it's the holy grail of softball umpiring to be in these SEC venues with this kind of pressure."

One area of women's college softball distinctly non-gendered is the umpiring. Umpires wear blue uniforms, and so they're just "Blue." As in "That's terrible, Blue" coming from the stands. Or "C'mon Blue, call that pitch both ways." Fans don't really care if the umpire is male or female, which on one hand seems like a kind of progress for women, but then again, when you turn a real human being into a color, you are more likely to verbally abuse that person.

Karen Weekly is the Co-Head Coach at the University of Tennessee. In 2017 she was president of the National Fastpitch Coaches Association, which meant that she delivered the presidential address at the annual convention, which I was attending for the first time. I have sat through such addresses for many different organizations, but in that darkened ballroom I witnessed something surprising, something revealing about softball's culture. A president of an organization can speak about anything to do with that organization, and most addresses are self-congratulatory and uninspiring. Weekly chose to talk about umpires, and she began with self-criticism: "I had two conversations this off-season, conversations that really made me think about who I am, who I want to be, and how I'm contributing to what I believe is a major problem in sports and our society." The first conversation, she went on to say, came about because her husband (Co-Head Coach Ralph Weekly) has told her that umpires tell him that she's difficult. While her impulse to this had always been defensive, she decided that she wanted to know what umpires really thought about her, so she asked one. She asked him to be candid and to speak for umpiring crews in general. He told her that umpires respected her as a coach, but that her only interactions with them were when she was criticizing or complaining. The second conversation Weekly had was with a conference umpire assigner, the person responsible for finding umpires to work games throughout the season. This assigner told Weekly that it was becoming difficult to find umpires to work games in certain conferences because of how they were treated by coaches.

Though a head softball coach works hard in the summer, primarily out recruiting, Weekly chose to spend some of her hours researching and thinking about the situation of umpires. She discovered that country-wide there are referee and umpire shortages across all sports; she discovered that only about half of the umpires or referees who complete their first year come back for a second year, and that the five- to seven-year attrition rate is 80 percent. The primary reason why so many umpires and referees choose to quit? The verbal abuse, she told this large audience of coaches, received from coaches and parents.

The problem, Weekly went on to say, is not confined to sports. It's a national problem, in that our entire country is uncivil, to the detriment of civic life. People are nasty on social media, in blog responses, at ball fields. The problem is big and, she said, can't really be solved by one person or one group. What can be done? All that she can do, Weekly said, is to change how she acts; she can stop trying to get an edge by criticizing and complaining. "Didn't we enter this profession as coaches so that we could impact young lives in a positive and lasting way, not just to win a game today by any means possible?" she asked. Being civil, respectful, and a good sport, she concluded, should be the end goal, not the means to a goal.

*   *   *

For those of you not already fans of women's softball, some context might be useful. Softball umpires aren't actually berated the way they often are at a baseball game. No one is screaming "Kill the ump!"—even Alabama fans when they're playing Florida. And while softball coaches might disagree with a call and say so, they almost never do the dog-and-pony show that baseball managers do when they get angry at an umpire, jawing at him from an inch away, spitting in his face, scuffing dirt over the umpire's shoes. Baseball players and managers are supposed to look as if they have everything in control, but when they don't, they swing the pendulum completely to the other side and go berserk. Softball isn't like that. It's a testament to Karen Weekly and the majority of coaches who would agree with her that winning at all costs—arguing with an umpire for some perceived edge—is not what you want to do.

I'm not nearly one of the loudest at a game, but on occasion I'll yell at an umpire, "Call that pitch both ways," or some such thing, a comment that almost always gets me a dig in the side from my wife's elbow. Meredith doesn't believe anyone should yell at umpires, and I've come around to her view. "Do the right thing because it's the right thing to do," Weekly said, and she was addressing coaches but it pertains to fans as well. Her presidential address got me thinking about umpires, and led me to interview an umpire crew at the Mary Nutter Classic in February. I also talked to supervisors and mentors in the stands, and others over email, and the more I've learned, the less I want to yell at dedicated people who are crucial to the game.

No one goes into umpiring to get rich or famous. The umpires and former umpires I've talked to have been modest, hard-working, forthright people. To me, umpires blend idealism and pragmatism—idealism in that they continue in the profession because they believe in the power of sports and know that without umpires the games couldn't go on; pragmatism because they have come to expect that they will get little praise from the participants and fans who count on them. Motivation and reward, to a large extent, come from within. As veteran umpire Liz Hammerschmidt put it, "we strive for perfection, to get every call right. We want that one game where we walk off the field and celebrate that the coaches didn't know that we were there."

Like most jobs, umpiring has entry-level positions, usually the younger travel ball leagues or high school games. Before umpires get assigned to any games, however, they go to rules clinics, they study, they have to pass a test. Many beginning umpires, as former players, have a feel for the job, though they still have to call games for years to acquire the experience and expertise necessary to be promoted to the college level. But if you demonstrate work

The plate umpire has a more-than-difficult job, one exacerbated by the second-guessing that comes from television's use of replay, super-slow motion, and multiple camera angles—none of which the umpire has. In this crucial play at the WCWS in a game between Florida and UCLA, home plate umpire Brandon Bluhm made a call of "safe" that UCLA fans agreed with and Florida fans saw the other way. Courtesy Tim Casey and Florida Athletic Department.

ethic and talent, you will be instructed and mentored as you climb the various levels.

Umpires are constantly being evaluated, of course, by fans, coaches, and parents. More useful evaluation comes from on-field colleagues. Senior, highly skilled umpires will be partnered with those less experienced, to serve as a role model and to give informal feedback. Various umpire associations have more formal evaluative and educational processes. At the Mary Nutter Classic, I found myself sitting next to a "mentor" umpire (who modestly said that he wasn't important and that I didn't need to write down his name), who was making notes and would be meeting with the umpire crew after the game to give them each a report. The umpire evaluator was being instructed every few minutes by another advisor, Jim Sanderson. During the course of the game, listening to the two of them and asking questions, I had my umpire consciousness raised considerably.

A highly respected teacher and mentor, Sanderson is one of four advisory staff for the national NCAA Softball Umpire Program. In 2000, the NCAA DI Softball Committee created a program to assist the conferences in implementing a formal training program that would standardize softball umpiring throughout the country. The mission expanded when the Softball Umpire Program was given the responsibility to identify, observe, and evaluate umpires for assignment to NCAA tournament games, as well as to provide continuing instruction. The Softball Umpire Program set up umpire camps and regional clinics. They set up priorities for each year about some part of the game that needed to be called uniformly. They began an educational and inspirational web site for umpires, that includes a weekly letter about how things have gone that week, as well as numerous articles about bats, testing, concussions and wellness, and the like. There's a "rules" section. It's all impressive.

A goal of the Softball Umpire Program is to is promote better communications between umpires and coaches. Another goal of the program is to recruit, and to recruit women. "We'd like to see some players extend their careers by becoming umpires," Sanderson told me. "Some of our best umpires are former players."

Liz Hammerschmidt, one of those former players, began umpiring part-time when she was playing at Kent State University. She quit when she got a full-time job and had children, but she wasn't happy with her job, and then a serendipitous moment occurred. "I met an umpire eight years ago," Liz recalled, "who I knew from my playing days. She came into the building in her umpiring uniform, and I asked her how I could get back into the game because I needed some extra cash. She told me to meet her and she'd bring me a uniform. I began with some recreation-level games, and then I went to some tournaments, in Michigan, in St. Louis, and then Atlanta. I began realizing that I wanted to umpire as a vocation. I gave up my full-time job. Just growing as an umpire and umpiring more tournaments got me involved in showcase camps for the college level. And when I went to this clinic at Clearwater Florida to get more training, there I was, sitting in front of DI and DII assigners. It was nice because an evaluator is on each field, and they evaluate you based on each position [behind the plate, at first base, and so forth]. You get feedback in between games. And you'll have it in writing and they'll go over specific details. It's really helpful and you learn a lot. That was seven years ago. They saw potential in me and believed that I could manage a college game. They looked not only at what I did but at my style, how I dressed, my body language, and how I interacted with the coaches and the players."

Hammerschmidt started getting assignments from the Mid-American Conference, and then got picked up for the Big Ten, the Missouri Valley, and the Summit League. She has to travel frequently for games, and her life is more than full. "I coach two softball teams, I work part-time for a freight company, I'm getting my Master's degree, I'm umpiring, and I have two kids. My family at home is truly understanding. I love it all."

Hammerschmidt met Trish Treskot at the DII nationals in 2014. "We hear about an umpire," she said, "and then we get to work with him or her down the road. It's amazing how relationships grow." Like Hammerschmidt, Treskot is a former player; she played for Saint Joseph's University outside of Philadelphia. She started umpiring after college for some extra money, but quit when the demands of her full-time job increased. But about 2009 some things in her life changed, and she began umpiring some recreation league softball, and then, like Hammerschmidt, met up with an umpire who knew her from her college playing days.

"My mentor, Sonny Pompelli," Treskot recalled, "saw something in me and said, 'Yo, this is how we're gonna do this.' We would go out and do summer stuff, and he would nitpick me [give feedback], and then I went to a camp and eventually started doing some college ball. I was driving a lot and calling DII and DIII games, just working my way up. I'd be at camps, and meet different umpires, there and at games. This community wants to help you. The reason I ended up out here at the Mary Nutter Classic was that I did the DIII national championship, and Greg Schmidt, who was the umpire-in-chief, said I should come to California. And I did and met some wonderful people, and I said to Liz, you should come to California, and she said ok."

John Baca had a different route to calling games at the highest level of DI softball. He began umpiring at the age of thirteen in an adult slowpitch league. When his umpire-in-chief told him that he should get involved in fastpitch softball, he began a long but steady climb up the ranks: from youth level to college, from calling DII games in the Rocky Mountain Athletic Conference to working for the Western Athletic Conference and the Mountain

West, mid-major DI leagues. Baca now regularly umpires for the Pac-12 and the SEC, for NCAA tournament games, and for the professional league.

Baca officiates multiple sports (football and basketball, in addition to fastpitch softball), and so he makes his entire living from being the center of attention in disagreements. Most umpires have other jobs. Treskot mentioned that this season was the first ever when she hadn't owned a business at the same time she umpired—she sold it on December 31, 2017. All the umpires I spoke with said that balancing family and work life was difficult, as was the travel. They did not mention, perhaps surprisingly, difficulties with the participants.

When I brought up Karen Weekly's presidential address at the NFCA convention, only Baca had heard about it. But none of the three believe that coaches are much of a problem, that the coaches go out of bounds or make it personal. "Coaches have a job to do," Baca said, "and they do it, we take it, and if there's something inappropriate, we handle it."

Treskot echoed that view. "I think the coaches have to do their job," she said, "which is to advocate for their players, and some do a great job of advocating. It's not about yelling at umpires, because there are limits and rules for what coaches can say, and coaches know how far they can go."

Perhaps even more surprisingly, the umpires said that college crowds are not really an issue, though a travel ball crowd can be. Fans, parents, and coaches of the younger girls, the umpires say, often don't know the rules and the environment is smaller. And unlike at a college game, there is no one there to remove a person causing a problem. "But we don't interact with college fans at all," said Treskot. "We can tune them out. You hear things, but you're in a zone when you're umpiring and it doesn't get in your head."

Baca said much the same: "Fans are fans, and we can't let them get into our minds. Some of the things they say are funny, actually, and make us laugh."

Hammerschmidt: "We like to quote them."

As far as the third group at the games—the players—the umpires are generous with their opinions. "Rarely do we have player issues," Baca said. "I've never had a situation where there's been a fight or something."

Hammerschmidt agreed. "Respect from players is important," she said. "I think this might have to do with the gender that we're officiating. When I was a player, it was the same. We did not question the umpire's call. That was the coach's job to do. You accepted whatever was said and let your coach deal with it. I still see that today." She believes that the players are often excited to have a female umpire, because they see her as a role model and she has an opportunity to show them something that they can do.

Treskot likes to interact with the players a bit, trying to recruit them to her profession. "I think a lot of umps do this," she said. "I'll be calling a game, and I talk to the catcher and say 'you should be an umpire, you know the strike zone.' So I'll have the catcher make the call with me. I'll even say 'you call the next one,' and I can play at that level and let them do it. It's fun to have that rapport with the kids and encourage them to start umpiring. If kids come back from college, they can have a job."

I asked the three umpires what the satisfactions were in making this a profession. They all agreed that they have an important job, because without them the game couldn't be played. They all said that they strive to make every call right, to be better each time they step on the field. And most of all, they mentioned the camaraderie. "No matter where you are in the U.S.," Hammerschmidt said, "everyone knows you'll have a place to stay. We have friends all across the country." Treskot said that umpires at this level are one big crazy family that all take care of one another, and they'd be happy if more people wanted to join that crazy family.

Umpires know that in the court of public opinion, they always lose. They take this in stride, knowing what their talents, preparation, and hard work make possible. So why do coaches and fans get upset at games? Jim Sanderson had a great line about this, and he uttered it with humility and understanding: "A few people see with their eyes and their brains, but most people see with their hearts." If you're a fan, and you have a side angle, and your team's pitcher throws it four inches off the plate, your heart sees it as painting the corner for a strike. The umpire calls it a ball, and wouldn't really expect a home-team fan to see it any other way.

NINE

Life Lessons

On April 18, the NCAA Division I Council passed legislation that will likely have far-reaching effects on the college softball world. Known as the "Early Recruiting" legislation, the new rules were intended to halt the spiral of girls committing to programs as middle-schoolers. The legislation set September 1 of a prospective player's junior year as the beginning of the recruiting cycle.

For years various groups had been lamenting early recruiting, including many college coaches and travel ball coaches. Some college coaches had been arguing that making an offer to a young girl, getting an acceptance, and then trying to hold that girl to her commitment was unethical. A choice of a college is a life-changing event—often cited as one of the two most important life decisions, next to who you marry or partner with—and making that decision when you're a young teen is often not best.

The practice of early recruiting didn't start with evil intentions, nor did it become an issue overnight. Like many processes, incremental change leads to results that few really want. And like many processes, even the people opposed end up having to participate as a way to not be left behind. So how did this practice become widespread? Imagine you're a college coach and a talented girl and her family come to your camp or you see them at a tournament, and they tell you that they've always dreamed of playing in your program. Nothing stopped you from offering a scholarship at that point and a girl accepting that offer, though neither the offer nor acceptance was binding. The only true binding commitment is when a high school senior in November signs a National Letter of Intent (NLI) to accept a particular scholarship offer from a school. Between eighth grade, let's say, and twelfth grade, nothing really stopped that early recruit from considering or taking offers from other schools, *except that they rarely did*. In college men's sports, early recruiting has been less of an issue, in large part because teenage boys change their mind numerous times before settling on who they will sign with. There have been instances where a coveted high school athlete told ten schools that he would sign with them and ended up going somewhere completely different at the last minute. If you spent a lot of time on that athlete, you wasted that time. The culture of teenage boys made early recruiting less viable. But girls' sports culture prizes loyalty, and these young recruits were honoring their own commitments, even if they weren't necessarily in the girls' best interests a few years later.

If a young softball player has the talent to play at a particular level, and wants to play for a particular school, and she could know that she has a scholarship offer and could therefore relax about the entire recruiting process, might that not be a good thing? In some instances, yes, but when early recruiting became the norm, numerous problems arose. For the coaches, these offers as made couldn't always be honored. DI coaches have available, at the most, twelve scholarships which they have to apportion among a roster that is usually around twenty to twenty-two, and coaches can't really know, years ahead, what their exact scholarship fractions will be. Coaches also might not know who will make up a future recruiting class. If they've offered a pitcher, let's say, and a year later an even better pitcher from the same class wants to come, a coach won't say no to recruit number two—jobs, after all, are on the line. Because girls *could* change their minds about a verbal commitment, coaches felt pressured to offer more non-binding scholarships than they truly had available, which often meant they had to cut someone they had earlier offered.

Hours of recruiting a player and getting a verbal commitment didn't end the process; coaches needed to keep the young recruit happy, a process often called "babysitting," where coaches show up at a recruit's travel ball games and answer phone calls and emails, thereby reassuring everyone involved that they are still interested. Some player-coach relationships lasted at least nine years, in that a girl would be recruited and babysat for five years and then come play for the coaching staff for four more. The entire process had its own internal logic but had also become a downward spiral. Despite the problems for coaches, early recruiting became the norm because schools getting these early star youngsters to commit were succeeding with them later—coaches, like suburbanites, have to keep up with the Joneses.

The NCAA surveyed prospective student athletes, and with more than 15,000 responses, the NCAA learned that over 40 percent of student-athletes in women's basketball and softball reported their first recruiting contact in ninth grade or earlier, and that in general, the later that recruiting began, the more positive the experience was for students being recruited. The National Fastpitch Coaches Association campaigned hard for the new legislation after a survey of its DI members revealed that over 84 percent of the coaches were in favor of making September 1 of the junior year the beginning of recruiting contact for softball.

The *disadvantages* for prospective college softball players committing early seem obvious: one, by the time you sign your NLI in November of your senior year, the offer may have changed, from a full to a half scholarship, for example; two, you're a catcher, let's say, and you discover that your school has two young catchers on their roster and you'll get no meaningful playing time in your first several years; or three, the coaching staff that you verbally committed to has been fired or left for another school. There are further scenarios. But the most basic argument against such commitments remains that a young girl is in the process of learning who she is and what she wants. So why did girls and their families keep a system going that did not really help them? Like many responses to complicated questions, the answers are multiple and particular. But in general, an early commitment had become a source of pride—for the girl, her family, and the travel ball organization. And not having an offer was a source of anxiety.

Morgan Smith's story of playing travel ball and being recruited is, by everything I know, a fairly typical story for a talented young athlete. When I first saw Morgan and met her parents, Paige and Kevin, she was just finishing her eighth grade year and living in Carson, California, near Los Angeles. She played for a high-powered, well-coached travel ball team, the Orange County Batbusters Mascarenas. Though this was a 14U team (fourteen-year-olds and under), a number of Morgan's teammates had already been offered a scholarship and verbally accepted, which, according to Paige, made her daughter feel some self-doubt as well as anxiety. Various showcase events during the summer after eighth grade helped give Morgan exposure to coaches of top programs, and a number of them expressed interest. In September of her ninth grade year, Morgan went with her parents on an unofficial visit to LSU and fell in love with the school.

Paige Smith said that her daughter responded to LSU for understandable reasons: for the vibe she got from the coaching staff and players, from the "fantastic superficial things that you get to see while on campus for a visit—tailgates, football games, and so forth." But parents see a school in other ways. Paige and Kevin met at UCLA, where they were both undergrads. Kevin played college football and went on to play four years in the NFL; Paige pursued a medical degree and now practices neonatology. Kevin wanted Morgan to consider UCLA, and to stay, perhaps, closer to home; Paige was interested in the academics of a university, how difficult travel is to the school, what the city and surrounding areas are like, what regular daily living is like. But a young teen whom you have parented to be strong and forthright believes that she knows her own mind and knows what is good for her. "Morgan essentially refused to even go visit any other schools," Paige said. "Her father and I wanted her to see more places to have a better frame of reference. She only went to UCLA out of respect for her father. We even had other visits scheduled, like Tennessee. Oregon came out to California to watch her pitch, but she was completely apathetic about seeing any other schools. She was sold on Beth Torina and LSU." Morgan committed to LSU a few months after that visit and has, her mother said, "been ecstatic ever since." Both parents believed, ultimately, that a girl makes her own decision, and peer pressure and the culture of travel ball determined that the decision was ready to be made.

Morgan Smith's story, thus far, is not really a cautionary tale, because she moved through the process rather quickly and is going to a superb program and coaching staff. Only time will tell if her choice made as a 9th grader will work out, on her end or LSU's end. But her story is a revealing one, where being showcased and then invited for unofficial visits by programs is the norm and you're just reaching high school. The new rules for recruiting establish that players can't be in contact with DI college coaches until the beginning of their junior year, which will give the girls a better sense of where they are as athletes, as students, as persons. The new model will also help generally in other ways. Girls who mature a bit later won't be at a disadvantage, in that most everyone by 10th grade is closer to where they will be at physically when they enter college. And rather than middle schoolers believing that they need to focus on softball because decisions about college are getting made early, these girls can play multiple sports and can develop their general abilities as athletes.

The emphasis on travel ball rather than high school competition makes more difficult the college opportunities for girls who come from lower income families. Travel ball can be expensive, particularly when tournaments are seen as a site to showcase the players to college coaches, which often means traveling nationally to the most prestigious gatherings of teams. The later recruiting model should allow 14U and 12U travel ball teams to play more regionally or even locally, which will reduce the cost for families. The new recruiting model should change the team dynamic for the young players, placing the emphasis back on developing the girls' skills and fostering their love for the game. Rather than a game being an event where you might get seen by college coaches—which emphasizes an individual's goals—the team experience and simply playing can most matter.

* * *

It had been a cold and snowy April in Minneapolis, so I was glad to get outside and enjoy some live softball when Nebraska traveled northward to Minnesota to play a crucial series in the Big Ten. On the first truly beautiful spring weekend of the year, with temps in the low sixties, the college students swarmed campus and nearby streets in shorts and tank tops, hopefulness trumping reality. It was the annual Spring Jam celebration, which the university bills as "the perfect welcome party for warm weather" and includes live music, carnival rides, and food. The fraternities, of course, provided the beer parties. Older fans in the softball stadium, though dressed in jeans and sweatshirts, were likewise all smiles, happy to know that spring was finally here and summer would follow, something all northerners know but still relearn emotionally each year.

In the press box, I ran into Nate Rohr, who I had met in February at the Mary Nutter Classic when he was calling a Nebraska-UCLA game for Nebraska radio. His deep knowledge of the Husker softball program, his command of statistics about the UCLA players, and his vivid play-by-play of the softball action, which he made visual, impressed me. As a teen, Rohr was the public address announcer for his high school's football and basketball home games in Beatrice, Nebraska, a small town forty miles south of Lincoln. In 2003 he made his way north, enrolling at the university to study broadcast journalism. In 2016, Rohr got the dream job for a former high school football player who had no career playing the sport—he became the public address announcer for the University of Nebraska's football team. Rohr is the Memorial Stadium voice saying to ninety thousand fans who ran the ball for how many yards. Given how passionately Nebraskans feel about their football team, the job comes with high stakes, but Rohr had been prepping for the job for years, as a long-time spotter and statistician for Nebraska football and as a full-time employee of the Husker Sports Network. The story that's much more unusual is how he became the radio voice of Nebraska softball.

In 2004, as a freshman at Nebraska, Rohr did public announcing for softball. That year the radio network did a twelve-game package with six students each calling two games. When it came time for the Big 12 tournament—Nebraska only joined the Big Ten in 2011—none of the announcers wanted to commit to being away for five days. Rohr jumped at the chance. Nebraska had a strong team that year, led by its All-American pitcher Peaches James, and in Rohr's second game that he ever called, James threw a perfect game against Oklahoma. Head Coach Rhonda Revelle liked Rohr's work, and the next year he did the entire twelve-game package. Over the next few years, the radio network began airing all home games, then all games that they could bus to, and finally the entire schedule.

Like Nebraska, more softball programs each year are doing radio broadcasts of their games, which might seem counterintuitive in an era when everyone has their eyes glued to screens. I asked Rohr what, in particular, he thinks radio brings to the sport. "Radio keeps a more consistent connection with one team," Rohr said. "TV has been very good to women's softball, but a crew parachutes in to do a weekend's games. With radio there's a constancy. Broadcasts of games become a part of people's lives. Even as people go through their days or work in the office, they can have the radio on and keep up with the team." Radio broadcasts of women's softball games certainly aren't a money-making scheme, but in addition to being a medium for some

Our current age seems defined by the ubiquitous screens that Americans gaze at for their entertainment or work; college softball programs, nevertheless, have turned increasingly to broadcasting their games on the radio. University of Nebraska's play-by-play radio announcer, Nate Rohr, is shown here. Courtesy Scott Witty.

fans, the broadcasts serve Nebraska athletics in a specific way. "Our broadcasts," Rohr said, "keep parents and recruits connected to the university. I love doing it. I'm a Cornhusker through and through."

It was a difficult weekend for Husker softball fans, as Minnesota, third in the Big Ten standings, swept them easily in three lopsided games. Nebraska came into the weekend fourth in the Big Ten and well-regarded in the polls and RPI rankings, so Minnesota's performance suggested that the Gophers might be jelling. Their outstanding pitcher, Amber Fiser, won all three games, and Kendyl Lindaman and Maddie Houlihan homered on both Saturday and Sunday. The games moved quickly; the sun shone; the Gophers won. Nice weekend for a softball fan in Minneapolis.

* * *

Who was not partying Saturday night in Minneapolis at the Spring Jam? Minnesota softball players, who after winning in the afternoon had to get ready for the next day's game. Being an in-season athlete cuts back on the weekend's socializing as well as adding to the work during the week. One of those Minnesota players, Sydney Dwyer, gave me a better sense of softball's demands when I talked to her on the following Tuesday. I asked her, first, about her daily schedule.

"I woke up this morning at 6:45," Dwyer said, "and we lifted from 7:30 to 8:15, which we do twice a week in-season. Then I went to a two-hour lecture from 9 to 11. When I'm done talking to you I'll have lunch, and then we have practice from 1:00 to 4:15. Then I have class from 4:40 to 7:20. This night class is just once a week, however, which opens up the other days for me."

Last year Dwyer was an NFCA All-American Scholar Athlete. A senior Kinesiology major, she has a 3.49 grade point average. In the Kinesiology major, students take courses such as "Human Anatomy," "Introduction to Biomechanics," and "Sport and Exercise Psychology" in order to examine the physiological, biomechanical, and psychological principles and mechanisms of movement, all of which can be applied in numerous ways to human health. "I came in to the university knowing I wanted to do Kinesiology," Dwyer said, "but I didn't know what direction I would go with it because I didn't know what I might want to do after college. But in my junior year I got interested in the strength and conditioning side, in part by watching our team's strength coach, Sara Wiley. I decided to work at my high school last summer, helping the athletes, and I thought, 'Yeah, this is what I want to do for now.' And I've always wanted to coach. My high school softball coach, Lori Duncan, has been one of the most influential people in my life, and so I thought I'd like to do that for others." Dwyer's plans are to intern at a training facility after she graduates, and then go to graduate school next fall at St. Thomas University in St. Paul. She imagines a future working with high school students and staying in the Twin Cities area, rather than pursuing a college position that likely would mean she'd have to move around the country.

Most people, when asked to imagine a coach, think of a man, a gendering even more likely with strength and conditioning coaches. But Dwyer will be one of a growing number of female coaches who supervise a weight room, instruct female and male athletes on correct techniques, and make team and individual plans for how to improve athletic performance, which usually means improving athletes' speed and power. For the first decades after Title IX passed, only a small percentage of female athletes made weight training a regular practice. That has changed. Dwyer grew up in Bettendorf, Iowa, and attended Pleasant Valley High School. "Athletes at my high school were lucky," Dwyer said. "We had a really strong conditioning program, so if you were in a sport you lifted from 6:30 to 7:30 three days a week." Many high school softball players aren't used to intensive weight training or the focus on working the explosive muscle groups; when that first fall ball season begins and they lift on a MWF schedule and do speed and conditioning the other two days, they have a big psychological and physical adjustment. The adjustment extends to getting everything done in a day. Dwyer mentioned that she got good at being productive and studying between classes.

After playing sparingly as a freshman, Dwyer emerged as a regular in her

Weight room training for female athletes has changed over the past fifteen years, with its emphasis now on lifting heavy weights and building the explosive muscle groups. What's also changed is the number of female athletes interested in becoming strength and conditioning coaches and running a weight room. Sydney Dwyer, who played for University of Minnesota, is one of those. Courtesy Sydney Dwyer.

sophomore season, one highlighted by her game-winning home run off Oklahoma's Paige Parker, one of two Minnesota wins in 2016 over the eventual NCAA champions. Last year, as a junior, Dwyer had a record-setting year; she and teammate Kendyl Lindaman both broke the Minnesota all-time record for RBI in a single season, with seventy-six. A two-time All-Big Ten

Minnesota *football* player would be expecting to get drafted by the NFL, but Dwyer was coming soon to the end of her playing career. "It's bittersweet," she said. "I've been playing since I was eight, and each week I'm getting closer and closer to it being the last time. In the years I've been here, I've seen seniors graduate and seen that it's a bit of an identity shock to find out what life is like without softball. But I'm also ready to be coaching, to helping athletes with their strength and conditioning work. I want to give back to people like those who gave to me."

* * *

Professional softball in the United States has always struggled, with few teams, with players earning minimal pay, and with few fans in the stands or watching on television. Japan has the world's best financed and attended professional league, with 2018 marking the fifty-first season of the Japan Women's Softball League (JWSL). Players from around the world are in the JWSL, players from Japan, Australia, the Netherlands, and the United States, including such stars as Monica Abbott and Keilani Ricketts.

Opportunities for college softball stars to play after graduation are limited, which is one reason why fans were excited in 2016 when the International Olympic Committee voted to return softball to the 2020 Olympic games, hosted by Japan. In 2016 the World Baseball Softball Confederation (WBSC) launched the first-ever world rankings for softball, across both men's and women's national teams. The ranking system tracks the performance of a country's National Team in the Softball World Championships, including junior and top-tier levels, over a three-year period. "These new softball world rankings mark another major milestone in the history of our global sport," said WBSC Softball Division President Dale McMann. "These rankings not only provide a benchmarking tool for nations to construct and evaluate their strategic development plans, but they also give the players and fans a new and exciting way to express the pride of their country through sport." At the beginning of 2018, the United States sat atop the women's softball rankings, displacing long-time leader Japan. Canada was third, followed by Australia, Chinese Taipei, Puerto Rico, Mexico, Netherlands, Italy, and at #10, the Czech Republic.

The United States National Team that plays in the Tokyo Olympics will likely have few collegians, being largely made up of players a few years older who have been playing professionally here and abroad, as well as playing for Team USA. Collegians may actually contribute substantially to other national teams; for softball, if you have a grandparent born in a particular country, you can play for their national team. So Florida State's Meghan King, Washington's Taran Alvelo, and Florida's Aleshia Ocasio have all played for Puerto Rico in summer tournaments. Numerous Latina college stars, including Tori Vidales and Cielo Meza, have been invited to play for Mexico.

Extending a softball career by playing for a national team or playing professionally is possible for only a tiny percentage of college players. A slightly larger percentage of college players will stay involved with softball by coaching, as Sydney Dwyer hopes to do, while another small percentage will give private lessons. Playing softball, like any activity that takes concentrated effort over a period of time, can be enhanced for young people by having instruction from someone who knows the game and can teach fundamentals as well as a mindset. For decades in American life, middle-class parents made their children go to private music lessons, not because the child was going to become a gifted musician but because parents believed that studying an instrument was useful life preparation. More recently, middle-class parents enroll their daughters in sports lessons, with some of the same aims—though many parents are also hoping for that college scholarship.

Sara Moulton's story is typical of how former players stay in the game by teaching. After Moulton graduated from Minnesota, she went immediately to play in the pro league for the Chicago Bandits. When the summer ended, she had to figure out how to support herself. Having excellent grades and a business marketing degree, she imagined that she would do some kind of marketing in a sports context. But then she got a call from Michelle Harrison, Moulton's own private pitching instructor from when she was young. Harrison asked if Moulton would be interested in opening an indoor training and lessons facility with her. "I said yes," Moulton recalled. "We looked at numerous buildings, and ended up converting a warehouse in Eagan into an awesome softball space for Strike Zone Sports, and I became a full-time instructor." That was back in 2014. A few years later when Harrison moved east, Moulton took over as owner and primary instructor.

I asked Moulton what she finds most satisfying about giving private pitching lessons. "Some girls I teach are eight years old," she replied, "and some former students come in even after they go to college, so I say that I instruct girls eight to college age. I love giving lessons. I don't feel like I'm going to work every day—I'm going to teach softball. What's really wonderful is giving instruction about something and watching the player's face light up. And then seeing them when they do it right and how excited they get about that. I try to get them to improve one percent each time they walk through the door."

Moulton's Strike Zone Sports is one of thousands of such facilities in the country, where girls come in and work privately or in pairs with an instructor. The most widely known is probably Club K in Nashville, founded by Cheri Kempf, long-time star pitcher who is now the commissioner of the National Pro Fastpitch league. Other former players teach in a clinic setting, such as Emily Allard and Kristin Scharkey with their company Be the Momentum, which teaches slapping and the speed game and will travel around the country to do occasional clinics for groups of girls. Though Allard and Scharkey have additional jobs that earn them a living, some clinic companies are national and do clinics regularly. One such company is The Packaged Deal, who claim—probably rightly—to be the #1 softball clinic company in the world. The Packaged Deal is a partnership of Jen Schroeder, Katie Schroeder, Amanda Scarborough, and Morgan Stuart, who focus on catching, hitting, pitching, and defense, respectively. With an aim "to empower girls and to inspire them to be better versions of themselves," the four former players made a standard curriculum for their clinics, one designed to teach girls to be better on and off the field. The Packaged Deal's success with their clinics and in the social media space even led Nike to sign them, in December 2017, to a three-year apparel and footwear contract.

The vast majority of former college softball players will not play, coach, or give private lessons after graduation; they will, instead, work in a public or private sector job unrelated to softball. *The Chronicle of Higher Education* has some good news for these players and what their athletic careers might do for them. The 2017 report "The Future of Work: How Colleges Can Prepare Students for the Jobs Ahead" argues that many valued attributes for college graduates have little to do with deep disciplinary knowledge or technical skills, and are difficult for colleges to teach because those attributes connect to character. The "soft skills" that employers are looking for—as opposed to hard skills such as engineering training or computer coding—include grit, resiliency, and initiative, all learned in spades by female softball players.

The Chronicle of Higher Education asked corporate recruiters what skills they ended up helping with most often, and those recruiters responded that "teaching young employees to bounce back from failure—and even encouraging those employees to expose themselves to the possibility of failure—has been a huge challenge." Social constructions of gender create a binary of masculinity and femininity that suggests "feminine" girls should not be competitive and aggressive and should not put themselves in situations where they publicly win or fail. All softball players, countless times, have experienced situations where their particular efforts led to winning or losing. Claire Shipman, television journalist and co-author of *The Confidence Code*, emphasizes the value of these oft-repeated moments: girls who play sports "embody the experience of not just winning, but the critical experience of losing.... [Sports is] an incredibly useful proving ground for business and leadership." An espnW survey of 400 female executives in large companies around the world showed that 94 percent of them played sports and over 80 percent played team sports.

Former athletes make more money because their competitive nature, their ability to overcome adversity, and their self-confidence leads them to choose jobs with higher salaries. Programs in finance and banking, for two examples, are trying to directly draw in people who are competitive and aggressive such as female athletes. But the story isn't simply that former athletes enter higher paying jobs or perform better. A recent Gallup-Purdue Index, a national study of college graduates, discovered that former female athletes outperform other college graduates, including male athletes, on career and life outcomes.

College softball's emphasis on a culture that promotes academic achievement, community service, and team-first ideas translates well to the business world. Jen Goodwin is the head coach at Yale University, and she told me that her players get recruited regularly for graduate schools and corporate positions. "The grads of our programs," Goodwin said, "go in many different directions, due to all of the different opportunities available to them. There is an event in the fall that targets varsity athletes, who know how to manage their time, prioritize, compete, fail, and perform under pressure. These are some of the intangibles that show up on paper as 'Four Year Player on the Yale Softball Team,' but recruiters know what is behind that."

The success of a job hunt for a graduating senior may depend on her ability to convey in interviews how playing softball at the collegiate level has set her up to be a valuable employee, has taught her these soft skills such as learning from failure. Kayla Bonstrom played at Stanford, graduated in 2016, and currently works in Washington, D.C., as a consultant for a defense contractor, helping her company optimize business strategies and processes. Although interviewing, she said, is scary at some level, "the good thing is that whether you realize it or not, softball has prepared you for such a moment." Being a former softball player, Bonstrom said, sets you apart from other applicants: "Skills like teamwork, drive, commitment, hard work, resilience, decisiveness, bouncing back from failure, and staying calm under pressure are all second nature to former softball players. I can say from personal experience that emphasizing these things helped me successfully navigate many interviews."

Graduates preparing for interviews do need to know what skills or situations they should talk about or even emphasize. Bonstrom suggested that former players should emphasize their abilities to manage a complex, demanding life: "Planning and organizing are things that come to student-athletes not because we are born with the ability to do so, but because it is a necessity. Being a student-athlete is a constant balancing act, and prepares you better than you think for life after softball. It's not a skill everyone has avidly practiced throughout college, which sets former student-athletes apart." Nancy Altobello, the EY (Ernst Young) Global Vice Chair-Talent, offers numerous reasons that businesses should hire athletes, and at the top of her list is that athletes know how to see projects through to completion.

Society celebrates the seemingly overnight success stories, Altobello said, but in business, like sports, success comes from long preparation: "The work is done behind the scenes, with weeks and sometimes even months of preparation going into the teaming, strategy and execution. It takes a strong work ethic to spend countless hours preparing for competition that's often measured in seconds." Organizing a complex and demanding life, seeing projects through to completion, knowing how to use particular examples to demonstrate teamwork and communication—softball players are ready to take these skills to the work world. To get that first job, however, players have to learn something that is difficult because it counters softball culture. The women are often excellent at explaining success as a team effort, but such talk only goes so far in an interview; the task for them when they prepare to interview is to shift the mindset from "we" to "I," and to claim their own skills and achievement, on and off the field.

TEN

It's an SEC World

By the early 1990s, Fresno State's softball program had achieved great success—nine Women's College World Series berths—leading to fan support that outgrew the capacity of their field, which didn't even have lights. Head Coach Margie Wright formed a committee of business people in Fresno to begin fundraising for a new field. "We met once a week for a year," she recalled, "and when we had enough seed money, we did a presentation to the president of Fresno State to ask him to give his blessing for us to begin the fundraising project. He refused to support us." But then the softball program, and all players and coaches who would follow, got a break.

Fresno State had randomly been reviewed on Title IX by the Office for Civil Rights (OCR). The administration turned in some false answers. When the OCR found out, they declared the university out of compliance with Title IX. Fueled by her belief that female athletes should have comparable resources to male athletes, Wright argued to the administration that building a softball stadium comparable to the baseball stadium would show compliance. The OCR supported her stand, and the university fell in line.

In the decades following the passage of Title IX in 1972, a softball team typically played on fields sub-standard to the school's baseball facilities. Fresno State's Bulldog Diamond, the modern forerunner to today's softball stadiums, debuted in 1996. The $3.2 million softball stadium featured nearly 1700 permanent seat-back chairs, sunken dugouts, lights, concessions stands, restrooms, practice areas, enclosed batting cages, a press box, and scoreboard. Even more fans came than before, with Fresno State setting attendance records for a season and for individual games. With temporary bleacher seats erected, the team drew more than 5,000 fans when they played host to UCLA in 1996 and again in 1997, a year when the team's average attendance was 2,557. In 1998 Fresno State's softball team won the national championship.

Fresno State's Bulldog Diamond, in 2014 re-named Margie Wright Diamond, arose from Title IX pressures and Wright fighting for her female athletes against the desires of a male administration. A story of a second stadium describes a different model for the building of softball facilities and symbolizes the sea change that happened in the 1990s—when fastpitch softball became truly national, expanding throughout the South; and when softball got a huge boost in its exposure to casual fans through the 1996 Atlanta Olympics.

In the mid–1990s Baylor University, a top-flight academic university whose sports teams rarely won, had woefully inadequate facilities for the Big 12 conference. Deciding to step up their fundraising for athletics, Baylor hired Tom Stanton as athletic director in 1995, luring him away from the American Broadcasting Company (ABC) where he had worked for twenty-five years, rising to the position of Executive Vice-President of Operations and President of Sales and Marketing. An alumnus of Baylor, a winner of three basketball and two baseball letters, Stanton had name-recognition among donors. He brought to his new job a business plan from the corporate world—rather than fundraise generally, he would appeal directly to specific interests. He also brought with him an appreciation of the numerous talented women he worked with at ABC. "It's hard to turn around a football program," Stanton said, "because you have to spend so much money. I wanted to create an athletic program competitive in all sports. I focused on women's facilities first. You need far less money to make a difference, and I always believed that Title IX was important."

Niche fundraising in the mid–1990s for major men's sports worked because donors were often former athletes or current fans; women's sports were less widely accepted and had a shorter history, making for a small list of potential donors. Early in his athletic director tenure, Stanton ran into what he calls a "wonderful Baylor family," Ted and Sue Getterman, who were alumni of the university and had stayed in Waco after graduation. Ted and Sue had owned a 7Up bottling facility, and Ted had been mayor of the city in the 1970s. Now eighty-eight years old, Sue Getterman is a "Regent Emerita" for Baylor, having served three terms a decade ago. She remembered well when she became involved with Baylor fundraising: "My late husband, Ted, and I decided that it was time to give Baylor a big gift, and we told them that we'd do what no one else wanted to do. Tom [Stanton] called us not long after and asked if we'd be the lead donors for a new women's softball stadium. Now, we were an all-male family. We had two boys and four grandsons, and we had never really followed women's athletics personally. But we said that we'd go ahead and help fund the stadium."

The Gettermans' million dollar gift was leveraged to raise two million dollars more. Ted and Sue had never even seen a women's softball game; that happened in spring of 2000, at Baylor's first game in the new facility that was dedicated that day as Getterman Stadium. "We threw out the first pitch," Sue recalled, "and we were excited to attend, but we didn't know that we'd become such fans of the sport."

Tom Stanton wanted to turn around athletics at Baylor sport by sport,

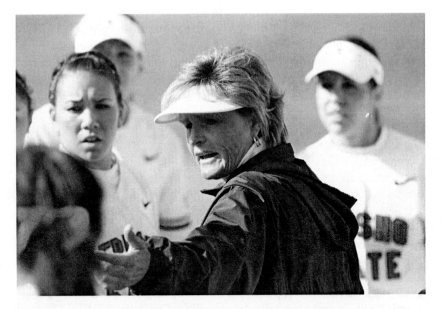

Hall of Fame coach Margie Wright led Fresno State to numerous Women's College World Series berths and the national title in 1998. For many years Wright held the record for all-time wins. Her fight for gender rights was instrumental in getting Bulldog Diamond, the forerunner to today's softball stadiums, built at Fresno State. The field has since been re-named Margie Wright Diamond. Courtesy Fresno State Athletics.

with an equal commitment to women. And that attitude and the new stadium paid immediate dividends in softball. In the summer of 2000, Baylor hired Glenn Moore, who in two years at LSU had won two SEC season titles. When he arrived in Waco to interview for the job, Moore was impressed not only with the new facilities but with Baylor's commitment to women's sports, measured in part by the softball program's budget that was a substantial increase over what he had at LSU. Moore has led Baylor to its position as a nationally elite program, and the athletic administration, Moore said, has approached him throughout his tenure to see what improvements the softball team has needed.

The Gettermans' commitment to donate to "whatever needed doing" for Baylor became a love story, an older couple's surprising relationship to softball and to female athletes two generations younger. "We went to all the games," Sue said, "and we always had the team to our house for a barbecue. Baylor softball has been a big part of our lives and we've just loved it." Stanton suggested that the Gettermans through the years have talked as if all the players were daughters. The first year that Baylor went to Oklahoma City to the Women's College World Series, the Gettermans went with them. When it came time to add on to the stadium, to keep the facilities in line with other stadiums that had been built or renovated, the Gettermans gave a gift so that Baylor could build an indoor practice facility. "I'm 88 years old," Sue Getterman said, "and my husband has been gone three years, but I still get in my car, drive to the stadium, sit with the fans, and watch the girls play. I'll do that as long as I can get there."

*   *   *

New state-of-the-art stadiums visually represent the influx of dollars coming into college softball programs. The Southeastern Conference has been the leader in this, pushing for commitments from each school, who then in turn fund-raise along the lines of what Baylor did to build Getterman Stadium. Tennessee in 2008, Arkansas and LSU in 2009, Kentucky and South Carolina in 2013, Mississippi State in 2016—all have gotten quality new stadiums for their programs. Ole Miss has updated its softball complex several times. The John and Ann Rhoads Softball Stadium, built in 2000, serves as Alabama's home field, and has been renovated three times since then. The seating capacity of 3,940 allows Alabama to lead the nation in fan attendance; the 2011 renovation added a new locker room, an expanded training room, a player's lounge, and a new team video room, all connected to the new indoor practice facility that includes three batting cages and a bullpen. Florida's upcoming $11 million renovation will turn Katie Seashole Pressly Stadium into

Texas A&M's luxurious new stadium, Davis Diamond, is the latest SEC entrant in the facilities arms race. Courtesy Texas A&M Athletic Department.

one of the finest facilities in the country. You get the idea—the SEC builds it, and the athletes do come.

Outside of the SEC, a few prominent programs have kept pace. Oregon's Jane Sanders Stadium debuted in 2016 with a $17.2 million price tag. Oklahoma and Arizona recently announced major renovations to their stadiums. But the facilities race in the world of softball has been run largely within the SEC, and the latest entrant came when Texas A&M's softball team stepped onto the field in 2018 in their new $28.6 million stadium, Davis Diamond, a facility comparable to the baseball team's Blue Bell Park. Davis Diamond seats 2,000 fans and includes club level seating and two luxury suites. Coaches have offices and a locker room in the facility, and the players have a locker room, player lounge, training room, video room, and computer lab, as well as a 6,744 square foot indoor hitting facility with four batting cages. Though it's difficult to imagine a future stadium with even more amenities, it will happen.

In DI softball, this was conference championship week—I was attending the SEC tourney, being held at the University of Missouri's stadium which came on-line in 2017 at a price tag of $17 million. I had not yet been to any of the newest stadiums and was curious as to what that amount of money could build. With its architecture of brick and iron, the stadium combines the traditional and contemporary. Its facade and entry are impressive: a tall iron fence with landscaping inside surrounds the field; the media area sits on pillars, floating above the concourse level; a stairwell tower sports a big SEC sign; above the four gates that serve as entrance to the stadium, two signs with three-foot high lettering say Mizzou Softball, and two more oval signs have the Tigers logo.

After walking up twenty two steps, I came out on the concourse level, which is wide to allow fans room to move around. Concession stands and restrooms line the back; the field sits below. Fourteen rows of chair back seats encircle home plate; bleachers with back supports go up and down the first and third-base lines, ending with each team's bullpen. Covered hitting cages sit under the stands. An expansive berm in left and center fields has room for hundreds to sit on blankets and watch the game. The stadium is gorgeous.

For the conference championship, the SEC had added a pavilion behind the right field fence, where on a raised dais sat an open-air version of its SEC Now studio. Around a long curved desk, former SEC stars Madison Shipman and Kayla Braud and a regular host of the studio show, Laura Rutledge, gave pre- and postgame analysis, and conducted postgame interviews with the winning coach and players. Imagine, if you shift the sport and network, Chris Evert and Hannah Storm interviewing Serena Williams after a U.S. Open tennis match—that was the vibe.

Star treatment for college teams and players once was the realm only of the Women's College World Series, beginning a decade or so ago when ESPN recognized that they had something good going with women's softball and began expanding their coverage. So why was this star treatment happening in Columbia, Missouri, at a conference tourney televised by the SEC Network? The network, which began in 2014, is owned by ESPN, who uses the SEC tourney as a dress rehearsal for the NCAA tournament. Games from the first two days of the SEC tourney are broadcast on the SEC Network; the semi-finals and championship game appear on ESPN. The channel may change, but the process, on-air talent, and approach are the same for all four days, and are replicated throughout the NCAA tournament and into the Women's College World Series. ESPN producer Beth Chappell said that her company treats every SEC game as it treats an ESPN game: "We have the same philosophy to document the game the best way we can and to bring to it great story-telling."

All major conferences have some kind of television network deal for their sports programs. The rather small MountainWest Sports Network began in 2006 as the first network devoted to a single conference. The Big Ten Network (BTN) followed in 2007, a launch which shook up the landscape of television sports deals by using a cable subscription service to pay for getting its content—the conference's sporting events—in front of the public. The BTN was created to provide the conference with more national exposure, improving distribution, for example, for football and men's basketball games that were previously available only on a local or regional basis. The BTN stated that they also wanted to increase exposure for women's sports, which they did follow through on. Other major conferences, such as the Pac-12 in 2012, have followed this independent model, though the Pac-12 has been far less successful in getting their product on cable or satellite providers.

The SEC went a different route—they threw in with ESPN. What is good for SEC sports programs, therefore, becomes good for ESPN, and vice versa. Their synergy produces a combined effect greater than the sum of their separate efforts. That the SEC Network is owned by ESPN doesn't make each school more money; the Big Ten Network distributes about the same amount to each of its conference schools. But the relationship between ESPN and the SEC Network facilitates a high quality product and increases the number of eyes on that product.

Think of it this way. The SEC championship gets ESPN resources: this means who is in the production truck, as well as the fourteen cameras capturing the action. And it gets top-flight on-air talent: Adam Amin and Amanda Scarborough, Beth Mowins and Michele Smith. ESPN's influence isn't important only for this championship tourney, moreover, because these events set a standard for everything the SEC Network does.

Football may be the most visible example of the synergy between ESPN and the SEC, but the effects for women's softball are many and crucial. The

Big Ten Network doesn't cover softball particularly well. They show only a handful of games on their cable channel during the season, rotated evenly between schools, so you often have inconsequential match-ups. Games that you watch on their subscription service, BTN2Go, are student-produced and have only a few cameras—the production values are mediocre. While it might be admirable to give college undergraduates experience in manning cameras or announcing games, you're not creating a product comparable to what the SEC Network provides on its digital broadcasts. The disparity extends to choices made on the networks' websites. Right now, in May, BTN on its website was featuring football. The SEC Network was leading with softball. Such choices demonstrate priorities.

Jill Skotarczak is the Assistant Director of Communications for the SEC. She made clear to me that a product's quality is tied directly to choices made by the conference and by the universities. "Our schools have made an investment in their production crews," she said, "so when a game doesn't have a linear broadcast [traditional television channel] they have the ability to do a quality digital broadcast. That's helped with the growth of the sport." Actually, these numerous high-quality games being broadcast *most* help the SEC

SEC Now is SEC Network's flagship news and information show that usually airs live from a studio set in Charlotte, North Carolina. During the SEC softball tourney, the show moves to the host site and does pre- and post-game analysis, as well as interviews, giving star treatment to the players and coaches. From left to right, Madison Shipman, Kayla Braud, and Laura Rutledge. Courtesy ESPN Images/Emily Merritt.

footprint. So why has the SEC, the SEC Network, and ESPN made the choices it has? They believe strongly in the appeal of women's softball. SEC Assistant Commissioner for Championships Byron Hatch says that women's softball is made for television: there's exciting action on the field; the games take two hours; the athletes are great. "We committed ourselves," Hatch said, "to the sport."

While ESPN owns the SEC Network, decisions on programming are a collaborative effort. "ESPN has staff," Hatch said, "who work directly with our conference office. We'll look at the upcoming season and collaborate on what games to televise, which ones to put on the channels and which ones on the digital platforms, what times they should be televised, and then we'll work with our schools, so we can minimize any conflicts that they might have. We'll come up with a proposed schedule, and then we'll reach out to our schools. We try to have some balance, some representation for everyone—but it won't be equal, because in a particular sport some schools will have something televised more than others." ESPN, as a business, cares about its TV ratings, so a marquee matchup will be featured.

College programs who spend substantial money on the sport aren't getting a financial return on their expenditures, even with growing on-field attendance and television ratings. I asked Hatch how the SEC thought about the non-financial benefits. "The benefits are to our student athletes," he replied. "When you look overall at the deal that the SEC has with ESPN, it gives all of our athletes, including female athletes, the opportunity to showcase their talent in front of a national audience. ESPN has made a financial commitment to our conference as a whole, and our institutions have done a good job in allocating revenues to their softball programs. It takes more than saying certain things, you have to practice what you preach. When you look at the facilities that we've built and the coaches we've hired, all of that takes a financial commitment, and our institutions have definitely done that. We're seeing the benefits. All thirteen SEC schools made the NCAA tournament last year."

Great stadiums, great coaches, tremendous exposure—SEC softball programs are very attractive to prospective student athletes. Recruiting success breeds on-field success, which breeds recruiting success, and so on, into the near and perhaps the far future. "We're in a society today where everybody kind of wants the bells and whistles when it comes to recruiting," Ole Miss coach Mike Smith has said. "The SEC by far has the best bells and whistles of anybody in the country."

*   *   *

Thirteen teams in the SEC have softball programs, which makes for awkwardness when it comes to the conference championship tourney: one team gets left out. Going into the final weekend of conference play, the race for the bottom was tight. Ole Miss was at 5–16; right ahead of them, with six wins, were Mississippi State, Kentucky, and Missouri. On the final weekend, Kentucky and Ole Miss won twice, Mississippi State once, and Missouri lost all three games to Florida. More awkwardness: as this year's tournament host, Missouri got to show off its new stadium but not its team.

Who would be left out was one SEC story entering the tournament, and another was the recent scheduling decisions of Missouri. To make the NCAA tournament as an at-large team, you can't have lost more games than you won. Fearing that their overall record would dip under .500, Missouri paid to cancel a mid-week doubleheader against a good Wichita State team (#31 in the RPI) and paid the University of Arkansas–Pine Bluff (#262 in the RPI) to come to Columbia and get crushed twice, as a way to add two wins to the Missouri overall record. The move was legal but many people thought it unethical, and the move simply added to the turmoil surrounding the program—Missouri had fired its successful but abrasive coach, Ehren Earleywine, on January 26, less than two weeks before the season opener; Gina Fogue, the team's assistant coach, had been given the difficult job of interim head coach.

Even though all thirteen SEC teams were expecting to make the NCAA tournament, given their RPIs, the conference championship can influence the NCAA tournament seeding, which the 2017 SEC tourney dramatically demonstrated. Ole Miss came into the tournament 36–18, with a 10–14 conference record and an RPI ranking in the 20s. With some luck in that Tim Walton didn't start either of his two aces (Kelly Barnhill or Delanie Gourley) when Florida played Ole Miss in the quarterfinals, the Rebels rode Kaitlin Lee's pitching to a tournament title, and then to a #12 seed in the NCAA tournament, which meant they got to host a regional in Oxford.

The SEC was a great conference this year, once again, but also a surprising one. In the pre-season coaches' poll, Georgia and South Carolina were in the bottom five, but their strong showings in league play had them in the top four of the conference, with byes on opening day. In the opening game on Wednesday, Mississippi State shut out Texas A&M 2–0, behind Holly Ward's three-hitter. Arkansas continued its strong season by beating Kentucky 3–1; Arkansas didn't hit much, all their runs being unearned, but Mary Haff pitched out of a bases-loaded jam in the sixth to hold the lead. Ole Miss and LSU had played that epic nineteen inning, 2–1 game back in April, but this time around, LSU catcher Michaela Schlattman hit a grand slam in the bottom of the second to put LSU ahead 4–0. Allie Walljasper, LSU's First Team All-SEC pitcher, closed it out 4–1. The evening's marquee matchup pitted Auburn and Alabama and two Second Team All-SEC pitchers, Alexis Osorio for Bama and Kaylee Carlson for Auburn. In a back-and-forth game, Alabama prevailed 6–4. Unlike most tournaments which are double elimination, one loss here and you fly home. Four teams were confirming airline reservations.

The opening game of Thursday's quarterfinals matched Mississippi State, a team who came into the tourney 2–8 in their last ten games, against a streaking South Carolina team who closed 8–2 to finish in third place in the SEC. South Carolina has been slowly improving year-by-year under Head Coach Beverly Smith, and this year they took a jump. Smith was attributing the excellent play to the team's belief in each other. "You can talk about this as a coach," she said, "and the players can say the right thing, but when they actually believe it and live it, great things can happen." A team such as South Carolina who exceeds expectations is always compelling, in part by demonstrating that intangibles matter.

In the bottom of the third inning, South Carolina scratched across two runs, and they added a third run an inning later when Alyssa Kumiyama homered. Cayla Drotar was a bulldog in the circle for South Carolina. "She grinds it out," Coach Smith said of her pitcher. "She doesn't concede to the hitter. She's willing to throw the change-up on any count. The special thing about her is that she bats third for us, and when she's not having a great day in the circle, she can change things at the plate." South Carolina won 3–1 and moved on to the semi-finals.

I asked Coach Smith when she believed her team could be really good. "I believed the entire time," she said. "Well, perhaps not back in fall ball. We were talented but inexperienced, and so it's hard to know exactly what you're going to have. But things started coming together in January practices. And during the season, if we've had losses, we just set them behind us and moved on. Our low points have been short-lived. This team has done nothing but develop and improve."

Coach Smith also pointed to something that can be important, particularly for young teams. "There were a couple of games early that we didn't deserve to win, but we found ways to win, and that's when I thought that this could be a special team. We beat Texas at home in the bottom of the 8th, and it felt like a springboard moment." She also mentioned the importance of two losses to Oklahoma where her team played well and realized that they could compete with anyone.

South Carolina had no superstar, but they did have solid pitching and hitting and played excellent defense, leading the SEC during conference play in fielding percentage, a position usually held by Florida. I asked Coach Smith how she and her staff approached the tourney and how they were imagining post-season play. "As a coach, I think big picture and seedings," she said, "but I don't talk to the team about them much. A few times this season I've stepped back, taken that 10,000 foot view with the players, and we've discussed goals. We talked about being a top-four seed in the SEC so that we could have a bye in this conference tourney. We accomplished that. We got to be here yesterday and have the day off, come to the ballpark and just take everything in, and now we've done our job in terms of winning this game and getting to the semi-finals. Now we'll approach things one game at a time."

The second game of the quarterfinals matched two teams who also surprised prognosticators this year. The Georgia Bulldogs were picked ninth in the pre-season poll after finishing last in 2017, but they got on a hot streak early, winning 25 games in a row in February and March, and won every SEC series until their last, against Ole Miss. With the big bats of Alyssa DiCarlo, Justice Milz, Alysen Febrey, and Cortni Emanuel, Georgia led the SEC in four offensive categories. Arkansas was picked tenth, but the team that was once a doormat in the league went 12–12 and finished seventh. Head Coach Courtney Deifel, in her third year, has led the Arkansas rise. "I'm so proud of this team," she said. "They've come into their own as the season has gone. They have a ton of character. Our players are not intimidated. And that's the big difference between last year and this one. They don't care who's in that other dugout. They'll battle for each other."

Arkansas got on the board early, scoring four in the top of the third, with the big blow being a two-out, three-run homer by A.J. Belans. Autumn Storms was the starter in the circle for Arkansas. Though Georgia chipped away with single runs in the third and fourth by piling up the singles, they missed an opportunity when they left the bases loaded with one out in the fifth. Mary Haff came in to relieve Storms and held the Bulldogs to one more run. With an 8–3 win, Arkansas moved to the semi-finals to face South Carolina.

Perennial powers Tennessee and LSU, who expect each year to make deep runs in the NCAA tournament, squared off in the day's third game, which also matched fan bases. Tennessee fans, who call themselves the Locos, are a hoot. They dance to "Rocky Top," sing "She'll Be Coming Round to Score (When She Comes)," and keep up nonstop cheering. They've been known to dress in hula skirts or squid heads, or to show up as Skittles. LSU has the loudest individual super-fan, the brother of third baseman Shemiah Sanchez, who yells encouragement on every pitch to the team and on occasion runs up and down the stairs in his excitement. The game was as much fun as the fans. LSU's Allie Walljasper gave up a run in the first inning on a Meghan Gregg double, but then shut down the powerful bats of Tennessee. Caylan Arnold sparkled in the circle for the Lady Vols, throwing an efficient three hit shutout, and Tennessee advanced with a 1–0 win. Their fans also came out on top, unofficially of course.

In the nightcap, league champion Florida faced off against arch-rival Alabama, who came in with a five-game win streak. The Tide got two runs off Kelly Barnhill in the top of the first on a groundout and a sacrifice fly, but then she got her rhythm and began shutting Alabama down. Courtney

LADY VOL
SOFTBALL

Some softball fan bases emulate the players in cheering on the team. Seen here having great fun are "The Locos," self-named Tennessee fans who dress up in various costumes for games. Courtesy Tennessee Athletic Department.

Gettins got the start for the Tide and held on several times when the Gators threatened. But in the bottom of the fourth inning, Aleshia Ocasio homered with Janell Wheaton on base to tie the game 2–2. Alexis Osorio, Alabama's senior ace, came in to relieve Gettins, and when in the top of the sixth Florida Head Coach Tim Walton brought Ocasio out of center field to relieve Barnhill with a runner on, it looked like two fresh and excellent pitchers might keep this tie game going a long time. But in the Gators' sixth, a walk to Ocasio and a perfect bunt by Sophia Reynoso put runners on first and second, and two outs later, SEC Player of the Year Amanda Lorenz smashed a long three-run homer to put the Gators up 5–2. Ocasio closed the door and Florida advanced, concluding a long Thursday of excellent softball in Columbia, Missouri.

The first game of the semi-finals on Friday matched South Carolina and Arkansas, teams happy to have gotten this far in the tourney. Only one would now be moving on. Cayla Drotar, set to start in the circle, was a last-minute scratch for South Carolina. Dixie Raley had to step in, warm up quickly, and psychologically adjust to being handed the game ball. South Carolina scored first, on a two-out infield single by Kenzi Maguire that she beat out by a whisker. Head Coach Beverly Smith said that all season different players had stepped up, something demonstrated in the fourth inning when eight-hole hitter Tiara Duffy hit a two-run homer. Arkansas got two walks and five hits, but only in the sixth inning could they push a run across, falling to South Carolina 3–1. Raley was superb, going the distance.

In game two, Matty Moss got the start in the circle for Tennessee. Some pitchers are stoical, epitomized by Alabama's Osorio. Moss is the opposite. She points. She gestures. She emotes. She has been a big-time pitcher for Tennessee for three years, particularly as a sophomore in 2017 when she went 26–3. Tennessee's opponent, Florida, did in the first inning what it excels at: Amanda Lorenz walked, and Nicole DeWitt followed with a two-run bomb. During the season Florida had scored more runs on fewer hits, I'm guessing, than any team in the country. Not only had the batters drawn a great number of walks, but they had been hit by pitch frequently. Their hits often had gone for extra bases. Their on-base plus slugging percentage was high, which usually translates into a lot of runs scored. While in batting average they were ranked only fifty-sixth nationally, they were eighth in runs scored.

Moss had trouble hitting the outside edge of the plate, which made for a short day, as Caylan Arnold relieved her with just one out and two more runners on via walk. Things didn't get much better, Janell Wheaton singling in a run to put the Gators up 3–0. In the bottom of the second, DeWitt hit a second bomb, her thirteenth of the season, this time a three-run shot. Wheaton followed up her earlier RBI by doubling in another run. In classic Florida fashion, in two innings they had scored seven runs on just four hits. The game moved along at a baseball pace, meaning slow. Both teams' batters fouled off a lot of pitches. Both teams showed plate discipline. The umpire had a tight strike zone. At the end of the fourth inning, the game was already over two hours long. But in the bottom of the fifth, Jordan Matthews singled in a run and Florida run-ruled Tennessee 10–2.

Winning the SEC *league* championship is a grind, twenty-four tough games over nine weeks. A slump, even a relatively short one, can cost you. Winning the SEC *tourney* can happen if you play your best on this one weekend. Sometimes teams do both, playing well all season and elevating their game in the tourney, and that was true for the 2018 Florida Gators. South Carolina took a 1–0 lead in the first inning on an RBI sacrifice fly from Cayla Drotar, but Aleshia Ocasio shut them down from there, and in the third inning, Amanda Lorenz hit a three-run homer for Florida, which closed the scoring. The Gators were SEC tourney and regular season champs.

*   *   *

The SEC was not the only league playing their conference championship this weekend, of course, and for many of the nation's leagues and teams, the stakes were actually higher. In the America East Conference tourney, Maine won two games but couldn't get to the conference championship; top-seeded University of Albany came through the loser's bracket to claim the league's automatic NCAA tournament berth by beating University of Massachusetts–Lowell twice on the final day. Top-seeded Monmouth University cruised through the Metro Atlantic Athletic Conference, not dropping a game, punching their ticket to the tournament; Quinnipiac, who I had seen play several games at the Clearwater Classic in March, lost a tie-breaker and didn't make the conference tourney. Teams from small conferences throughout the country were celebrating championships that ensured they would be in the spotlight, the NCAA tourney, the following week. For those teams losing in the America East or MAAC tournaments, and their compatriots in similar leagues, the year was done. There would be no at-large berths to the NCAA tournament. Seniors had ended their careers.

The Pac-12 doesn't hold a conference championship. Oregon claimed the league title and the automatic bid when they swept three games from Cal. UCLA closed their strong season with two wins and a loss against Arizona State, a team also likely headed for a top-eight seed in the NCAA tournament. Washington, one of the nation's best teams, was using their bye weekend to get healthy. In 2017 after a six year absence, the Big 12 reinstated its softball

Conference tourneys usually conclude a senior's softball career, as there are few opportunities professionally. Schools celebrate with Senior Day for the final home game. Florida's Aleshia Ocasio is shown here about to get a hug from her pitching coach, Jennifer Rocha. Courtesy Tim Casey and the Florida Athletic Department.

championship, though the small number of teams in the conference who play softball meant that the league chose to do pool play, which turned out strangely this year when all the teams in pool B went 1–1 against each other and they had to choose a team to play against, and lose to, Oklahoma for the title.

The Big Ten tournament saw the regular season second-place team, Minnesota, beat everyone convincingly to win their third straight tournament championship. Regular-season champ Michigan went out in the quarterfinals to rival Michigan State. What caused Minnesota the most problem was the weather in Madison, Wisconsin, where it rained off and on during the entire tournament—the Gophers endured numerous rain delays and muddy cleats, and, in a one-of-a-kind moment, a "chopper delay" of forty-five minutes, when the Big Ten brought in a helicopter to hover over the outfield grass in an attempt to dry things out enough to resume playing. The attempt worked.

The most exciting Power-5 conference tournament was the ACC's in Atlanta, where second-seeded Pitt made a strong showing. Though their non-league play was so-so, they won the Coastal Division of the ACC and, entering the tournament, were on the proverbial bubble for making the NCAA tournament as an at-large team. They cruised through the first two rounds of the tournament and in the championship game led powerhouse Florida State University 4–2, with two down and two on in the seventh inning. But FSU's Anna Shelnutt hit a game-winning, walk-off homer, and Pitt would now have to wait until Sunday night to learn if the selection committee would include them in the tournament without the automatic bid.

* * *

In 2017 the SEC placed all thirteen of its teams into the NCAA softball tournament, a result that had conference representatives and ESPN announcers glowing. Eight of those thirteen were chosen to be regional hosts, a great advantage to moving forward in the tournament. For decades the Pac-12 dominated women's college softball, in part because California was the hotbed of travel ball but even more because the SEC didn't play the sport until 1997. Even when the conference did begin, it took years to get to the level of the Pac-12 and the Big 12, the SEC not winning its first national championship until Alabama broke through in 2012. Florida followed, winning in 2014 and 2015. Only Oklahoma interrupted the forward march and, in Oklahoma's three title years, the SEC had the runner-up team.

Was it a good thing for softball—for the sport as it is played nationally—that the SEC hosted half of the regional tournaments in 2017? The mathematical formula of the RPI favors the strongest conferences, and even then, Minnesota and James Madison had top-fifteen RPIs; on the eye test, as well, both teams were certainly deserving to host. But the selection committee was chaired by a senior administrator from Conference USA with little knowledge of softball, and the most powerful member on that committee was from Ole Miss who likewise had no background in softball. The committee's choices clearly looked biased, with little logic or consistency, unless you count consistency as rewarding SEC teams. Many fans of the SEC might believe that the game is served well by having eight SEC teams host. Our teams deserve it, they might say. We have the best coaches, and the best stadiums. We get the best talent, and we prove it on the field. We're the best fans, too.

In recent years, in part because of police shootings, of the visibility of BlackLivesMatter, of the rise of white nationalist movements, and the like, cultural commentators have argued vehemently about privilege, which has often been equated to only one kind, a racial privilege. Race privilege is real in the United States, certainly, but numerous other kinds of privileges sometimes slide out of sight, privileges of gender, able-bodiedness, country of origin, or class, to name a few. Those who feel defensive about discussing privilege often point out that much of what gets named privilege has come about through hard work, good habits, and sacrifices. And they are right that accusations of privilege in our culture are often simplistic and used as a cudgel to beat certain groups. But that doesn't mean that privilege doesn't exist.

When a group has privilege of whatever kind, the privilege is often hard to see—privilege blinds you by making "normal" what is not necessarily so. Having some version of privilege—being born a middle class American, let's say, in a safe suburb that has the resources to build good softball fields—does not make you immune to life's hardships. It does not guarantee that you won't have tragedy strike your family, or that you won't have dyslexia to make school difficult, or that you will excel in anything. The privilege does make it easier, however, to become a college softball player than someone who has a different kind of life.

This book is not about the tremendous complexity of the United States, and I want to keep the focus on women's softball. But those who admire the sport and are glad of its growth might well consider how privilege leads to a widening gap between haves and have-nots. Economist Joseph Stiglitz's May 2011 article "Of the 1 percent, by the 1 percent, for the 1 percent" in *Vanity Fair* is credited with being the first mainstream article to use such language in criticizing the economic inequality present in the United States. "The top 1 percent have the best houses, the best educations, the best doctors, and the best lifestyles," Stiglitz wrote, "but there is one thing that money doesn't seem to have bought: an understanding that their fate is bound up with how the other 99 percent live. Throughout history, this is something that the top 1 percent eventually do learn. Too late."

The Occupy Wall Street movement of the 2012 political elections popularized the "1 percent" term, which has continued to be culturally useful. At the 2018 College Sports Research Institute's annual conference, John Barnes and Frederick Williams from the University of New Mexico made a presentation that equated the rich-get-richer trend in the United States to college sports. Their talk, titled "College Sports' 1 Percent: A Resource Based View of the Bifurcation of NCAA Division 1," gave statistics that showed the tremendous difference in resources for universities and colleges in different conferences, and how having more money ensures a competitive advantage. As an example, my own, the Alabama football program, the most successful in the country in terms of money-making, prestige, and winning, has an entire wing of an athletics building given over to employees who are not coaches and not considered part of the staff. What do these well-paid football enthusiasts do? They might watch recruiting film, make the first decision on potential recruits, and then edit film to get a cut-up that allows an assistant coach to come in and be very efficient with his time. These employees might put together game films on future opponents. How many such employees does Alabama have? Perhaps ten to fifteen, perhaps many more. The university won't say and doesn't have to. Alabama, through its money and desires, gains a competitive advantage.

Women's softball isn't men's football, of course, and no one handed the SEC its success in women's softball. They earned it. The conference administrators made good choices. Universities emphasized the building of quality facilities and offered outstanding coaches high salaries. The coaching staffs recruited well in California and kept the best young players in their regions. At Missouri this weekend, I was struck by a large banner that hung on the right field fence and sported a promotional logo for the league. The banner read "SEC: It Just Means More." If you're from the SEC, perhaps the logo's message is clear. If you're not from SEC country, the banner can have multiple meanings, and you can feel it as arrogance.

If you want to see the female softball athlete celebrated and showcased, as I do, then the SEC is the conference to follow. But I also want softball to flourish across the country. Contested issues about the calendar, how the RPI is constructed, and who makes the narratives that determine seeding in the NCAA tournament affect that flourishing. Privilege can make it difficult to see what you have that others don't, to see how you might have built-in advantages. Privilege can also make it difficult to acknowledge how you wield power.

ELEVEN

A Broken System

On Sunday night, May 13, the NCAA selection committee for DI softball announced their brackets for the upcoming tournament. On Monday May 14, Eric Lopez, the host of the popular "In the Circle," opened his podcast by saying, "We cover college softball, the sport that is run by the dumbest people in the world." Lopez and his co-host Victor Anderson are media members and devoted fans who watch innumerable games and talk frequently to coaches and players. They are knowledgeable softball junkies, unlike the selection committee, "who proved once again," said Lopez, "to be the most incompetent committee in all of sports." Anderson explained sarcastically that the committee appeared to be following an ABC model for their placings—A for achievement; B for brand name; and C for convenience—with "A" appearing often to be the lesser grade in this context. Lopez and Anderson, as well as fans across the country, were exasperated and angry by the softball selection committee's work, which in a sense trivializes the season. As Lopez proclaimed: "This crap doesn't happen in men's sports."

The softball selection committee, unlike committees in other prominent college sports, do not go before the national media to explain in depth how they made their choices. While nothing this year was as egregious as not seeding Minnesota and James Madison, as happened in 2017, the committee demonstrated a breathtaking inconsistency of judgment. Were you following the RPI? If so, then many of your choices made no sense, as when Baylor, #14 in the RPI and the second-best team in the Big 12, was sent to Texas A&M while Alabama, tied for seventh in the SEC and #16 in the RPI, was made a twelve seed host. And if you were following the RPI, you wouldn't have left out Florida Gulf Coast, who finished second in the ASUN conference and was #38 in the RPI, in favor of numerous teams behind them. Were you rewarding teams who appeared to be coming on strong late in the season, as the selection committee sometimes implies that they do? If so, you wouldn't make Georgia, #10 in the RPI but struggling after their ace pitcher Brittany Gray went out with a season-ending injury, a seven seed. Why wouldn't a northern team such as Hofstra, who won their conference tournament, climbed to #19 in the RPI, and only played fourteen games at home, get to host? And why might Arkansas, #17 in the RPI, be jumped to a thirteen seed? Might it have had something to do with the chair of the selection committee being from the University of Central Arkansas? If not, then what went into the committee's decision?

The SEC conference and their fans were pleased. Nine SEC teams were named as national seeds, more than half the number of hosts, with the attendant advantages of not having to travel, getting to play before a home crowd, and having a favorable draw in a four-team bracket.

To visualize the geography of softball's host sites, begin in the upper left of a U.S. map, with the University of Washington, come down the West Coast to Oregon and UCLA, head east to Arizona and Arizona State, stay in the Southwest but bump up to Norman, Oklahoma, and then zigzag through the South, through SEC country, with a final stop in Tallahassee, Florida, home of Florida State. Those are your sites. Not one in the Rocky Mountain area; not one in the Midwest; not one in the Ohio River Valley; not one in the mid–Atlantic region; not one in the Northeast. Not one, in other words, in areas of the country that don't have the built-in advantage of warm weather, an advantage that drives the accompanying built-in advantage of playing a large majority of games at home.

As an allusion to the ancient Olympic Games, the phrase "Let the games begin!" announces the opening of competition. In contemporary usage, the phrase is often used sarcastically, implying that "the fix is in," that the playing field isn't level. In *The Hunger Games* the announcer for The Capitol, Claudius Templesmith, says, "Let the games begin" and follows with "And may the odds be ever in your favor!" even while he knows that the games are controlled by President Snow.

If the NCAA softball tournament was one-and-done and played on neutral sites, like basketball and many other sports, then the outcry over the bracketing would be far less. If seeding was done for all sixty-four teams, or even thirty-two teams, then fewer schools would be upset because how you did in your season would matter more. But when sixteen hosts are chosen with little logic or consistency year after year, and the other three teams for a site are grouped sometimes for convenience of travel, sometimes not, there will be outrage. The principle of fairness, and the lack of it in the case of the softball selection committee, drives much of the argument and angst by softball fans around tourney time. They fear that a concentration of power in conferences such as the SEC and the Pac-12 will harm the game in the long run. They are critical of ESPN announcers who seem to be apologists for the powerful. They fear that a sport they admire and love becomes trivialized by the powers that be in the NCAA simply because it is played by female athletes.

Let the games begin!

* * *

In 2018, Nicole Newman was one of the best unknown players in the country. If you're wondering what team she played for, then you've helped prove my point. Newman was the ace pitcher for Drake, who played the first game of the NCAA tournament against BYU in the Eugene, Oregon, regional—BYU teams don't compete on Sundays for religious reasons, and so the regional kicked off Thursday night. Excluding the injured Brittany Gray from Georgia, Newman was leading the nation in ERA at 0.62 and leading in strikeouts per seven innings at 11.4 batters. She made USA Softball's list of Top 25 Finalists for Player of the Year.

Drake came in with the third-best team ERA in the country, behind Oregon and Washington. Against BYU, Head Coach Rich Calvert didn't start Newman, a rise-ball pitcher with high velocity; he threw, instead, Kailee Smith, whose best pitches are drop balls and change-ups. Calvert explained that his goal wasn't just to win a game. "It doesn't matter if you finish second, third, or fourth," Calvert said. "I thought, 'What's our best chance to win the regional,' and our best chance was to have Newman fresh on day two against Oregon, if we could win our opener. I believed that Smith would be a good match-up against BYU, and if we didn't win that game and dropped into the loser's bracket it would be a long haul in the regional, but we might have a chance in the game against Oregon if we had a fresh Newman."

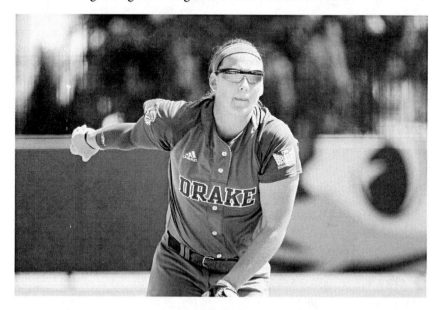

Drake's Nicole Newman pitches against Oregon in the Eugene regional. Newman came back from a severe arm injury in 2017 to go 22–5 in the circle with a 0.89 ERA, helping lead Drake to their first-ever wins in the NCAA tournament. Courtesy Drake Athletics.

In the third inning, BYU showed off its speed with three straight infield singles, and a fielder's choice scored Rylee Jensen with the first run of the 2018 tournament. Though Newman didn't start in the circle, she homered in the bottom of the third, the first home run of the tournament. She came on in relief in the fifth inning, struck out six of the seven batters she faced, and got the first win of the tournament, as Drake came from behind to beat BYU 3–2, Drake's first-ever NCAA tournament softball victory. The game was well-played, tense, and reminded everyone (including me) to stop complaining about the brackets and love the sport.

Success in a softball season may come in many ways, on and off the field. For several teams, on-field success in 2018 was measured simply by making the tournament, four programs doing so for the first time: Boise State University, Kennesaw State University, Monmouth University, and Prairie View A&M University. All these programs were likely to get a boost in their recruiting and fan base, but no newcomer won a game. Success can come, as with Drake, in making the step from newcomer to winner—though they lost to Oregon on day two, they came through in the loser's bracket to beat BYU again, before losing to Oregon in the regional final. Other teams also went further than they ever had in the tournament, such as Wichita State and Ohio University, who each got into their first regional final in program history.

On-field success can also come by fighting through adversity. James Madison University lost their superstar Megan Good for the year due to injury, but the setbacks didn't end there. Two players got concussions; one tore her ACL; another went out with a stress fracture; in all, JMU had seven injuries to contributing players. "When someone went down," Head Coach Loren LaPorte said, "the team didn't miss a beat, or freak out, or fold. Someone from the bench simply stepped up." JMU won their league, the Colonial Athletic Association, and won forty-three games. They didn't get as far in the tourney as they had hoped, losing to Ohio in the Knoxville regional, but given the adversity they faced, the season was certainly a success.

For the softball fan, the tournament has become a big viewing party. ESPN, for the second year in a row, covered every game from the sixteen regional sites, either on its channels or digital platforms. ESPN's production values at each site were first-rate, with camera crews catching the perfect angles to show a home-run robbing catch or a slide to avoid a tag. The announcing pairs showed the polish that comes from doing women's softball throughout the season as well as for years. And ESPN's tournament studio show, Bases Loaded, deftly took viewers from game to game—showing action from various regional sites throughout each day, providing analysis of the tournament as it was unfolding, displaying great athletic feats.

* * *

People who want to empower girls stress the importance of role models coming from the political, business, academic, or sports worlds—that is, girls who view powerful women imagine such possibilities for themselves. On ESPN's television channels and digital platforms, girls were seeing powerful and skilled young women everywhere. And many of the athletes were women of color.

Just as sexism is part of our culture and affects media coverage and representations of female athletes, matters of race and ethnicity affect the softball world. Any communal activity such as a sport exists within the culture at large and is subject to cultural reverberations. Tyler Walker is African American, grew up in San Jose, California, and starred for Minnesota from 2012–15, graduating with numerous top-five marks in program history, including runs scored, home runs, doubles, and batting average. Walker remembers playing on culturally diverse teams when she was a young girl, but as she moved through travel ball, softball became more suburban, white, and well-to-do. "As I started getting involved with other organizations in the Bay Area," Walker said, "it became common to see that some girls had the newest gear at all times. It also became more common than not that I was the only person of color on the team. I even had a college coach ask me on a visit how I would feel playing on a predominantly white team. It was a bit offensive. I remember wondering how that conversation would have gone if she had asked a white player how she would feel about having a black teammate."

Walker played in the Twin Cities, which due to its immigrant settlement is largely German and Scandinavian. For members of a minority culture within an identifying activity, selfhood is complicated. I asked Walker whether she felt seen as a student and softball player foremost (as Caucasian players would expect), or as an African American softball player. "Fans and teammates," Walker replied, "viewed me as a student-athlete. But when it came to some media coverage, I felt like my cultural background made for a 'good read' so it was often mentioned." Walker said that she always thought of herself "as just another student-athlete," but now, post-softball, she considers her identity more through gender and race, as a black woman. Walker hopes that over time there will be more women of color who play the game. "Softball has gotten me so far in life," she said, "and it would be amazing to see the game change the lives for more multicultural athletes."

Most coaches I talked to about race and college softball, including the head coach for Duke, Marissa Young, who is bi-racial, pointed to the progress that has been made. "Compared to when I played [2000–03]," Young said, "you see a lot more diversity in the game, from coaching staffs to players, which is fantastic." At a micro level, two of the three freshmen who made USA Softball's Top Ten Finalists for Player of the Year demonstrated such diversity: Aaliyah Jordan from UCLA, an African American, and Jocelyn Alo from Oklahoma, a Hawaiian Islander, were having phenomenal years. At a macro level, Young's assertion is borne out by the general numbers.

The NCAA compiles statistical information regarding various demographics for its sports, including specific numbers of players within ethnic groups, as well as changes over time. In general, efforts to increase opportunities in softball for female athletes of color have been succeeding. Within the decade from 2008–2017, Asian-American softball players in the three NCAA divisions increased their numbers by 27 percent, Polynesian and Hawaiian Islanders by 43 percent, and Latinas by over 55 percent. The greatest increase was in those declaring themselves mixed-race, a number that jumped nearly 1,000 percent, though that increase is likely due in part to changes in reporting. African American softball players were the only group who saw their overall numbers decrease, though at the DI level there was a 10 percent rise.

Opportunities in particular endeavors are shaped in part by culture—that is, ethnic and racial communities create their own particular cultures that reflect what the communities emphasize and value. Chinese-American parents steer their children more toward learning a musical instrument, often the piano or violin, than learning a sport; commentators note the prestige that basketball has among African Americans. Black women, for example, are six times more likely to play DI basketball than softball; Latinas, however, are more than four times likely to play DI softball than basketball. "I don't think racial barriers are the issue," Young said, "as much as it's young people falling into whatever is around them, what opportunities are available."

Kelly Inouye-Perez is serving her thirtieth season in the UCLA softball program: joining as a player in 1989; then becoming an assistant coach in 1994 and head coach in 2007. She has acquired a long-view perspective. "I was born and raised in Los Angeles," she said, "and we're very diverse here, and so is UCLA. The sport was predominantly Caucasian back when I played in the late 1980s. But that's changed." UCLA's softball roster, with numerous players of color, certainly reflects a demographic shift. When I asked what she thought had spurred the progress, Inouye-Perez pointed to changes in how various ethnic groups understand what softball can offer. "These groups realized what an opportunity in softball means," she said. "A girl can earn a scholarship, can have a college degree paid for fully or partially. The parents are supportive and push their children not only to play but to go above and beyond, because it's going to connect to their education and ultimately to how they succeed in the world. Parents are giving their kids an opportunity in travel ball so that coaches can give them an opportunity for college, which can set them up for life. Being part of team culture and learning how to play a role and deal with adversity is part of the opportunity."

"We recruited a girl from a neighborhood in Los Angeles where the people there say, 'You're never going to go to college,' and she worked at softball and defied what her community said. And now she's going to graduate from UCLA, and she'll be part of that first generation in her family with a college degree. There's opportunity if you're an athlete. Playing softball can just help someone with their admission into college."

Young believes, like Inouye-Perez, that communities of color are more likely now to push their daughters forward in their ambitions, and she attributes some of that to the game's growing popularity. "Just seeing more players of color on television," she said, "inspires young kids to stay involved in this sport. When these girls say, 'I want to go play college softball,' everybody around them recognizes that this is a great thing, not an off-the-wall dream."

Although communities of color may now be more accepting of girls striving to excel in softball, economics matter in who plays the sport. It's easier for college coaches to recruit at a travel ball tournament that brings multiple teams to one site and runs games all day long than it is for coaches to drive to a high school field and watch one game. Travel ball teams, therefore, not high school teams, give prospective college players the desired exposure. But travel ball is expensive, beyond the financial means of some families.

While fastpitch softball is played throughout the country, the much-touted growth of the game has not occurred evenly. Towns and cities that

Economic and cultural factors have contributed to women's softball being a predominantly Caucasian sport, though this is changing as opportunities grow. Shown during a pregame warm-up, Duke Head Coach Marissa Young, who is bi-racial, says that "seeing more players of color on television inspires young kids to stay involved in this sport." Courtesy Reagan Lunn, Duke Athletics.

build and maintain facilities are much more likely to have a thriving recreational and travel ball program. Large cities usually have inadequate facilities, as the amount of land needed to build a set of fields for tournament play is rarely available—it's cheaper to build and maintain soccer fields or basketball courts. Rural areas often don't have enough population or funds to build multiple fields for recreation leagues or travel ball teams; only the area high school may have a field. Some towns and cities located in northern climates will fund development of facilities for leagues, but the weather issues that affect college play have the same effect on youth league play. So what do you need for accelerated growth? Expanding suburbs in warm climates. If it doesn't rain much or is temperate in winter, as in Southern California or Florida, cities will build beautiful fields as a tourist attraction, as a way to host large tournaments whose players and parents spend money in local businesses. The local softball community and its players benefit. But new facilities in developing suburbs are not racially neutral, because suburban growth, demographically, is largely middle class and white.

Opportunities in softball link to beliefs about gender roles as well as economic factors. Texas, Florida, and Southern California have been a hotbed of girls softball, all areas with a large Hispanic population. Many of the sport's best players are Latinas, a development noticeable enough that ESPN reporter Andrea Canales wrote in 2017 about the "Latina wave in softball." There have been great Latina players in the past, but a cultural shift in attitudes about gender roles was needed to enlarge the number of players. Latino culture, emphasizing traditional gender roles, didn't encourage girls to attend college and pursue careers, but that has slowly changed. The increasing ambitions of young Latinas and their desires for equal opportunities have allowed more girls to pursue highly competitive sports. One of my favorite teams to watch in recent years was the 2016 University of Michigan team that went 52–7, was ranked #2 through most of the year, and reached the Women's College World Series. That team had swagger and style, and they also had one of the best infields in college softball history: second baseman Sierra Romero (the national Player of the Year), first baseman Tera Blanco (like Romero, a First Team All-American), third baseman Lindsay Montemarano, and shortstop Abby Ramirez.

Michigan's head coach, Carol Hutchins, recruited that all-Latina infield. I asked her how college softball is doing with opportunities for players of color. "Clearly we're not doing well enough," Hutch said, "The percentage of women of color has increased over the years, but we certainly wouldn't be considered a very diverse sport. The question is 'what do we do about it?'" Hutch also mentioned that female coaches of color were tremendously under-represented.

Duke's Marissa Young, who played for Hutch, is particularly proud that she can serve as an inspiration in this regard. "I've gotten a lot of positive feedback being a minority female head coach," Young said. "I know that when I played there were almost no female coaches of color for a role model. We'd be naive to say that barriers don't exist now for women or women of color, but that's the challenge to overcome." Perceived barriers are, to Young, something that can be used for motivation: "Women need the mindset that I'm going to show people what I'm capable of doing, that I can be excellent in all areas of life. That is what I tell my team. Excellence is a way of life, it's not compartmentalized in softball. What we want to do on the field we also have to do in our conduct: how we dress, how we show up and go to class, how we interact with people in the community. Excellence is a way of life, and if someone can achieve that in softball they know they can achieve anything in any realm."

*   *   *

For three years Kylee Hanson achieved excellence in the circle for her Florida Atlantic University teams, particularly in 2016, her junior year when she led the nation with a 0.76 ERA on her way to being named a Top-10 Finalist for USA Softball Player of the Year. Coached by softball legend Joan Joyce, that FAU team went 51–9 but lost twice to the University of Central Florida in the Gainesville regional hosted by Florida. In 2017 Hanson's senior season was cut short by a severe ankle injury, though she received a medical redshirt. After graduating from Florida Atlantic, Hanson transferred to Florida State University for her final year of eligibility, entering their master's program in public health.

"I made a list of pros and cons of all that I had at FAU," Hanson said. "I wasn't unhappy there at all, but I always felt like there was something more for me, that I was ready to step up to some stronger competition." Her decision wasn't only about softball. "Transferring," she remarked, "was a way for me to grow, to experience new things, to step out of my comfort zone. I have been so happy to try this new academic program and make new connections, which will be huge for me later in life. Tallahassee is the state capital and the Department of Health is located here." No player this weekend looked any happier than Hanson. She had returned to competition without missing a beat—she came into the weekend 25–4 with an ERA just over 1.00—and now here she was getting the ball in the circle and playing in a regional at home. She threw a five-inning no-hitter on Friday against Jacksonville State, and in the regional final against the same team on Sunday, Hanson didn't allow a hit until the sixth. Her weekend pitching line consisted of eleven innings, twenty-four strikeouts, and one hit. When I remarked on how much she was smiling, on how she appeared to be playing with so much joy, she said, "I've been told that this is the happiest I've ever looked out on the field. I don't know if that's just generally being happy, or it comes from the great comfort level and confidence I have in my teammates."

Florida State's pitching staff, Hanson and Meghan King, gave up a single run and five hits total in their three games, one of many impressive team pitching performances of the regionals. Alabama, behind Alexis Osorio and Courtney Gettins, swept its three games, allowing only one unearned run. Paige Parker and Paige Lowary dominated in the circle, showing why Oklahoma looked capable of three-peating, as they gave up no runs on the weekend, a feat matched by Oregon's duo of Miranda Elish and Megan Kleist.

While numerous pitchers continued their brilliant seasons in their tournament games, a handful of great hitting teams upped their production in the regionals. Georgia scored twenty-seven runs in its three wins and looked like a WCWS contender if the bats were to stay hot against Tennessee, their super-regional foe, who themselves looked ready to do some damage when they scored twenty-six runs in their regional. Kentucky outdid both of them, run-ruling opponents three games in a row, only the third team in the modern era of regionals to do that. Kentucky outscored its opponents 28–1 on the weekend. Could they continue that run production against Oregon's staff, their upcoming opponents in the super-regional?

While the ESPN announcers were talking on-air about the success of the SEC and Pac-12 teams, they didn't address what happened to teams from those leagues who didn't host. California, in the Athens regional, lost twice to Northwestern. Oregon State lost its opener to Wisconsin, beat them the next day in an elimination game, but got shut out by Alabama 6–0 in the first game of the regional final. The SEC's non-host teams fared no better. Ole Miss did make the regional final in Tempe, but they got crushed 7–1 and 9–0 by Arizona State on the weekend. Mississippi State, in Tucson, lost to North Dakota State to drop into the loser's bracket, beat the Bison in an elimination game, and lost to Arizona in the regional final. Missouri got a #2 seed in the Norman regional from the selection committee, despite buying its way in with a last-minute scheduling change; they lost to Tulsa to drop into the loser's bracket, beat them the next day, and then got trounced 7–0 by Oklahoma. Auburn didn't even make it to the regional final, losing to Florida State and then Jacksonville State.

If you host it, you will win—that is almost always the case in the NCAA tourney, but in 2018, as in 2017, it was *always* the case. All sixteen hosts won, and collectively they went 48–3, a dominance far beyond what won-loss records and RPI rankings would suggest.

There are two issues here. One concerns the built-in advantages for a regional host: not having to travel; playing on a field the players know; having fan support; and opening with the #4 seed in their site, which allows the host to save their ace pitcher to be fresh on day two. The second issue might be far easier to address, and that's the issue about the fairness of the selection process and the seeding itself. In 2016 and 2017 the selection committee released several potential seedings in the weeks leading up to the tournament, along with brief reasons for their choices—in effect imitating what other NCAA selection committees, particularly in men's sports, do. But the selection committee embarrassed themselves in 2017 when they changed the narrative on the final weekend about what was important, as a way to exclude Minnesota and James Madison and to get Ole Miss as a regional host. In 2018 they declined to release any preliminary seedings and declined to do anything that would lift the veil of secrecy about their decisions. Anyone who cares deeply about women's softball, from media to fans to coaches, realizes that the criteria that the selection committee uses varies from year to year. Members of the committee make arguments that are self-serving for their region or their teams, and so from the outside looking in, the process looks like a crap shoot—who is in the room speaking on a program's or conference's behalf makes all the difference.

If the NCAA wants to keep a format of sixteen teams hosting a four-team regional, then the least they could do is to seed thirty-two teams, so that the match-ups in the regionals are more equitable and so that a team's play during the season matters more than just getting you in the tournament or not. If the NCAA is still looking to save money on travel, then they could use geographical proximity for the #3 and #4 seeded teams. But don't just make up odd groupings for no discernible reason. For example, Auburn, a bubble team to host, was sent to Florida State, the #6 national seed. Was this for geographical reasons? Why not then send Mississippi State, who finished behind Auburn in the RPI and the SEC, to Florida State, and send Auburn to #14 seed Arizona, which would be an easier draw? Why privilege Mississippi State over Auburn? I could go on with numerous examples, but I'm sure you understand the point. Seeding only sixteen teams and then making arbitrary regional groupings lessens the importance of the entire season's achievement for many teams.

Who gets seeded and who doesn't matters greatly; for the very good programs, getting to the super-regionals regularly is a goal. Recruiting certainly is helped when your program gets chosen to host a regional and you advance to week two of the tournament. Coaching jobs can depend on it, as coaches do get fired if expectations aren't met. Coaches may also leave a particular conference if they believe that they will be treated unfairly by the selection committee.

Glenn Moore, at Baylor, is unlikely to be fired or to leave his school; he's generally happy there. But he's not happy with the seeding process, and examining what the committee has done in recent years with Baylor suggests why. In 2016, his Baylor Bears team was thirteenth in the RPI. Not only did they not host, but they were sent to Eugene, Oregon, to play the #4 seeded Ducks. In 2017 with a similar RPI, Baylor not only hosted and won their regional, but they upset a highly regarded Arizona team and went to the Women's College World Series. In 2018, they were fourteenth in the RPI, weren't chosen to host, and again lost a regional final.

Moore has been frustrated by the selection committee's lack of transparency in decision-making, because if they don't follow established principles, or explain how they come to decisions, a coach can't do much to change the outcome. He is tired of the illogical reasons he has been given when he has asked about the seedings. "We have a broken system," he said to me when I asked him about Baylor's snub. Moore is only one of many coaches I've spoken to who feel this way.

A marquee men's sport would never have its championship treated so cavalierly.

TWELVE

Champions Crowned, Supers Won

The pinnacle of interest for women's softball, the DI Women's College World Series, was still a week away, but for softball fans who follow all levels, this was the most exciting week of the season. DI was presenting its super-regionals; DII and DIII were conducting their championships.

Unlike DI softball, where the selection committee chooses sixteen national seeds from any region or conference, DII softball has created eight regions across the country which hold, in essence, their own regional tournaments. Rather than creating an RPI ranking that is supposed to evaluate teams mathematically across different conferences and strength of schedules, DII softball creates an RPI only within each region. The selection committee then forms two four-team sub-regionals, with the winners squaring off in a super-regional. Each region, therefore, sends one representative to the national championship, a format that helps northern teams who are competing for the most part against each other in the post-season. If you're from a northern region, you like this system because it doesn't discriminate against you for geographic reasons of weather and home games: everyone who practices indoors, travels to tournaments down south, and has few home games is in the same boat, more or less. That seems fairer. But if you're in other regions—this year, let's say, the South Central, which had five teams ranked in the top fifteen nationally but could advance only one—you tend to dislike this model.

For the tenth time in the 21st century, the James I. Moyer Sports Complex in Salem, Virginia, hosted the DII softball national championship. Kylee Smith threw the first pitch on Thursday morning, May 24, for the #1 ranked University of North Georgia. The sophomore Smith had repeated as a First Team All-American; with her 35–1 record, her nation-leading strikeout total of 320, and her 0.65 ERA, she was also named the DII Pitcher of the Year and Player of the Year. Opposing Smith was Jen Leonhardt of the University of Southern Indiana, who had led her team in 2017 to the national championship tourney for the first time in program history, going 29–4 in the circle during her superb freshman season. But in 2018 Leonhardt's ERA had jumped a run a game, her losses had climbed to twelve, and her team was coming in a big underdog.

Southern Indiana was ranked #6 in the pre-season poll, but their season had been full of ups and downs. "We had exceptional talent returning," said Head Coach Sue Kunkle, "but we had also graduated some key players and had to figure out how to put the pieces together. We'd get back on the bus after losing to a team we should beat, and we'd be scratching our heads. When we found ourselves near .500 and in jeopardy of not even making the conference tournament, we decided that we needed to start having fun and to not pressure ourselves anymore." Their record at that point was 17–15, but the team did start playing better. The sixth seed in their own conference tournament, they won it to advance to postseason. In the sub-regional, they beat Grand Valley State, the region's one seed, and then beat the two seed, Illinois-Springfield, in the super-regional. On to Salem.

After a superb freshman season for Southern Indiana, Jen Leonhardt's sophomore season was up and down. But she pitched brilliantly in the national tourney, including one-hitting top-ranked North Georgia and no-hitting highly regarded Angelo State. Courtesy Dan McDonnell and University of Southern Indiana Athletic Department.

Though Southern Indiana entered the national championship tournament with momentum, facing North Georgia was formidable. But Southern Indiana was the upset winner 1–0, as Leonhardt allowed only one hit and singled in the winning run herself. Pitching dominated in this game, as neither team had a baserunner until the fifth inning. Smith was an unlucky loser, giving up only an unearned run, enough to drop North Georgia to the loser's bracket.

Watching two evenly matched teams in a high-stakes game was every bit as exciting as watching DI rivals compete. The game wasn't on television—I streamed the games on my computer, via the NCAA's LiveVideo feed—and I didn't know all the players, as I do for top DI teams. But the next day, I was familiar with Leonhardt to some extent, and I watched her throw a no-hitter against Angelo State, as well as add two hits and a run scored. DI softball will likely continue to be the level covered by media, but seeing a player elevate her game on any national stage is breathtaking.

While the sixteen seeded teams in DI last week all won their regionals, upsets had been prominent in DII regional play. The trend continued in Salem. The top three teams by national rankings that made it—North Georgia, Chico State from the West region, and Angelo State, who had emerged from the tough South Central region—all went out before the semi-finals. Southern Indiana wasn't the only surprise team. Saint Leo University was making its first appearance ever in the national tournament, and they had to get hot at the right time to do so. They finished a distant fourth in the Sunshine State Conference, ten games behind Palm Beach Atlantic. But in their region, Saint Leo beat #22 ranked Embry-Riddle, #4 ranked North Alabama, and #16 Alabama-Huntsville. Coming to Salem lightly regarded, they defeated Chico State, lost to Saint Anselm, and then knocked North Georgia out of the tournament.

By Saturday, four teams were left, and Southern Arkansas, the highest ranked team coming in, had played its way there through the loser's bracket. The Lady Muleriders—one of my favorite names for a women's softball team—had been strong all year in the circle and at the plate, led by two finalists for Player of the Year, pitcher Victoria Taylor and all-time career DII home-run leader Brooke Goad. 2018 was a year of remarkable hitting performances: Goad had thirty-two home runs and seventy-two RBI; Colorado Mesa's Brooke Hodgson had a .508 batting average to go with seventeen home runs and 105 RBI, the second-highest single-season total in NCAA DII history; Texas A&M-Commerce's Mariah Jameyson might have bettered both, finishing the regular season among the nation's leaders in all offensive categories, when she hit .510 with twenty-three home runs and eighty-nine RBI. But only Goad, of the three sluggers, was in Salem, and Saint Anselm's Morgan Perry shut out Southern Arkansas 3–0 in the semi-finals, which sent Goad and her Lady Muleriders home and sent Saint Anselm into the finals.

Saint Anselm is a northern school, located in Goffstown, New Hampshire, and its team was making, like Saint Leo, its first appearance in the national championship tourney. DI softball will likely never have a finalist from New England, but DII's format for post-season play means that a northern team coming into its own later in the season has a chance to prove that it belongs—as Minnesota State (Mankato) demonstrated by winning it all in 2017. Saint Anselm's Head Coach Jill Gagnon had done a remarkable job with the program. In 2016 the team won twelve games, followed that up in 2017 with an 18–16 overall record, before smashing all program marks in 2018 by winning forty-four games and getting to Salem.

The two-out-of-three final series matched Saint Anselm with the University of Southern Indiana, who was undefeated in the tournament but had needed two days to get their semi-final win. USI faced Saint Leo in their semi-final, a game that began Saturday morning with Leonhardt giving up four runs in the top of the first, her only runs so far in the tourney. But slowly USI chipped away at Saint Leo's lead. In the fifth inning with the score 4–2,

Caitlyn Bradley was the hitting star for Southern Indiana in the championship series. Here, her teammates congratulate her after her three-run homer in game one. Celebrations such as this at the plate are standard in women's softball after every home run. Courtesy Dan McDonnell and University of Southern Indiana Athletic Department.

heavy rains swept into the Roanoke Valley, postponing the game's conclusion until Sunday. When the game resumed the next day, USI scored a single run in the sixth, and then Claire Johnson, on her twenty-first birthday, hit a solo home run in the bottom of the seventh inning to tie the game. Her personal and team celebration got even better when she drove in the winning run in the eighth, as USI beat Saint Leo 5–4. Leonhardt earned the win for her two days of work, allowing just one hit and no runs over the final seven innings of the game.

The Saint Anselm-Southern Indiana finals matched two teams whose season statistics didn't suggest that they would make it to the championship series. Neither team had been ranked nationally in the top twenty-five in the final regular season poll. Neither team was among the top forty in the country in team batting average or ERA. Saint Anselm's ace, Morgan Perry, had had an excellent year, going 26–4 with a 1.57 ERA and pitching her best in the post-season, while centerfielder Amanda Bickford had batted over .400, but neither was their conference's player of the year. The only player for Southern Indiana who made first-team all-league in the Great Lakes Valley Conference was third baseman Mena Fulton. But both teams had gotten excellent pitching, as well as clutch hitting and fielding, in the tourney.

In the opening game of the final series, Southern Indiana's Caitlyn Bradley hit a three-run homer in the top of the third, more than enough runs for Leonhardt, who threw five innings of one-hit shutout ball before Coach Kunkle brought in Haylee Smith to save a few pitches for Leonhardt's arm. Saint Anselm loaded the bases with two outs in the seventh, but a grounder got the Screaming Eagles the 4–0 victory. The next game resembled the earlier one. Bradley hit a two-run double as part of a seven-run second inning, Leonhardt shut down Saint Anselm's bats, and the University of Southern Indiana won 8–3, sweeping all five games they played.

Southern Indiana was the new champion of DII softball, and Jen Leonhardt was named Most Outstanding Player of the tourney, developments that would have been inconceivable four weeks earlier. "Now that I look back on it," Leonhardt said, "I appreciate the times that I struggled, as it helped me grow as a person. And our team struggles helped us as a team once we got to Salem. 100 percent. We were low seeds all the way through the post-season, but we were playing and having fun. And entering the championship we absolutely believed that we were going to win it." When I asked her what was most memorable about the week, she mentioned how proud she was to be on the first national champion in school history for a women's team sport.

* * *

DIII softball has more teams than the other divisions, as well as more conferences. Automatic bids go to forty-two conference champions, and so the competition to receive an at-large bid is high. While DIII ranks teams in regions during the year, the selection committee doesn't choose, necessarily, two teams from each region to host, as DII softball does. Instead, DIII has sixteen host sites, scattered fairly proportionally through the country. Some regions can be geographically large because they have few DIII colleges, like the West, which includes Texas, the Southwest, and the West Coast. This year, that region had come up strong, as Texas Lutheran at 37–1 and the University of Texas–Tyler at 38–1 were in the same region and ranked second and third in the country, while Linfield at #9 and George Fox at #12, two Oregon schools, were matched. Only one team from those pairs would be making a super-regional, and only one from the foursome would make the national championship. That team turned out to be UT-Tyler.

Unlike in DII, the DIII teams making their appearance in Oklahoma City, the site of the national championship, had been powerhouses all season. The top half of the bracket featured defending champion Virginia Wesleyan University, led by pitcher Hanna Hull, the reigning Player of the Year. Despite playing the toughest schedule in the country, Virginia Wesleyan and Head Coach Brandon Elliott came into the championship 50–2. In their opening game, they were matched against Ithaca College, a frequent national championship participant out of the Northeast region, Deb Pallozzi having built the Bomber softball program into a perennial contender. Joining them in the top half of the bracket was #4 seed MIT, in the national tourney as recently as 2016 and led back this year by Jen Williams, entering her eighth year as the head coach. Completing the foursome was Luther College from Iowa, who regularly contends in the Midwest region; Head Coach Renae Hartl took Luther to four consecutive appearances in the national championship tourney from 2010 to 2013.

University of Texas–Tyler was favored in the bottom half of the bracket. Head Coach Mike Reed began the softball program in 2005 and proceeded to coach the Patriots to the national championship around six times in a ten-year stretch, culminating with a national title in 2016. UT-Tyler was matched up with the lone surprise team. In for the first time, Case Western Reserve University was led by Josie Wilson, who had engineered a remarkable turnaround in her eight years coaching the program. Joining them were Rowan College and Illinois Wesleyan University. Rowan and their long-time head coach Kim Wilson were advancing to the national finals for the sixth time; they finished tied for third in 2016. Illinois Wesleyan and second-year head coach Tiffany Prager had played in last year's tourney, winning their first game but then going out with two losses.

The story of the top half's bracket was written primarily by Hanna Hull, as she marched Virginia Wesleyan into the championship series by throwing consecutively a no-hitter with one walk, then a three-hit shutout, and then

Virginia Wesleyan University head coach Brandon Elliott led his team to the 2017 DIII national title. Despite playing the most difficult schedule in the country, VWU came into the 2018 championship tourney with a 50–2 record, making them the favorite. With Elliott are assistant coaches Jenna Wilson and Chris Smith, and players Carla Hall (l) and Julia Sinnett. Courtesy Virginia Wesleyan Athletics.

a one-hit shutout. Virginia Wesleyan looked intimidating and was taking a far easier route than in 2017, when they lost their first game and had to win four consecutive elimination games to make the championship series. The most thrilling game in the bottom half of the draw came in the second round, when Illinois Wesleyan outlasted UT-Tyler 3–2 in ten innings. Julie Josten homered in the bottom of the seventh inning to tie it for Illinois Wesleyan, and Shelby Fulk knocked in Jillian Runyon in the bottom of the tenth inning to win it. Illinois Wesleyan dropped a game to Luther in the semi-final round, but advanced to the championship series when they beat Luther 5–1 in the deciding game.

John Wesley never played women's softball, of course, but three hundred years after he lived, he was exerting an influence on the sport. Wesley was an 18th century English cleric who through his life and teachings inspired the Protestant denomination that came to be known as Methodism. In the United States, the United Methodist Church owes him its origin, and two of the many colleges that the Methodist Church helped found and still supports are Illinois Wesleyan and Virginia Wesleyan.

Illinois Wesleyan had a slow start to their season. In their opening tour-

As a freshman in 2017, Hanna Hull led Virginia Wesleyan University to the national championship and won, along the way, DIII Pitcher of the Year and Player of the Year honors. She repeated the honors and the title as a sophomore. Courtesy Virginia Wesleyan Athletics.

nament in Tucson, they lost 15–11 to St. John Fisher and 21–4 to Berry, both highly ranked programs who at that point in the season were far ahead of Illinois Wesleyan. "We are a team in a cold-weather area," Head Coach Prager said, "and so success is going to happen later in the season. When we arrived in Arizona, we hadn't had one day practicing outside. And we started off playing really high-caliber teams. We knew our team was good, and as the season went on, we were confident in our progression. It's a long season, and we were trying to peak later in the year." Illinois Wesleyan hit their stride in league play, going 14–2 to win the College Conference of Illinois and Wisconsin (CCIW). They lost the opening game of the conference tourney, however, which meant that they would need to win three games on one day to claim the title. And they did.

Illinois Wesleyan's sophomore shortstop Sam Berghoff had been brilliant all year hitting and fielding, winning Player of the Year honors in the CCIW; Jillian Runyon showed off her athleticism at the plate, in the field, and on the bases, stealing fifty of fifty-two. Ally Wiegand, a transfer from South Dakota, was Illinois Wesleyan's pitching ace. Voted Most Outstanding Player in the regional and Most Outstanding Pitcher in the super-regional, Wiegand won the opening game in the national championship 5–1, threw the first eight innings of a ten inning thriller to help beat UT-Tyler 3–2, and then in the deciding semi-final game shut down a high-scoring Luther team 5–1. On the year, Wiegand only walked seven batters in 152 innings. Her strikeouts to walks ratio was an incredible 34.83–1, nearly triple the next best ratio in the country.

Despite having star players and success so far in the tourney, Illinois Wesleyan came into the championship series an underdog to Virginia Wesleyan, led by their two First Team All-Americans: sophomore Hull in the circle and powerful senior first baseman Cassetty Howerin, who hit .424 with eight home runs and sixty-two RBI. Complementing Howerin's power was senior speedster Kiersten Richardson, who hit for average and power while scoring sixty-three runs and stealing forty-seven bases, and a third senior, Amy Large, who had a solid season in the outfield. But Coach Elliott was attributing much of the season's success to three other senior players—Alana Peters, Teresa Cardamone, and Amanda Archer—who were willing to be role players and leaders in the dugout. "You didn't see their contributions often in the box score," Elliott said, "but they were just loyal to the program. Their work ethic didn't change. Their impact in the dugout was tremendous. It's hard when you think you're going to play a lot and instead a freshman comes in and starts. It would have been easy for them to quit or complain or be a distraction. But they swallowed their pride and opinions and helped lead us." Elliott was also savvy in getting those seniors in for pinch running, pinch hitting, or even the occasional start.

Though both teams had dominant pitchers, the opening game of the best-of-three championship series began with runs: Madison Glaubke hit a solo home run in the top of the first for Virginia Wesleyan, which was answered by Illinois Wesleyan when Runyon tripled and Berghoff singled her in, the first run that Hull had given up in the tournament. In the fourth inning, Virginia Wesleyan's Julia Sinnett hit a two-run home run; in later innings Howerin twice singled in Richardson. Virginia Wesleyan took the first game 6–1, behind Hull's five-hitter.

As in DII, teams play a double-header on the first day of the championship series, and so after a short break, Virginia Wesleyan and Illinois Wesleyan got back at it. Virginia Wesleyan scored twice in the bottom of the first inning, which had often been enough runs to win. But Illinois Wesleyan came up with two runs to tie in the third, and then went ahead in the sixth when two controversial calls at home plate went their way. Down two runs going into the bottom of the seventh, Virginia Wesleyan rallied, scoring one on a sacrifice fly and then plating the tying run on a blooper down the right field line from Teresa Cardamone, one of those seniors who had played sparingly all year. But in the eighth inning, Maggie Graham doubled in Shelby Fulk for Illinois Wesleyan, and the run stood up as the game winner. Brea Walker got the complete-game, 5–4 win for Illinois Wesleyan, while freshman Carla Hall, in relief of Hull, lost for the first time all season.

Game three of the championship series, the following day, began as if it might emulate game two's dramatic twists and turns. Illinois Wesleyan scored in the top of the first when Runyon was hit by a pitch, stole second, moved to third on a grounder, and then scored on a wild pitch. Virginia Wesleyan took the lead in the bottom of the inning on a two-run blast by Glaubke. Then Hull got into her rhythm, allowing only one more hit and a walk. Virginia Wesleyan won the deciding game 3–1, earning their second title in a row and setting a DIII record with fifty-five victories. Hull won all five games in the championship to earn the Most Outstanding Player award. But as is often the case in women's softball, she deferred praise: "Teammates are a big part of success, and this team really came together—our motto was 'love your teammates, love your sport.' I think we did a really good job with that."

*   *   *

On May 23, USA Softball, the national governing body, announced its four finalists for the USA Softball Collegiate Player of the Year award, considered the most prestigious honor in women's collegiate softball. Oklahoma's Paige Parker, UCLA's Rachel Garcia, and Florida teammates Amanda Lorenz and Kelly Barnhill, who won the award in 2017, made the list. Their on-field achievements spoke for themselves, but wanting to know what the players were like off the field, I talked to those who know them well, including their parents.

Parker, the lone senior in the group, was also a finalist for the Senior CLASS Award, which combines athletics, academics, character, and community service. I asked her parents how they would describe her. "She is a sweet, sweet girl," her mom, Kim, replied. "She is very family oriented, loves dogs, loves to bake."

"She's respectful, and polite, and hates to disappoint someone," her dad, Terry, added. Certainly the hitters that Parker has faced throughout her career *may* disagree, since she has disappointed pretty nearly all of them.

One measure of softball culture is that its stars don't behave as if they're entitled. "Rachel Garcia won Freshman Player of the Year and made the national team," her head coach at UCLA, Kelly Inouye-Perez said, "and yet the one word that I would use to describe her is 'humble.'" Numerous people I talked to echoed this assessment.

Chris Garcia, Rachel's mom, said of her daughter that "[Rachel] made parenting easy. She's kind, caring, and sensitive—she competes, but she doesn't have to let you know that she's competing." Rachel began a donation drive at her high school during her senior year, where the team set up a bin at their field and asked for donations for a local women's shelter. After Rachel graduated, the team continued the event and Rachel has gone back to her high school to help present the donated items and money to the shelter.

The four stars are excellent teammates, which was something that got brought up again and again when I asked various people about the players. Susie Lorenz said of her daughter, Amanda, that she doesn't like attention. "She will distract any attention that she gets," Susie said. "She can hit a home run in a crucial moment but she'd rather praise the batter before her who drew the walk to extend the inning. She's probably more happy for her teammates' success than her own." Lorenz is outgoing in front of a camera, but not off the field. "She's really different there," her mom said. "She's quiet. She's a homebody."

Lorenz took extra classes to challenge herself academically and will graduate in three and a half years. In spring of 2019, when she's playing her final year of softball, she will be in Sports Management graduate courses at Florida. Star male athletes are notorious for not achieving in the classroom, or not even going to class. In women's softball many of its biggest stars are equally high achievers in the classroom.

Barnhill is an Academic All-American, as well as one of the more decorated on-field performers in recent years. She reads. She's a bit of an introvert. Her close friends are a tight group. Her dad, Jeter, emphasized that Kelly's strong work ethic is not for individual accolades. "The team spirit," Jeter said, "she's about that." One unusual way that Kelly celebrates her teammates is that on each of their birthdays, she bakes them their favorite cake. "To me her love of baking is really surprising," Jeter said, "because I don't cook at all, and Susie [Kelly's mom] doesn't bake. For Kelly's twenty-first birthday we got her a really fancy mixer and bowl. It's what she wanted."

Paige Parker, Rachel Garcia, Amanda Lorenz, Kelly Barnhill. All four finalists for USA Softball Player of the Year are, not surprisingly, fierce competitors. All were also described—by teammates, parents, coaches, and sports information directors—as sweet young women off the field.

* * *

All the Player of the Year candidates had led their teams to the super-regional round. Three games kicked off on Thursday night. Only one went to form, when UCLA easily beat Arizona 7–1; Garcia threw five innings of one-hit shutout ball and added a two-run home run. In Oregon, the Ducks' excellent pitching staff got rocked—Kentucky's Alex Martens hit a three-run homer in the first off Pac-12 Pitcher of the Year, Megan Kleist, and later in the game Abbey Cheek duplicated that feat. Oregon's Maggie Balint relieved Kleist but got tagged for a two-run home run by Cheek, Kentucky surprising fans around the country by winning 9–6. The most dramatic opening game occurred in Gainesville, Florida, where the #2 seeded Gators were looking to extend their mastery over Texas A&M. Using just one hit, the Aggies scored three runs off Barnhill in the top of the third, when she couldn't find the plate.

Florida's Amanda Lorenz was named a DI Player of the Year finalist by USA Softball. Lorenz hit for power and average and walked frequently. Her on base + slugging percentage average was an amazing 1.335. She is shown here rounding third after a home run and doing a fist bump with Head Coach Tim Walton. Courtesy Tim Casey and the Florida Athletic Department.

A&M took a 4–2 lead into the bottom of the seventh, but their misery against Florida continued when, with two outs, consecutive errors followed by two walks led to Florida's come-from-behind 5–4 win.

On Friday night, the other five super-regional sites began, so that all sixteen teams were competing. Texas A&M stayed alive, turning the tables on Florida with their own 5–4 comeback victory, highlighted by a three-run home run from Tori Vidales. Oregon, likewise, evened up their series, beating Kentucky 6–1 behind a strong effort from Miranda Elish, who gave up only two hits and no earned runs. UCLA closed out their series with Arizona, Garcia going the distance in a 3–2 victory, making the Bruins the first qualifier for the Women's College World Series.

The Pac-12's two other teams in the super-regionals also won on their opening nights. Arizona State cruised to a 5–2 win over South Carolina. The Sun Devils got eleven hits and scored early runs, while G Juarez baffled the Gamecocks, taking a no-hitter into the seventh before giving up a single and home run. The outcome never looked in doubt. Not so in Seattle, where Alabama had a two-run lead going into the bottom of the seventh before the Huskies tied the score on a Sis Bates two-run single. In the ninth, Washington's ebullient third baseman, Taylor Van Zee, singled in the game-winner. Two strong pitchers dueled throughout the nine innings, with Gabbie Plain ultimately besting Alexis Osorio.

The Tallahassee site matched two strong pitching staffs and two teams who have become regulars in the super-regional round, but this year, as in 2017 when they met, only one could move on. Last year LSU upset the Seminoles, who many experts felt had a good chance to win the national championship. LSU was the underdog again, but they jumped in front of Florida State on early home runs from Amanda Doyle and Michaela Schlattman, and the Tigers won 6–5 despite a seventh inning three-run home run by FSU's Jessie Warren. While experts predicted low-scoring games in Tallahassee, the opposite was true for the Athens super-regional, where great hitting teams squared off in Georgia and Tennessee. The game turned, however, into a pitcher's duel of sorts, with Georgia building an early 4–0 lead and then holding on in the seventh, when Tennessee narrowed the gap to 4–3 and left the tying and winning runs on base.

Of the sixteen teams who competed in the super-regionals, fifteen usually make the NCAA tournament. The one exception, Arkansas, was making its first-ever appearance in a super-regional. Arkansas had been led all year by their freshmen, and they won their regional in the same way, with Mary Haff throwing 4 2/3 shutout innings in the regional final, and Hannah McEwen hitting a two-run homer and scoring another run. But in the super-regional round, Arkansas looked a bit overmatched in their opener against two-time defending champion Oklahoma. They made three errors; Oklahoma's Jocelyn Alo and Shay Knighten hit long home runs; Paige Lowary started in the circle and gave up only three hits; Oklahoma won easily, 7–2.

*   *   *

On Saturday, May 26, seven super-regional sites had games, with only UCLA, who began on Thursday, having earned a place in the WCWS. Two of those seven sites had little drama. In Norman, Oklahoma's Paige Parker started in the circle and shut down Arkansas; behind Parker and Falepolima Aviu's four RBI, Oklahoma swept the series with a 9–0 win. In Tempe, Arizona State's Breanna Macha gave up one earned run in a 5–2 win over South Carolina. Oklahoma and ASU had joined UCLA as participants in the Women's College World Series. Five of the seven sites were playing only game two in the best-of-three series, but by Saturday night, or actually early Sunday morning, all of the super-regionals were over. No one expected that outcome—everyone was looking forward to more softball on Sunday—and no one, likewise, expected the day to feature so many dramatic, game-changing home runs.

Here's how the homers went down, or out.

In Seattle, Washington's Taylor Van Zee homered on the second pitch of the game, extending the momentum that the Huskies earned in their come-from-behind victory the night before. Washington outhit Alabama 13–3 in a game that seemed never in doubt after that second pitch. Final score was 6–0. Huskies into the WCWS.

In Eugene, Oregon's DJ Sanders hit a grand slam in the bottom of the second inning as part of a seven-run inning, and Oregon routed Kentucky 11–1. Ducks in.

In Athens, Georgia's senior star Cortni Emanuel, a slapper and speedster, came up in the top of the eighth inning against Tennessee with nobody on base and two outs; facing an 0–2 count, she lined her third *career* home run over the right field fence, putting Georgia in front 2–1. Mary Wilson Avant held off Tennessee in the bottom of the inning, helped by center fielder Ciara Bryan's game-saving catch against the wall. Bulldogs off to OKC.

In Gainesville, in the top of the seventh inning with Florida leading 2–1, Texas A&M was down to its last out. But then Sarah Hudek singled and Tori Vidales homered to put Texas A&M up 3–2. In the bottom of the inning, Florida's freshman Jordan Matthews got down to the final strike of the game. Two runners were on, having coaxed walks from A&M's pitcher Trinity Harrington. Matthews fouled off two, two-strike pitches before hitting a walk-off home run. Final score, 5–3. Gators in.

In Tallahassee, LSU, up one game in the series, dropped behind early in game two but tied Florida State 5–5 in the fifth inning on a grand slam by Shemiah Sanchez. The game went to extra innings, and four times LSU batted with a chance to win the game and advance to the WCWS. But Florida State's Meghan King, despite being hit early, settled into a groove, and in the top of the eleventh inning Carsyn Gordon hit a solo home run and Anna Shelnutt added a two-run home run. King shut down the Tigers batters in the bottom of the inning and Florida State beat LSU 8–5 to force a deciding game.

Subtropical Storm Alberto was due to hit the Florida Panhandle some time on Sunday, so the decision had been made at the start of the day to play game three immediately following game two, even though that resulted in a 10:50 p.m. start time after the earlier, eleven-inning game. In the bottom of the third, the Seminoles' Jessie Warren continued the FSU power surge, homering with a runner on base, two runs that were enough for Kylee Hanson. Despite being outhit five to two, Florida State held on for a 3–1 win. They were the last of the eight teams celebrating an upcoming trip to Oklahoma City.

What a week of women's college softball. And one more still to come.

THIRTEEN

Drama on the Big Stage

In 1999 Meg Aronowitz graduated from Emory University and began a news career with CNN. Soon after, she joined ESPN, working with major league baseball before helping launch in 2005 the all-college sports network, ESPNU. Aronowitz has been, in her news career, a behind-the-scenes champion for expanding women's sports broadcast coverage. As a coordinating producer for ESPN and the SEC Network, she oversees coverage of multiple sports and multiple championships, but a career highlight has been her role in increasing exposure of college softball and the Women's College World Series. It has been a privilege, she has said, to help grow the game. The championship used to be tape-delayed two weeks. Now we produce every pitch of the postseason.

Aronowitz's passion, skills, and salesmanship to her ESPN bosses has helped make possible the spectacle of the Women's College World Series. The television coverage has created a shrine for American softball devotees: OGE Energy Field at the USA Softball Hall of Fame Complex in Oklahoma City, where every year the WCWS is played. Where every year fans can see—in person or on television—an event that is both a fierce competition and a celebration of the female athlete.

On Thursday, May 31, the 2018 WCWS opened with Arizona State playing Oregon before 8500 passionate softball fans. Young women who hadn't been in this tournament before had never played in front of such a large crowd, nor played at the venue that they had seen so often on a screen. "All the years I've watched on television," Arizona State's Kindra Hackbarth said the day before, "it's just surreal to be in OKC at the Women's College World Series." Her feeling was shared by many players here. Would the venue and event be overwhelming for the newcomers?

When a junior or senior player produces in the clutch, a commentator or coach will note her experience. When a freshman doesn't come through, they will talk about her inexperience. When it comes to the WCWS, such talk is amplified, because not only does experience (or lack thereof) in the women's college game matter but experience at this tournament—that is, an upperclassman coming to OKC for the first time might show nerves being on a stage this big.

UCLA Head Coach Kelly Inouye-Perez, who was starting three freshmen at the WCWS, doesn't believe that a player needs experience at this venue. "We have a saying at UCLA," Inouye-Perez said, "that 'the game doesn't know how old you are.' They've all been playing since they were seven or eight years old. If you act like a freshman, and act like you're inexperienced, then yes, it will definitely show up, but as you get more experience, you learn how to manage those things." Inouye-Perez recruits athletes who have been go-to players throughout their careers, and she believes that they've always played with high expectations and learned how to deal with those expectations. UCLA doesn't have team captains or say that seniority leads. "I want everyone to understand," Inouye-Perez said, "that when it comes to softball, the expectation is that you're ready to compete from the first."

In the first at bat of the first game, Arizona State's Hackbarth, a newcomer to the WCWS, singled; her freshman teammate, Denae Chatman, followed with a home run. No apparent nerves there. But Arizona State gave up their 2–0 lead with some sloppy, or perhaps nervous, fielding: two errors and misplays of five balls that could have kept them in the game, or even ahead, if they had made the plays. Morgan Howe, newcomer to the WCWS, hit a three-run home run in the top of the fifth to close the gap to 6–5, but Oregon pulled away in the late innings.

The day's second game matched Washington against two-time defending champion Oklahoma, a favorite to win again. Huskies Head Coach Heather Tarr handed the ball to a freshman, Gabbie Plain, who not only was throwing against a line-up that led the country in runs scored, but who had the majority of the fans rooting for them. Pressure? You wouldn't know it, watching her stay calm in the circle. She kept pitch counts low and her defense—particularly the left side with Taylor Van Zee and Sis Bates—played great behind her. Taran Alvelo relieved Plain in the sixth and combined they shut out Oklahoma. I asked Plain what her emotions were like before the game and then in that first inning. "There were definitely nerves," she said, "but that's a healthy thing. It keeps you on your toes. I was just going out there thinking it was any other game." A cool customer.

I watched the four games on opening day keeping in mind whether players had been here before or not. Georgia wasn't in OKC last year, and sophomore Justice Milz came up for her first time in the WCWS and hit a deep bomb in the first inning, putting the Bulldogs ahead. Florida's freshman Jordan Matthews answered with a two-run double off the center field wall in the bottom of the inning. Freshman Hannah Adams later homered for the Gators, who run-ruled in five innings their rival from the SEC.

After being held four innings without a hit, Florida State broke a scoreless tie with UCLA by scoring four runs in the fifth inning, getting three of their runs on a fairly routine fly ball that was misplayed by a freshman for a bases-clearing double. In the sixth inning, the Bruins struck back, plating six runs, which included freshman Aaliyah Jordan's triple down the right field line to drive in what would prove to be the game-winning run. Not all the freshmen or all the newcomers excelled on opening day, but many of them did. The importance of experience is complicated and individualistic. It's difficult to know how this particular pressure will affect even an experienced player. Florida State's Kylee Hanson was in the final week of an outstanding career; she relieved Meghan King in the fifth inning and took the loss, allowing five runs on five hits. "Kylee transferred here for this opportunity," her coach, Lonni Alameda, said after the game. "Sometimes when you get the chance for something you dream of and wish for, that kind of gets a lump in your throat. I think at every level we've gotten to, the reality hits her and the lump is there. Then when she settles in, she's outstanding."

*   *   *

Day two of the WCWS featured the winners from day one. The opener matched Washington, the Pac-12 school who spent most of the season's first

UCLA's Rachel Garcia was awarded national Player of the Year from USA Softball, in part because of her dual talents. Garcia had an outstanding season not only in the circle, where she went 29–4 with a 1.02 ERA, but at the plate, where she hit .356 with eleven home runs and fifty three RBI. Courtesy UCLA Athletic Department.

half ranked #1, against the conference rival who swept them in Seattle and assumed the #1 ranking for the rest of the year, Oregon. Could Oregon win a fourth straight time? The answer turned out to be no. Washington defeated Oregon 6–2 behind Gabbie Plain, who gave up zero earned runs for the second straight day. Plain had an excellent drop ball, as she did against Oklahoma, measured in part by twenty-seven of her thirty-two outs so far in the WCWS having been groundouts. The game was scoreless until the fifth inning, when Washington broke through for four runs off Oregon's Megan Kleist, keyed by Van Zee's two-run single and Bates' run-scoring double.

In game two, between Florida and UCLA, Kelly Barnhill and Rachel Garcia struck out twenty-eight batters between them, which suggested that these All-Americans had great stuff, which they did. But they didn't always have command of the zone, and the game featured five home runs, key walks, and a few costly errors. Florida jumped on top, scoring in each of the first three innings to take a 4–0 lead. But like the previous night, UCLA came back with one big inning, scoring five runs in the fourth. One run was walked in, one scored on a sacrifice fly that featured a bang-bang play at home that the umpire ruled in UCLA's favor (a call that Florida fans felt robbed by), and the last three came on a home run by reserve catcher Taylor Pack. The teams traded late-game solo home runs—by UCLA's Bubba Nickles and Florida's Jordan Roberts—and UCLA moved forward with a 6–5 win.

*   *   *

Elimination Saturday. After day three of the WCWS, half the teams would be packing their bags. Elimination Saturday began with two-time defending champion Oklahoma playing Arizona State. In 2018 Oklahoma, with Jocelyn Alo's big bat added to their already formidable hitting, had scored the most runs in the country; their pitching staff, with Paige Parker, Paige Lowary, and Mariah Lopez, was arguably the best big-series staff in the country; they led DI schools in fielding percentage. Sweeping through their regional and super-regional match-ups, Oklahoma came into the WCWS looking like the most dominant team in the country with their 55–3 record. But they lost their opener to Washington, and to make the championship series, they were now facing four elimination games over the next two days. A tall task.

Head Coach Patty Gasso was welcoming the challenge. After Thursday's loss, in the press conference afterwards with four of her key players sitting with her, she began getting her team ready to compete. "I know this might sound crazy," Gasso said, "but this road was meant to be for us and we embrace it. We've been very fortunate to win the first game the last couple years, and it sets you up nicely, but this road is a different road and we're embracing this." Gasso spoke with both steeliness and great emotion. "We are good at learning lessons," she said. "So maybe this is necessary. When we lose games, this team bounces back like none I've seen. This road is different, but it's welcomed, because this group has it in them to make a run. As long as we have one pitch left, one out left, we're going for it with all we've got."

Against Arizona State, Alo opened the scoring for Oklahoma with a homer in the third inning; the Sooners added a second run in the sixth on a Lea Wodach single. Parker was superb, baffling the Arizona State batters as she threw a two-hit shutout on only seventy-eight pitches. The second team out in the WCWS, after Arizona State, was Georgia, who lost 7–2 to Florida State. The Seminoles' Meghan King gave up only two unearned runs, and Florida State bunched their hits in the fourth and fifth innings to take command.

The evening session, matching the winners of these early elimination games against the losers on Friday, began with Oklahoma and Florida. Many had picked these two schools to play in the championship series, as they had done in 2017. In the bottom of the first, Alo hit a long homer for Oklahoma to put the Sooners up 1–0. In two later at bats, Florida Head Coach Tim Walton chose to walk her intentionally and pitch to Shay Knighten. It worked once, but the second time, with the bases loaded, Knighten struck out only to have the ball get away from the catcher on a wild pitch, Knighten reaching first and Caleigh Clifton scoring to give Parker a cushion. Parker exhibited mastery over the Gators hitters, who all season had been very good at taking pitches just off the plate and fouling off two-strike counts. Parker got ahead in the count on twenty of the twenty-four batters she faced; scattering two hits and two walks, she shut out Florida 2–0. Walton praised her after the game. "There's not a whole lot you can do when you've got a pitcher, strike one all day long," he said. "Not strike one with one pitch, but strike one inside, outside curve, changeup, bounced the changeup when she wanted to, featured a little bit of a rise. She was good. I give her all the credit."

Patty Gasso had alternated her big-game pitchers all season, throwing Paige Lowary, for example, on opening night of the super-regional. Few media members were expecting her to hand the ball to Parker a second time on Saturday. After the game, Gasso explained: "When Paige Parker says, 'I would like to have the ball,' you listen to Paige Parker and you give her the ball."

A reporter asked Parker if she had "adamantly" told her coach that she wanted the ball. "I don't know if it was adamantly," Parker replied. "I just told her before the game."

"Kind of whispered it," interjected Gasso.

"Yeah, I did kind of whisper it to her," Parker said, as the press room cracked up.

Did Parker wake up on Elimination Saturday and think, "I'm going to throw two complete game shutouts, against Arizona State and Florida, and then we're going to go on and win this championship"? Don't bet against it. The Oklahoma fans—the majority of those in the stadium—were over the moon after the game, not only because the Sooners were advancing but because they defeated arch-rival Florida. Some artistic sort was likely already composing a song about a new Western gunslinger with nerves of steel, "The Ballad of Paige Parker." Gasso's "We're going to do it" speech seemed to be working.

In the evening session's second game, Florida State against Oregon, the Seminoles got on the board first when freshman Elizabeth Mason, who had rarely played since game two of the regional, doubled home Cali Harrod in the third inning. Kylee Hanson had the ball for Florida State, and she was in command of all her pitches. Head Coach Lonni Alameda had said two days earlier that when Hanson settles in, she's outstanding, and her pitcher was backing up her coach's statement.

In the enclosed press box, media members are shielded from the noise of the crowd. Wanting a better sense of the stadium's atmosphere, I sat down behind home plate in the fourth inning, where there were open seats because some Sooners fans had gone home. There the noise was loud, sometimes deafening, as the Florida State and Oregon rooting sections kept up constant cheers. Though I could hardly hear the players or coaches talking, I could hear the crack of the Florida State bats, as they started barreling up the Oregon pitchers, even when they were making outs.

Florida State bunched three sharply-hit line drives in the fifth, with Mason again getting an RBI. More hits and runners in the sixth led to a third run. Freshman star Sydney Sherrill bombed a solo home run in the seventh. Hanson scattered five hits and two walks, not giving up a run until the sixth inning; when she walked two batters in the seventh, to bring the tying run up to the plate, Alameda brought in Meghan King, who quickly got a flyout and strikeout to end the game. FSU advanced with a 4–1 win. Elimination Saturday was over. Both top seeds, Oregon and Florida, as well as Arizona State and Georgia, were going home.

Florida's loss meant that the SEC teams were eliminated. As a conference, the SEC did not have a good post-season, despite getting to host at nine regional sites. In the super-regionals, all the SEC teams lost unless they played another SEC team—Florida and Georgia beat conference rivals Texas A&M and Tennessee. And once in Oklahoma City, the lone SEC win was Florida over Georgia in the opening round. Bragging rights for a conference were going to the Pac-12. Only Arizona lost in the super-regionals, and that was against fellow member UCLA. And in the WCWS, Washington and UCLA were in the semi-finals without dropping a game.

* * *

If you read your local sports pages, you've likely seen quotes from an athlete or coach that gave a view not directly the writer's. If you watch ESPN SportsCenter or even your local news stations, you've likely seen innumerable press conferences that generated sound bite quotes. At events that are big enough to have numerous media members—professional sports, college football or basketball, conference championships—press conferences are arranged so that players and coaches don't have to respond repeatedly to the same questions with each member of the media. These press conferences are usually boring, with athletes and coaches giving rote answers, saying as little as possible.

At the USA Hall of Fame Stadium, press conferences are held in a sterile and unattractive room meant to be simply functional. The ceilings are low, the walls concrete. A few photos of former winning teams or great players hang in no apparent design. A table along one wall is filled with team guides, box scores, and play-by-plays from earlier games. In the back, cameramen from the NCAA or television stations film the proceedings. In front of them, print media sitting at four rows of tables have their computers out, trying to put together the beginnings of a story. In front of them, media members who rely more on their tape recorders sit in three rows of chairs. If you watch police procedurals or shows that feature the CIA, you can easily imagine the scene: think interrogation rooms.

At the Women's College World Series, about twenty minutes or so after a game ends, players and the head coach from the losing team are brought to the press conference room, where they are seated on a raised platform and asked questions. The first press conference is followed by a second, with players and the head coach from the winning team.

On Elimination Saturday four teams came into the press conference room minutes after having their season, and this year's dreams, end. The emotions in the room matched the program's expectations coming in to the WCWS. Arizona State was a long shot to even make it to Oklahoma City, and going out in two games to Oregon and Oklahoma—favorites for the title—didn't seem like failure. No one in the room was upset or sad. Everyone seemed happy that, as they put it, ASU softball was back. The seniors talked directly about how much Head Coach Trisha Ford and their teammates meant to them. Coach Ford talked about how proud she was of her team and how exciting the future looked. Questions got lengthy replies. Georgia's final press conference was similar. The players and Head Coach Lu Harris-Champer were proud of what they had accomplished, proud that even after their pitching ace, Brittany Gray, was lost for the season, they continued to play well, making it to OKC. Smiles filled the room.

Not so for Oregon and Florida. These two heavyweight programs had expectations of winning the championship. Disappointment was evident, in the body language, in the comments. But the players and coaches did not become defensive, did not put up a wall to shield emotion.

Head Coach Mike White began Oregon's press conference by praising Florida State and then praising his team: "We fought hard at the end and just came up a little bit short. I'm extremely proud of this team. I'm proud of these four seniors, [who] left our program better than when they came in. They've been great representatives for the University of Oregon. I want to thank them all with all my heart." And then he turned to them, away from the media, and directly said, "Thank you."

Gwen Svekis, Oregon's All-American catcher, was asked about how tough it was to end her career this way. "We know what we've accomplished," she replied. "And it hurts right now, but I'm very proud of my career. I'm very proud to be a Duck. I feel like if we had come out and played the way that I know we can, we wouldn't be going home tonight. So that hurts. But I already know that we had a great four years, and to hear Coach White say that we left the program better than we found it is the greatest achievement of my four years."

Coach White didn't dance around his disappointment at once again bringing a team that he thought would do better, but he also accepted responsibility. "We're watching teams perform better than what they did in the season," he said. "Teams in our conference that we compete with, they're performing better than us. I'm pointing the finger at me right now. I've got to find a way to get this team to perform better in the big moments." The self-reflection quickly shifted, however, to further graciousness. "But before we go," he said. "I want to thank all of you in the media. All the support we've had from Eugene, all our fans coming down, they've made a huge difference to our program. The support from our athletic department, Lisa Peterson coming down. I want to thank everybody for the support we're getting." And he praised his team one final time. "We've had a lot of fun together. And that's what I talk about, a funeral is a celebration of life. They need to think about a celebration of a season here, being Pac-12 champions and being the #1 team in the country coming into this tournament. They've got to hold their heads high. It wasn't our week. But we've enjoyed this season tremendously."

Florida's press conference was similar in its style if different in its particulars. Head Coach Tim Walton congratulated Oklahoma and praised Paige Parker's outstanding pitching. Players congratulated the other team and complimented each other, even as great disappointment was evident. With one thoughtful reply at a time, they began turning disappointment into solace, into an understanding of all that had been accomplished.

When a reporter asked Amanda Lorenz what it meant to her having played her last game with the seniors who were sitting up there—Aleshia Ocasio, Kayli Kvistad, Nicole DeWitt, and Janell Wheaton—for about five seconds, Lorenz looked almost stunned. And then she began, with her voice quivering, to talk about how special it had been.

"They really just did anything that they could for the team," Lorenz said. "We were special enough to have a whole senior class that really did everything for the benefit of the team, trying to get the team better." And then she began naming each senior and saying something heartfelt. "Aleshia Ocasio, what an athlete. I'll never play with an athlete like that ever again." Praising Kvistad and DeWitt likewise with particular details, Lorenz last brought up her travel ball teammate Wheaton: "And Janell, I have the most history with Janell, so it's kind of crazy that it finally has come to an end. Seven years, eight years playing together, it's just been really superb, and I'm really thankful that I've had the opportunity to learn from her as a teammate. We've gotten a lot better together. We committed to Florida together. We wanted to win a national championship together. We won one at travel ball." Lorenz paused, everyone in the room understanding that they didn't, of course, win a national *college* championship together, and then she went on. "To play in the College World Series with someone who made me better growing up and is one of the reasons why I'm here is just really special." Lorenz was crying, her teammates were crying. I was tearing up, as were most of the media members. Lorenz transformed that sterile room with some alchemy mixing heartbreak and graciousness.

*   *   *

For the first time since 1990, all four semi-finalist teams playing on Sunday, day four of the WCWS, were coached by women. The day had turned into Rematch Sunday in that, like Thursday, Oklahoma was playing Washington, and Florida State was going up against UCLA. But the losers then would now have to win twice.

Though Gabbie Plain had thrown the first two games for Washington in the WCWS, Head Coach Heather Tarr started Taran Alvelo in the circle. For nearly three years, Alvelo had thrown the crucial innings for Washington. She was having an excellent junior year until late April, when a stress fracture in her ribs caused her to sit out for several weeks and then be rusty when she returned. But she had shut out Alabama in the super-regional final game, looking like the Alvelo of old, and it was to be her turn against Oklahoma. Tarr's explanation demonstrated one reason why her players love to play for her: "We are not where we are today without her. Gabbie Plain has had a phenomenal season. But we're not Washington without Taran Alvelo. She absolutely deserved to start this game today no matter what was going to happen."

On Saturday, Oklahoma came through the loser's bracket and looked like they could fulfill Coach Gasso's prophecy that this team, which all season bounced back after a loss stronger than ever, would win it all. But Alvelo and the defense shut down the Oklahoma bats, and Washington scored single runs in the first, third, and fifth to win 3–0, highlighted by an RBI single and a solo home run from their senior left-fielder and all-conference performer, Julia DePonte. After Thursday's loss, Gasso had said that she was tremendously impressed with Washington and their defense. "The left side of the field [Sis Bates, Taylor VanZee] was off the charts," she said. "They were outstanding and those are the kind of plays that you need to make to win championships and they did." The defense continued that superb play on Sunday.

Back in February at the Mary Nutter Classic, Tarr had told me that she thought Washington's defense was the best in the country. Oklahoma led the nation in fielding percentage—Washington was fourth—but it was hard to argue against Tarr's assertion watching their first three games in the WCWS. Not all conferences vote on a defensive player of the year, but the Pac-12 does and the coaches had given the award to shortstop Bates. She showed why: making running catches in the outfield on flared fly balls; going into the 5–6 hole, gloving a hard shot and throwing the runner out at first; taking away a base hit up the middle. Bates has a very quick release to her throwing motion, which allows her to play a deep shortstop and still nab runners at first. In the press box, which is usually quiet, there were frequent OMGs, "I've gotta see that on replay," for Bates. While she had the showy put-outs, the entire Huskies infield was more than solid.

Washington shortstop Sis Bates displaying her athleticism, as she charges a ground ball and gets off a quick throw. Bates was spectacular at the WCWS, following up her season-long play that earned her the Pac-12 Defensive Player of the Year. Courtesy Washington Athletic Department.

J.T. D'Amico has been on the Washington coaching staff for a decade, primarily serving as the defensive coach. He acknowledged that you have to recruit and get talented defensive players who want to be coached, but he stressed likewise that attention to details makes the difference. Even the details of throwing the ball around the horn after a put-out. "No one does it like we do," he said. "The consistency, the spacing, the way they move their feet, how they make eye contact. We practice basic catch and throw. There's nothing magical about it." My asking D'Amico about defense got him excited. He mentioned how important the timing of the stretch is for a first baseman: "It's the most under-coached thing, but it's so important. If they stretch too early, they limit their side-to-side mobility. If they're too late, they won't be fully stretched out. You have to practice this."

Because Plain and Alvelo are drop ball pitchers, the infield gets considerable action. But the most important defensive play of the game came from right fielder Trysten Melhart. With Washington up 2–0 in the fifth, Oklahoma got two runners on, bringing up Shay Knighten, who lined a shot to right. Melhart broke quickly on the ball, then used her speed and a full-out dive to make the catch—just as she did in game one against the Sooners, when Knighten had two runners on in a nearly identical situation. Oklahoma didn't threaten after that, and their chances for a three-peat at the WCWS came to an end with their second loss to Washington. The Huskies were moving on to the championship series. Playing with passion and joy, led by their vocal leader, Van Zee, they still had not lost all season to a team outside the Pac-12.

In Rematch Sunday's second game, UCLA didn't get behind as they had in their previous two games. Though Florida State was getting some hits, Rachel Garcia, who earlier in the week had been named USA Softball's National Player of the Year, was striking out batters with runners in scoring position. Garcia helped her own cause by singling in Kylee Perez in the third to put UCLA up 1–0. The game then turned on two pitches in the sixth inning. With runners on second and third and two outs, Florida State's freshman Elizabeth Mason, down in the count 0–2, laid off a Garcia rise ball at the letters—a nearly impossible pitch to hit. On the next offering, Mason homered to put the Seminoles ahead 3–1, which stood up as the final score. Meghan King gave up seven hits and two walks, but was tough in the clutch as UCLA came up with only one unearned run.

After an hour break between games, the two teams came back on the field—the winner would be going on to the championship series, the loser would be going home. Unlike the first game, this one was a slugfest. UCLA had eleven hits and scored six runs, but that wasn't nearly enough. Only Garcia of three UCLA pitchers was effective in the circle, and she looked gassed early in the game. Florida State kept hitting shots. Their outs were warning-track fly balls. They had three doubles and four home runs (the teams

Washington foiled Oklahoma's attempts for a three-peat by beating them twice in the WCWS, in part because of two great catches by outfielder Trysten Melhart, one in each game when Oklahoma was threatening with two runners on. Courtesy Joshua Gateley.

combined for seven homers, tying an all-time WCWS record for one game). Florida State romped 12–6, any hope for a UCLA comeback ending when Meghan King entered in relief of Kylee Hanson in the seventh and shut down the Bruins one, two, three.

Washington and Florida State, two teams not talked about much in the final weeks leading up to the WCWS, were in the championship series.

*   *   *

If you watched the Women's College World Series on television, then you are familiar with the commentators who reported the action. For the early games, play-by-play announcer Adam Amin paired with the analyst Amanda Scarborough; for the later games, Beth Mowins had the call with Jessica Mendoza and Michelle Smith providing insight. Laura Rutledge and Holly Rowe interviewed coaches and players. They are a talented and experienced group who prepare hard, have tremendous connections within the game, and understand how to celebrate the female athlete.

Fewer people know the name Graham Hays, and likely wouldn't recognize him, but Hays has been celebrating the female athlete for fourteen years through his writing gigs at ESPN.com and, in the past few years, with espnW. Hays writes on women's basketball and soccer as well as softball. When I asked if he sees himself as a champion of women's sports, he replied no, that he's simply a storyteller. Champions of something often speak loudly, generalize, get on their soap box. I understand Hays not thinking of himself that way; certainly his quiet and humble personality isn't made for a soap box. But he *is* a champion of women's sports as a storyteller who gets the details right, as a writer who gives women's sports their due.

The backstory of how Hays became the premier writer for women's softball is rather unusual. "I'm the third of three kids," he recalled. "I was born in Denmark and grew up mostly in England. My parents are Americans but were based over there for work. No one in my immediate family cared about sports at all. But my two grandmothers were huge sports fans, Sooners fans actually, who lived here in Oklahoma. So I learned about sports through my grandmothers, when I would come over to the United States in summers." Hays was a teenager when women's sports began emerging in the mid to late 1990s, with the 1996 Atlanta Olympics, the beginning of the WNBA in 1997, and the attention given to USA Soccer's national team that won the Women's World Cup in 1999.

In 1999, after two summer internships, Hays was hired full-time by ESPN. He's had a variety of roles there: working in and writing for the fantasy sports department; writing for ESPN's pop culture sites, "Page 2" and "Page 3." In 2004 he began focusing on women's sports. "I was putting in pieces on women's college and professional sports where anyone would take them," Hays recalled. "I did that for a number of years while also doing some editing. Eventually espnW began, and after a couple of years I moved over there—almost six years ago now."

In the press box during the tourney, any question about a rule or softball history got directed Hays' way. He's watched every game of the WCWS for fifteen straight years. No one has written more pieces about the tournament. I asked him about his career highlights covering softball over the many years. He told me two stories, about two games.

Hays witnessed the first one, an NCAA tournament game in 2009 at the Amherst regional, matching the third-seeded Washington team against the University of Massachusetts. UMass had beaten Washington earlier to force a second and deciding game, which began at 8:00 p.m. and lasted well past 1:00 in the morning. Washington's Danielle Lawrie and UMass' Brandice Balschmiter had matched up and thrown every pitch in the first game, and were to do so again in this fifteen inning game, with Lawrie throwing nearly 400 pitches on the day. "Seeing that in person was, as far as a game goes, as good as I hope to ever see," Hays said. "It was epic." Washington finally won, with Lawrie striking out twenty-four batters, and two weeks later the Huskies would claim their first and only national championship in women's softball.

Hays' other favorite game was one he did not attend, because it took place between two DII schools during their conference season. But Hays has helped make this game legendary, as he wrote the story that gained national interest. I'll let him set the stage. Here's the opening paragraph from his story of April 28, 2008: "*Western Oregon senior Sara Tucholsky had never hit a home run in her career. Central Washington senior Mallory Holtman was already her school's career leader in them. But when a twist of fate and a torn knee ligament brought them face to face with each other and face to face with the end of their playing days, they combined on a home run trot that celebrated the collective human spirit far more than individual athletic achievement.*"

Neither Western Oregon nor Central Washington had ever reached the NCAA tournament at the DII level. On that day, they were one-two in their conference standings. In a scoreless game, with two runners on, Tucholsky lined a ball over the center field fence; she excitedly rounded first base, thought she had missed the bag, and turned back to tag it. And then she crumpled to the ground, a few feet away from first base, unable to move. The umpires told Sue Knox, Western Oregon's head coach, that the only option available under the rules was to pinch run for Tucholsky and have the hit recorded as a single instead of a home run, because any assistance from coaches or trainers while she was an active runner would result in an out.

When Knox was about to substitute a pinch runner, she heard the Central Washington first baseman, Holtman, say to her, "Excuse me, would it be OK if we carried her around and she touched each bag?" Holtman somehow knew that an opposing player could give assistance. I'll let Hays finish the story: "*Holtman and shortstop Liz Wallace lifted Tucholsky off the ground and supported her weight between them as they began a slow trip around the bases, stopping at each one so Tucholsky's left foot could secure her passage onward. Even with Tucholsky feeling the pain of what trainers subsequently came to believe was a torn ACL (she was scheduled for tests to confirm the injury on Monday), the surreal quality of perhaps the longest and most crowded home run trot in the game's history hit all three players.*"

"'*We all started to laugh at one point, I think when we touched the first base,*' Holtman said. '*I don't know what it looked like to observers, but it was kind of funny because Liz and I were carrying her on both sides and we'd get to a base and gently, barely tap her left foot, and we'd all of a sudden start to get the giggles a little bit.*'

"*Accompanied by a standing ovation from the fans, they finally reached home plate and passed the home run hitter into the arms of her own teammates.*"

The story illustrates beautifully what is remarkable about women's softball culture and the female athlete, and choosing this story as one of his favorites reveals much about Graham Hays.

* * *

Day five of the WCWS was game one of the best-of-three championship series, the first championship series since 2010 that would not feature Oklahoma or Florida. On paper, the match-up looked like a test between Washington's pitching and defense and Florida State's hitting and speed. But the Huskies didn't get to the championship all year without scoring runs, and the Seminoles had an excellent pitching staff. You could imagine almost any scenario for any one game.

It was a pitchers' duel.

Meghan King started for Florida State. In the bottom of the third inning, Washington's Trysten Melhart and Taylor Van Zee singled, Sis Bates was hit by a pitch, and King faced a bases loaded, one out situation, with the Huskies sluggers coming up. But King fanned both Julia DePonte and Kirstyn Thomas to get out of the inning. Gabbie Plain had the ball in the circle for Washington. In the fourth inning she walked the bases full with two outs, but a routine ground ball that Bates handled unassisted retired Florida State. Through five innings, Plain had given up only two hits and no more walks. But Florida State broke through in the sixth when sophomore catcher Anna Shelnutt homered to left-center to put the Seminoles up 1–0.

As a freshman in 2017, Shelnutt seldom played, but when the starting catcher got injured late in the year, Shelnutt emerged in the ACC tournament and got hot offensively. This year, Shelnutt was the everyday catcher, and

There are amazing athletic plays and then there are amazing plays with the game on the line. In this screen capture, Florida State's Jessie Warren dives for a bunt attempt. She caught the ball and then doubled off the runner on first, protecting a 1–0 lead in the seventh inning of game one of the best-of-three championship series.

while her batting average hovered in the mid .200s all year, her defense made her indispensable. Her coach, Lonni Alameda, had praised her for keeping the pitching staff loose with her goofiness. In the ACC tournament, Shelnutt had picked up her hitting, blasting the walk-off homer against Pittsburgh in the deciding game. She continued to hit well throughout the regionals and super-regionals, earning the nickname "Postseason Anna." Shelnutt has a big chip on her shoulder and a love for her coaching staff, in large part because she came to Florida State lightly recruited—most schools told her that she was too small to catch. The FSU coaching staff, Shelnutt recalled, "saw past my size … saw that I actually knew what I was doing back there and that I loved it." They were now loving her clutch hitting.

Washington's Taryn Atlee opened the bottom of the seventh with a single. Jessie Warren then made the defensive play of the game from third base. On a bunt attempt by the speedy Melhart, Warren stretched out in a dive to snag the ball at ground level, and then rose to her knees and threw to first to double off Atlee. If the ball had dropped, Washington would have had two runners on with no outs. While the next batter, Kelly Burdick, singled, Van Zee grounded out to end the game. FSU won 1–0 on a home run by Shelnutt, a defensive gem by Warren, and stout pitching from King.

Before game two—day six of the WCWS—Washington could take heart, knowing that Plain had shut down the Florida State bats in a way that no one else had in the tournament, and knowing that they were on the verge of breaking through offensively. In a surprising move, Lonni Alameda started King again rather than going with Kylee Hanson. Van Zee smoked a single up the middle to lead off the game for Washington. An error on a bunt was followed by a short fly ball that got lost in the sun and fell between two Seminoles fielders, scoring two. A ground ball out plated a third run. Alameda's decision to throw King was looking questionable. Washington fans were feeling good, as their staff hadn't given up three runs yet in the nine games of the NCAA post-season.

Taryn Alvelo had the ball in the circle for Washington. She yielded a lead-off single to Warren, but came back and struck out the next two, pumping her fist each time, showing again why she's fire to Plain's ice. On a two-strike pitch to Shelnutt, Alvelo began to stride off, believing that she had strike three, but the umpire called the borderline pitch a ball. Shelnutt promptly lived up to her nickname, blasting a two-run homer.

In the bottom of the second, FSU's Elizabeth Mason, who had the game-winning RBIs against Oregon and UCLA, hit a single that scored two in a three-run inning. Washington left the bases loaded in the top of the fourth. In the bottom of the inning, Mason again came through, her line drive carrying over the center field fence for a two-run homer. Warren followed with her own, and FSU had suddenly opened an 8–3 lead. King was great from there, allowing only one baserunner in the final three innings, and Alameda's decision to throw her in game two looked like genius. King's pitching performance throughout the WCWS was one for the ages, literally—she compiled the lowest ERA in WCWS history, allowing just one earned run in 34⅓ innings. Rather amazingly, she didn't even win the Most Outstanding Player award, which was given to Jessie Warren, who tied the all-time WCWS record of thirteen hits and, of course, came up with the game-saving defensive play in game one of the championship series.

Florida State was led by their stars, Warren and King. They got solid contributions from players who had performed well all season: Kylee Hanson, Sydney Sherrill, Carsyn Gordon, Dani Morgan, Zoe Casas, Morgan Klaevemann, and Cali Harrod. But they got necessary and great performances all tourney long from their unknowns, Shelnutt and Mason. There was no nickname for Mason before her postseason heroics, but she was the biggest individual surprise, not having even played in the super-regionals. She didn't start game one of the WCWS, either, but she played like a star from then on. In a moment that caught national attention, ESPN's cameras focused on her parents just before Mason hit her two-run homer in the final game. As she rounded the bases, the cameras caught the parents in a big hug. And from the field, Mason, too, saw them.

"It really hit me today," Mason said at the postgame press conference, "when I looked up and saw my dad and my mom, they're jumping up and down. I'm sure every girl on the team, you have that moment where all you want to do—you love your team—but all you want to do is see your parents."

The biggest surprise from the 2018 Women's College World Series wasn't actually Mason's or Shelnutt's unexpected performances—the biggest surprise was simply Florida State, as a team, winning the championship. When they went through a 4–5 stretch in late February and early March, losing games to McNeese State and South Alabama among others, they dropped well out of the top-ten in the national rankings. A later twenty-game win streak hardly boosted their national profile. Perhaps it was because Florida State in past years had dominated a weaker conference in the ACC but then come up short in the super-regionals or WCWS. Or perhaps it was that last year's team, the 2017 Florida State Seminoles, was supposed to be their breakthrough group, when they had six players make first-team All-ACC, including power-hitting first baseman Alex Powers, who was ACC Player of the Year in 2016, Jessie Warren, ACC Player of the Year in 2017, and two-time ACC Pitcher of the Year Jessica Burroughs. That team was experienced, deep, strong in hitting and pitching. That team was ranked #1 for much of the year. That team lost, however, in the super-regionals to LSU and never made it to Oklahoma City.

Expectations can become burden. "Last year's team was amazing," Head Coach Lonni Alameda said. "We did everything right, but we forgot to cel-

Florida State's Meghan King takes off her pitcher's mask and begins celebrating a win. King's tourney ERA of 0.21 was the lowest in WCWS history. Courtesy Maury Neipris and Florida State Athletics.

ebrate the little things. So this year we celebrated everything and we had a blast with it."

Travis Wilson, Alameda's long-time assistant coach, echoed this point, saying that you don't have to treat softball like a business. "You can treat it as fun, as a game," he said. "And you can win." Florida State players looked loose out on the field, not loose as in unprepared or unserious, but loose and intense at the same time. The players had fun after games and in their press conferences. They exhibited strong feelings, crying not in shame or embarrassment, but out of joy and emotion. They talked frequently about how much fun they had with the coaching staff. About how much they loved playing for Alameda.

Expectations can become burden. It looked that way for several teams in Oklahoma City, who played a bit tight. FSU did not play tight. In the first inning of the final game, when Washington had scored three quick runs, Alameda called time and strolled out to the circle, gathering her players around her. On camera, you could see the players begin smiling and then laughing. Here's how Alameda remembered the moment: "You eye it up and you look around, walk in there with a big smile, and be like, 'Hey, we're the Cardiac Kids, we need to be down by three in order to perform. This is so much fun, right? We're right where we want to be.' And they laughed."

After the final out, Florida State players had their requisite dogpile in

Florida State's head coach Lonni Alameda and her team look loose. Alameda said that the coaching staff in 2018 emphasized celebrating all the little things and having fun with the game. The strategy worked. Courtesy Larry Novey and Florida State Athletics.

the infield. The streamers and confetti flew. The players and coaches were awarded their big national championship trophy and their individual small trophies. They had won the 2018 Women's College World Series for the first time, and they were the first team in history from the Atlantic Coast Conference to do so. The celebration moved to the outfield. Photographers asked the players and coaches to group for a team photo of the winners. But that customary *team* photo doesn't exist, actually, because Lonni Alameda waved in all the FSU supporters—families, administrators, and the like—and said that everyone should be part of the Florida State softball *family* photo.

Epilogue: Looking Back

Former player and coach Carol Bruggeman is now a part-time TV analyst and full-time Executive Director of the National Fastpitch Coaches Association (NFCA). When I asked her what makes women's college softball special, she said she had a simple answer: "The people are very different from people in other professions, or even other sports. We help each other. We have created a culture where we believe it's best to share information."

In Las Vegas in December of 2017, at the NFCA annual convention, I witnessed this sharing firsthand when I attended a session led by two of the most highly respected pitching coaches in the game, Oklahoma's Melyssa Lombardi and Florida's Jennifer Rocha. Lombardi began, and she took her audience of coaches, who numbered hundreds, through a slide by slide demonstration of exactly what she does in a bullpen session. She first discussed a "block session," one that emphasizes development and mechanics. Lombardi asks her pitcher to continually throw the same pitch, refining her mechanics, until she can consistently locate the pitch where Lombardi wants it. Lombardi then discussed a "variable session," where her pitchers will throw different pitches in different locations, competing as if it were a game. In fall ball, Lombardi said, Oklahoma begins with 80 percent block sessions; by spring, her pitchers will do variable sessions 80 percent of the time. Lombardi has a rating system in relation to location, speed, and movement, and she asks the pitcher to immediately rate each pitch. They then must "accept and adjust"—a psychological strategy that mirrors what she wants them to do when the season begins in February. All successful pitchers, she said, have to learn to eliminate judgment, to accept what they threw, and move on to make in-game adjustments. (I'm summarizing what Lombardi laid out in detail.) After Lombardi finished, Rocha laid out what she does to teach her pitchers how to "command the strike zone." She isolates zones, where every pitch has to be on the inner half or outer half of the plate, and her pitchers have to use the change-up in their mix of pitches. Like Lombardi, Rocha provided detailed information on what she does to help make Florida's pitchers so dominating.

As I watched the session, I marveled at how Oklahoma and Florida were giving out at a national convention the recipe for "the secret sauce." Businesses don't do this: they protect their computer codes; they keep to themselves their practices and strategies; they worry about protecting trade secrets.

Lombardi, Rocha, and the many coaches I've referred to in these pages are incredibly generous with each other. They do share, and again and again I heard that acts such as these are done *for the good of the game.* The generosity that marks women's college softball coaches is matched, however, by the chip on their collective shoulders. They believe absolutely in the greatness of their athletes and they don't think softball has gotten its due, nor women's sports in general.

*   *   *

In my year of being immersed in this game, what will I remember most? Certainly I have images in my head of the athletes performing amazing feats. On the field: Washington's Trysten Melhart making two diving catches to hold off Oklahoma and to send the champions home; Florida State's Jessie Warren laying out completely to catch the bunt in the first game of the championship series. At the plate: the sheer power of Oklahoma's Jocelyn Alo or Minnesota's Kendyl Lindaman. In the circle: the wicked riseball of Kelly Barnhill or Paige Parker's command of multiple pitches when it mattered most. I'll remember Rachel Garcia in the Los Angeles regional, bringing UCLA back through the loser's bracket by throwing over 500 pitches on the weekend and hitting a long three-run homer for a 6–4 win in the deciding game. The season had so many great individual plays; the season had so many dramatic moments.

But what I'll *most* remember are the press conferences at the Women's College World Series, when everything that makes softball special was on display: the emotions, the idealism, the graciousness. I would never have guessed, before that final week of the season, that performances off the field would make such an impression on me. But they did.

Patty Gasso's speech when she said that Oklahoma was going to come through the loser's bracket to win the championship made me believe her, and made me understand how leaders at certain moments find the words to motivate people to great feats. Amanda Lorenz' praise of her senior team-mates was such a display of naked emotion that everyone in the room under-stood immediately that more than sports had been on the line.

One final example. In Washington's press conference after defeating Oklahoma for the second time and punching their ticket for the champion-ship series, a reporter mentioned that it was the first time since 1990 that the final four teams had all been coached by women, and she asked Heather Tarr if she'd like to comment on that. If you know Tarr, you know that she's perky and intense. I watched her sit up even straighter, bigger, and she looked as if she were a sun shining light. "Yes, I will," she said, and then she talked about how proud she was of those coaches, and how proud she was that her university has a female president, Ana Mari Cauce, a female athletic director, Jennifer Cohen, and a female senior associate director of athletics, Erin O'Connell. "I just feel very prideful," Tarr said, "in proving to our women [players] that women can lead. You can lead with emotion. You can lead with wisdom. We have to continue to prove to the world that we can lead each other and we can be great with each other.

Bibliography and Resources

Many hundreds, if not thousands, of books have been written about baseball. Fastpitch softball, excluding the many how-to or coaching books, has had only a handful of books written about the game, including the following:

Finch, Jennie and Ann Killion. *Throw Like a Girl: How to Dream Big & Believe in Yourself.* Chicago: Triumph Books, 2011. The life-story of a famous softball player, Jennie Finch, used to give affirming messages to girls.

Reilly-Boccia, Cassie. *Finished It: A Team's Journey to Winning It All.* iUniverse, 2014. An account of the University of Alabama's championship winning season in 2012, as told by one of the key players on that team.

Westly, Erica. *Fastpitch: The Untold History of Softball and the Women Who Made the Game.* New York: Touchstone, 2016. When Title IX was enacted in 1972, opportunities for softball players at the college level grew, which spawned an accompanying growth in travel ball and high school teams. Westly provides research into the top fastpitch teams of the 1940s, '50s, and '60s, when town teams such as the Raybestos Brakettes gave female athletes employment and sport opportunities unavailable otherwise.

Many books have been written on Title IX and its effects on women's sports. Among those that have informed me and helped shape my understanding of the subject are the following:

Brake, Deborah L. *Getting in the Game: Title IX and the Women's Sports Revolution.* New York: NYU P, 2010.

Heywood, Leslie and Shari L. Dworkin. *Built to Win: The Female Athlete as Cultural Icon.* Minneapolis: The U of Minnesota P, 2003.

Mitchell, Nicole, and Lisa A. Ennis. *Encyclopedia of Title IX and Sports.* Westport, Conn.: Greenwood P, 2007.

Nelson, Mariah Burton. *The Stronger Women Get, the More Men Love Football: Sexism and the American Culture of Sports.* New York: Harcourt Brace, 1994.

Suggs, Welch. *A Place on the Team: The Triumph and Tragedy of Title IX.* Princeton: Princeton UP, 2005.

The work of Mary Jo Kane and Nicole LaVoi at the Tucker Center for Research on Girls & Women in Sports (U of Minnesota) has been enlightening and invaluable, particularly their studies of media, of sexuality and sports, and of coaches and gender. Likewise, I am indebted to the insights that Cheryl Cooky, Michael Messner, and Michela Musto have produced over the years; their longitudinal study of women's sports' media coverage, "It's Dude Time" (*Communication and Sport*, 2015, Vol 3 (3), 261–87), should be required reading for anyone wondering why interest in women's sports has so badly lagged behind men's sports.

As readers of *Women's College Softball on the Rise* will have already noted, I am indebted to the scores of people who talked to me about various matters related to the sport of fastpitch softball or to the events of the 2018 season. Most of these interviews were brief conversations after a game, short phone interviews, or email exchanges. Others were longer face-to-face interviews, with the interviewee responding to a set of questions. I appreciate all those who talked to me, including the following:

Lonni Alameda
Emily Allard
Victor Anderson
John Baca
Jeter and Susie Barnhill
Gayle Blevins
Kayla Bonstrom
Carol Bruggeman
Rich Calvert
Michael and Lynn Coutts
J.T. D'Amico
Mike Davenport
Mickey Dean
Courtney Deifel
Michelle DePolo
Sydney Dwyer
Ryan Ehlen
Kimberly Elchlepp
Brandon Elliott
Sue Enquist
Trisha Ford
Kris Ganeff
Ben Garcia
Chris and Joe Garcia
Sue Getterman
Jen Goodwin
Kindra Hackbarth
Liz Hammerschmidt
Kylee Hanson
Byron Hatch
Graham Hays
Kris Herman
Amy Hogue
Hanna Hull

Carol Hutchins
Kelly Inouye-Perez
Jill Karwoski
Dave King
Sue Kunkle
Lauren Lappin
Loren LaPorte
Nicole LaVoi
Amanda Lehotak
Jen Leonhardt
Emily Lopez
Eric Lopez
Susie Lorenz
Victor Martinez
Joe, Maryellen, and Mariah Mazon
Haylie McCleney
Tom Meyer
Cheryl Milligan
Glenn Moore
Jeffrey and Sara Moulton
Win Muffett
Kim and Terry Parker
Gabbie Plain
Tiffany Prager
Dot Richardson
Nate Rohr
Jim Sanderson
Chez Sievers
Jill Skotorczak
Bev Smith
Paige and Kevin Smith
Ally Snelling
Tom Stanton
Alison Strange
Heather Tarr
Bonnie Tholl
Trish Treskot
Mae Wadyka
Kirk Walker
Tyler Walker
Kelli and Troy Walljasper
Tim Walton
Karen Weekly
Linda Wells
Mike White
Margie Wright
Marissa Young

Index

Numbers in **_bold italics_** indicate pages with illustrations